Interacting with *Babylon 5*

FAN PERFORMANCES IN A MEDIA UNIVERSE

Interacting with

Foreword by Henry Jenkins

Babylon 5

Kurt Lancaster

UNIVERSITY OF TEXAS PRESS, AUSTIN

Printed in the United States of America
First edition, 2001

Requests for permission to reproduce material from this work should be sent to Permissions, University of Texas Press, P.O. Box 7819, Austin, TX 78713-7819.

⊗ The paper used in this book meets the minimum requirements of ANSI/NISO Z39.48-1992 (R1997) (Permanence of Paper).

Library of Congress Cataloging-in-Publication Data
Lancaster, Kurt, 1967–
Interacting with Babylon 5 : fan performances in a media universe / by Kurt Lancaster—1st ed.
p. cm.
Includes bibliographical references and index.
ISBN 0-292-74721-7 (cl.: alk. paper) —
ISBN 0-292-74722-5 (pbk.: alk. paper)
1. Babylon 5 (Television program) I. Title: Interacting with Babylon Five. II. Title.
PN1992.77.B24 L36 2001
791.45′72—dc21 00-064906

Dedication

For those with whom I learned and shared the art of role-playing games: Earl Cookson, Chris Davis, Steve Levin, Daniel Mackay, and Steve Wennerberg.

A montage of various objects comprising the *Babylon 5* imaginary entertainment environment.

The theater, the theater—what book of rules says the theater exists only within some ugly buildings crowded into one square mile of New York City? Or London, Paris, or Vienna? Listen, junior. And learn. Want to know what the theater is? A flea circus. Also opera. Also rodeos, carnivals, ballets, Indian tribal dances, Punch and Judy, a one-man band—all theater. Wherever there's magic and make-believe and an audience—there's theater. Donald Duck, Ibsen, and the Lone Ranger. Sarah Bernhardt and Poodles Hanneford, Lunt and Fontanne, Betty Grable, Rex the Wild Horse, Eleanora Duse—they're all theater. You don't understand them, you don't like them all—why should you? The theater's for everybody—you included, but not exclusively—so don't approve or disapprove. It may not be your theater, but it's theater for somebody, somewhere.

—Director Bill Sampson (Gary Merrill)
to aspiring actress Eve Harrington (Anne Baxter)
in Joseph Mankiewicz's *All About Eve* (1950).

Contents

List of Figures

All of life can be broken down into moments of transition or moments of revelation. This had the feeling of both. G'Quan wrote, "There is a greater darkness than the one we fight. It is the darkness of the soul that has lost its way." The war we fight is not against powers and principalities—it is against chaos and despair. Greater than the death of flesh is the death of hope, the death of dreams. Against this peril we can never surrender. The future is all around us waiting in moments of transition to be born in moments of revelation. No one knows the shape of that future or where it will take us. We know only that it is always born in pain.

G'Kar from the *Babylon 5* episode "Z'ha'dum"
by J. Michael Straczynski (1995)

Foreword

Henry Jenkins

Midway through *Babylon 5*'s first season, in an episode called "And the Sky Full of Stars," Security Chief Michael Garibaldi picks up a copy of the newspaper *Universe Today,* and the camera quickly pans over the various headlines on its cover. Some of the headlines refer to narrative issues raised on previous episodes; others introduce issues and topics that will surface more directly in subsequent episodes. What initially might seem to be a throwaway detail—a character reading a newspaper—becomes an important turning point when we return to it for a second viewing. Of course, these headlines are only fully decipherable if you freeze-frame the image for closer scrutiny, and their full importance was made clear only through the ongoing Net and Web discussions of the series.

For me, this moment is emblematic of why *Babylon 5* was such a remarkable experiment in television storytelling. First, it reminds us of the elaborate narrative planning that went into the production of the series. J. Michael Straczynski understood television as a long-form storytelling medium, and he planned and developed the basic story arc for all five seasons before the first episode was produced. His careful calculations certainly left him room to respond to shifting conditions (ranging from the loss of cast members to the perpetual threat of premature cancellation) and offered space for one-shot episodes. Such long-range planning also enabled him to build into the series elaborate foreshadowing and references to its history episode by episode. Not many television producers could have built plot details for the second season into a mid–first season episode.

Second, this moment suggests the degree of self-consciousness about media that ran through *Babylon 5*. The series' characters inhabit a world profoundly shaped by the flow of news and information across various channels of communication. They read about events that affect them in the newspaper or watch them unfold on television. They give interviews to reporters, and we watch as what they say is distorted to serve various agendas. They grumble over attempts to merchandise their identities as part of the ongoing propaganda and public relations warfare that shapes the complex intergalactic politics at the center of the series.

Third, the fact that these details are buried within the text, waiting to be discovered by tactical use of the VCR as an analytic tool and the collaborative efforts of Net discussion lists, points to the awareness and exploitation of fan competencies that transformed *Babylon 5* into one of the most significant cult television programs since *Star Trek*. Like *Star Trek*'s Gene Roddenberry, Straczynski understood the fans to be central to the program's success from the outset. Straczynski saw his fans as a group of opinion leaders to be courted through prebroadcast publicity and convention appearances, as a group of niche marketers and activists whose support could keep the program on the air during rough times, and as students in an ongoing classroom where he could share his views about the production process and the aesthetics of television storytelling. Straczynski's relationship with fans was rocky. He was worshiped for his extraordinary productivity and personal vision and feared for his slashing flames in response to some fan comments. He at once sought to facilitate fan discussion and to regulate fan speculations to avoid potential intellectual property issues. Yet whatever that relationship with his audience became, Straczynski sought to use digital media to directly and personally engage them, not just occasionally, but week in and week out.

Straczynski sought to validate the new styles of reading and interpretation that have been facilitated by the shifting media environment. The introduction of the videotape recorder and the Internet has significantly altered the informational economy surrounding American television. It is significant that Stephen Bochco's *Hill Street Blues* (1981–1987) was the first major success story of the videotape era and that David Lynch's *Twin Peaks* (1990–1991) was one of the first new cult television series to develop an important Internet following. These series, with their ever-more-elaborate use of story arcs and program history, rewarded a viewer who carefully scrutinized the images using the freeze-frame function, who watched and rewatched the episodes on video tape, and who used the Internet as a vehicle for discussion with a larger interpretive community and the Web as a means of annotation. The succession of new media technologies since the late 1970s has encouraged the emergence of a culture based around the archiving, annotation, transformation, and recirculation of media content. Straczynski's genius was in recognizing the shape and potential of that new culture and in producing a science fiction series that rewarded these participatory impulses. He trusted his audience to ferret out information craftily hidden within the text, awaiting our discovery; he trusted the audience to make meaningful connections from episode to episode and season to season; he trusted the fans to be invested enough in the series to watch his ambitious story unfold and flexible enough in their understanding to cope with the complex shifts in character alignment. He made demands on the audience almost unprecedented in American television history, and for those of us who stuck with him over the five-year run of the series, our patience and commitment were fully rewarded!

For these reasons, it is vitally important that media and cultural scholars look closely at *Babylon 5*, which seems, in retrospect, as rich an embodiment of what television storytelling can do in an age of media convergence as *Star Trek* represented the full potential of television storytelling in the network era. If you didn't watch *Babylon 5*, you missed something important.

Over the past decades, cultural scholars have come to recognize that fandom functions as an important basis for media activism and grassroots cultural production and distribution. Fans were often the first to recognize the participatory potential of new media technologies. They expressed frustration with the impersonal relationship network television sought to establish with its audience, and they demanded a more active role for themselves, insisting on their own sense of ownership of and involvement with cultural materials, and refusing to see consumption as a process that begins and ends at the point of purchase. The character of American television has been fundamentally altered as television producers have begun to incorporate a more sophisticated understanding of the active audience into their production decisions. The result has been the conscious production of cult-friendly programs like *The X Files, The Simpsons, Buffy the Vampire Slayer, Dawson's Creek, Xena,* and *Babylon 5,* among many, many others. These series build in opportunities for audience participation and elaboration, recognizing our pleasure in backstory, in-jokes, foreshadowing, and encrypted information; adding fuel to our Net discussions; providing rationales for rereading; offering raw materials for our cultural production; and using the online world to provide unprecedented access to the behind-the-scenes creative decisions shaping the series' development. The changing economics and cultural dynamics of the contemporary media environment (what I am calling media convergence) are generating new kinds of relationships between media producers and media consumers.

Media convergence has been a buzzword within the media industries for the past several years and has assumed a multitude of meanings and associations. Here I use it to refer to new corporate strategies pertaining to the movement of intellectual property across multiple channels of communication. The concentration of media ownership has resulted in horizontal integration: major media companies maintain interests in all of the various forms of media and seek to exploit synergistic relationships among their holdings. Within this system the most profitable forms of popular culture are those that move fluidly across different media, gathering diverse audiences and alternative markets along the way. In this culture of media "franchises," it is hardly surprising that the media industry responded to (and fueled) audience interest in *Babylon 5* through the production of a broad range of tie-in and other software, card games, role-playing games, comic books, novels, and Web sites. Many of these tie-in products actively encourage fan participation, invite us to take on avatars and alternative persona, and reward our mastery over program knowledge by creating opportunities to deploy it in complex simulations of *Babylon 5*'s fictional universe. In the 1970s, *The Rocky Horror Picture Show* urged spectators not to "dream it" but to "be it," actively encouraging us to sing, dance, shout comments, and perform in the aisles of the movie theater. Since *Rocky Horror,* media producers have sought more and more sophisticated ways to enable us to "be" part of the show.

Metaphors of performance seem uniquely appropriate for analyzing the new forms of media consumption that are taking shape around this intertextual, interactive, and immersive style of popular entertainment. We don't simply watch, read, or interpret these cult programs: we are invited to play a part in their production, circulation, and reception; we are encouraged to assume a role within their fictional universe and to stage our own versions of popular narratives. Let's face it, we would be performing elements of popular culture with or without official sanction. As I am writing this introduction, there are, for example, more than 250 amateur (and unauthorized) *Star Wars* movies on the Web; these are made when friends, neighbors, and family members get together to stage light saber battles, creating special effects on their home computers and distributing their productions to like-minded people around the world. We all know people who are gifted at impersonating not only the catch phrases but also the specific intonations associated with their favorite programs. Many of us have had to listen to bad Monty Python impersonations for decades, and whole books have been written about the elaborate costumes constructed by *Star Trek* fans.

At the same time, this new interactive culture encourages the commercial development of performance spaces for the audience as producers transform this participatory impulse into a new marketing strategy. From an early age, we are encouraged to play with the materials of our culture. Action figures are often our first avatars. Children use such toys to appropriate and restage central moments in their favorite popular fictions. As we grow older, we seek new means to enact cult television programs and movies through computer and video games, role-playing and card games, and MUDs (multiuser domains). These new gaming systems encourage collaborative storytelling and shared performances, and players make complex investments in the fictional personas they adopt for the duration of the play. It still astonishes me that so little has been written about the kinds of narratives that emerge from the fantasy role-playing community and how these alternative models of cultural production are shaping the scripting of science fiction television or the writing of popular fiction. A whole new generation of authors has emerged from the *Dungeons and Dragons* community, and it is clear that their play has had a substantial impact on the kinds of stories they write. (Not coincidentally, a whole new generation of scholars has come of age rolling dice in someone's basement and calculating their hit points, so we should expect these experiences to influence how they are theorizing interactive fictions.)

Kurt Lancaster provides a valuable service in demonstrating what the theoretical models and critical vocabulary of Performance Studies can contribute to our analysis of this new media culture. Using *Babylon 5* as a rich and compelling case study, he examines the place of role-playing within contemporary popular culture, responding to anxieties that such imaginative activity confuses the boundaries between fiction and reality or leaves the "player" subject to the ideological manipulations of the master text. He pays close attention to the various genres of games and immersive media that sought to open the fantasy of *Babylon 5* to popular participation, helping us to understand both how rules structure the roles we can play in its fictional universe and also what space remains for individual expression and subcultural appropriation. Games are, after all, systems of rules and procedures that enable pleasurable shared activity. When we transform the contents of television programs into games, those rules and procedures tend to make some meanings more accessible than others, to facilitate some fantasies more readily than others, and to enable some kinds of interactions while foreclosing others. To be pleasurable, these games have to be open-ended enough to enable us to do what we "want" with these fictional characters and their universes, and yet they also have to acknowledge producers' anxieties about controlling the circulation of their intellectual property and regulating the production of meaning.

In adopting a performance studies model, Lancaster poses and addresses a set of questions about audience-text interactions different from those that have dominated audience research within the cultural studies paradigm over the past decade or so. In its attempt to break through cultural hierarchies and to expand the critical examination of performance to include various forms of everyday theatricality, performance studies increasingly explores a space that closely parallels the concerns of cultural studies. Performance studies approaches, as presented in this book, help us to rediscover the question of popular aesthetics and to recognize more fully the creative and expressive potential of everyday people. Performance studies does not ignore the ideological and sociological dimensions of these phenomena, though it tends to focus more fully on personal rather than subcultural meanings, but its central focus is elsewhere—in understanding how the properties of different texts and performance contexts shape our improvisations. As someone who has made significant contributions to cultural studies discussions of audience activity, I welcome this fresh perspective. As our media environment changes, we need to constantly rethink our methodological assumptions and conceptual frameworks; we need to break out of old binary oppositions, for example, between active and passive audiences or between models that center around resistance and co-optation. Performance studies invites us to deal in a more complex way with the fusion of personal and cultural assumptions that occurs as we take on the task of performing a role within a preexisting cultural narrative. As performers, we are giving voice to the text, but this is never a simple act of ideological ventriloquism. As we enter into the world of the text, we necessarily change it to match our own needs and interests, sometimes in subtle ways, sometimes in bold and subversive ways. As practiced by Lancaster, performance studies proves especially effective at identifying the space for improvisation opened up by various forms of interactive entertainment.

As someone trained within the Cultural Studies tradition, I would hope to see future scholars push this model further, developing a more detailed ethnography of people at play with these materials, examining what fills those spaces they open up for performance and how the identities they adopt within their game play relate to their everyday lives. As we do so, Lancaster's careful, systematic mapping of the performance opportunities within these various game systems will prove foundational. The initial body of work on the television audience built directly upon a preexisting body of theory and criticism that sought to understand the specific properties of television as a medium and the narrative construction of basic genres of television entertainment. This process is perhaps most explicit in the Nationwide project, one of the landmarks of the Birmingham School, which combined two monographs—one a textual analysis of how the British news program *Nationwide* structured its meanings and the other an ethnographic account of how various focus groups responded to the program contents. Lancaster's focus on the genres of games that enable us to "perform" *Babylon 5* similarly lays the foundation for more precise work on the place of role-playing within contemporary media consumption. I hope that my colleagues in Cultural Studies will respond to its challenge, seeing what ethnography can contribute to the Performance Studies paradigm Lancaster presents here. I am convinced that a dialogue between the two approaches will be the most productive way of understanding the more immersive and interactive properties of contemporary popular culture.

Preface

From the Imaginary to the Performative

Simulacra and Science Fiction

The 1960s saw the fulfillment of humankind's desire to enter outer space, in the form of both Earth orbits and Lunar landings. Later plans—for colonies on the Moon and Mars as well as huge orbital space stations housing a micropolis representing a multicultural humanity—never came to fruition. With the Russian launch in 1998 of the first part of an international space station, and its subsequent construction, some may believe that a rejuvenation of the manned space program has begun. However, the station will house less than a dozen people at a pricetag of about $20 to $40 billion. For the same price, engineer Robert Zubrin contends, the foundation for a fully realized Mars colony is achievable. NASA, for now, has not made a human mission to Mars a priority. Those who dream of a reality of humanity's moving into space must redirect this desire into the fantasy of science fiction. *Babylon 5* is one such fiction that embodies this dream, depicting as it does a fairly realistic space colonization project.

Ultimately, however, fantasy becomes a simulacrum—indicating not the real but a desire to live within a representation of the unreal: the fantasy becomes the real, and, with it, reality becomes modeled on the simulation rather than vice versa, as philosopher Jean Baudrillard suggests in his essay entitled "Simulacra and Science Fiction": "It is no longer possible to fabricate the unreal from the real, the imaginary from the givens of the real. The process will, rather, be the opposite: it will be to put decentered situations, models of simulation in place and to contrive to give them the feeling of the real, precisely because it has disappeared from our life" (1994:124). The desire to enter imaginary environments is predicated on a desire to become what the simulacrum suggests. Such worlds as Middle-earth, and those depicted in *Star Trek* and *Star Wars*—based on words and images born of the imagination—offer simulated environments that people can enter. They evoke, for some, places of wonder—imaginary universes where fantasy is, at times, more desirable than the everyday reality of a Presidential impeachment, El Niño phenomena, school shootings, and third-world nuclear brinkmanship. Because of such events, or perhaps in spite of such events, imaginary entertainment environments beckon, giving participants a "feeling of the real, precisely because it has disappeared from" their lives, as Baudrillard suggests: a reality that lacks an ordered mapping and placement of self within a centered, predetermined social structure, which no longer offers transcendence into space as an imagined possibility.

Babylon 5, a 110-episode science fiction television series (which future cultural historians will quite possibly look back on as a masterpiece), presents an imaginary universe as visually suggestive as George Lucas' *Star Wars* series (1977; 1980; 1983; 1999), as politically and socially aware as the best of Gene Roddenberry's classic television show, *Star Trek* (1966–1969), and as historically detailed and intricately plotted as J. R. R. Tolkien's novel *The Lord of the Rings* (1954–1955; revised 1965). Using *Babylon 5* as a case study, I analyze how one can participate in simulacra of science fiction through role-playing games, war games, collectible card games, CD-ROMs, fan fiction, and online fan Web pages: the various nodes comprising the imaginary entertainment environment. They are concrete places where people can *perform*—make real—fantasies that they have only previously watched. In this project, I essentially describe what viewers can do with a television show off-screen. Exploring the performance significance of these various sites of fantasy, I describe each in detail and reveal the potential performance qualities evinced through it.

This project is not, however, an ethnographic study of *Babylon 5* fans. It is an examination of the scripts, the set pieces, the scenarios, the potential mise-en-scenes arising from these various sites. I do not examine the "actors," the participants. Instead, the work posits theories suggesting how prospective participants become immersed in this kind of fantasy play. It explicates the processes occurring if a player participates in these sites, without describing actual performances in progress. However, I do write from first-hand experience. Having played fantasy games for over twenty years, I speak with the knowledge not just of a scholar, but of a science fiction fan, avid gamer, and gamemaster.

A proper ethnographic analysis of *Babylon 5* fans and gamers would require another kind of book, one that is beyond the scope of this project. Someone interested in this sort of study is advised to look at the works of Henry Jenkins, John Tulloch, Gary Alan Fine, Sherry Turkle, Janet Murray, and Constance Penley, among others. This being said, there are some generalizations that can be made about science fiction fans and gamers. Millions of people do play fantasy games and immerse themselves in the kinds of environments discussed in this project, from *Dungeons & Dragons*–type role-playing games to the *Pokémon* collectible card game. Indeed, each year over twenty thousand people attend GenCon, a game convention held in Milwaukee, Wisconsin, in August. Although these participants tend to be educated, white middle-class males, that statistic itself is a stereotype, for women and nonwhites do play these games, though they are in the minority. In the final chapter I give my own analysis of the social function behind these games. In any case, I refer to the spectator-participants—the players—generically, as an amalgam of inferred assumptions garnered from over twenty years of playing the types of games described in this book. The specific details arising from individual game-play can be different, but the general principles comprising the experience as a certain type of performance are universal. For this project, what specific players do to create their own unique performances isn't as important as the analysis of the specific theories explaining how the process of an immersive performance occurs. The details and specific ways people play and make the culture their own, as they express their own particular desires through these games, are unique, but *how* this occurs revolves around the performance theories described in this book.

Briefly, my own history and experiences of these games began when I was in middle school, when a group of people decided to play *Dungeons & Dragons* (1974) during lunch hour. At the beginning of high school my brother bought the game. Throughout high school I went on many quests, read Tolkien, and eventually became a gamemaster, a person who prepares adventure quests for other players. I also played war games and computer games. These were more of the "hack-and-slash" type in which players increase power by killing monsters in dungeons and taking their treasure. In college I met a group of people who participated in a more literary form of role-playing through such games as *Middle-earth, Stormbringer,* and *Call of Cthulhu,* which were based on the works of Tolkien, Moorcock, and Lovecraft. Character interaction and development were stressed over violence and action. Role-playing action-oriented games became literally *role*-playing experiences focusing on characters.

From these game sessions—especially ones performed under the direction of gamemaster Steve Wennerberg—I remember scenes more palpable than those found in films or novels. I and my coparticipants were immersed in a shared fiction more enriching than that previously experienced in other limited-participatory so-called *literary* forms. Later, when I entered graduate school in theater and performance studies, much of my research dealt with participatory forms of popular entertainment, for I wanted to discover *how* they could be as much or more emotionally powerful than traditional forms of what is considered literature.

If role-playing sessions can be as cathartic as theater, then are they not as worthy of study and analysis as the conventional forms of culture studied by the academy—whether this be art found in museums, plays performed onstage, or works of the Western Canon? Indeed, popular entertainment forms have their roots in the participatory forms of art found in traditional cultures, including the oral performances of the *Odyssey* and *Beowulf* and the one-month-long Indian performance-mythology called the Ramlila of Ramnagar, to name just a few.

Performance scholar Richard Schechner lays out a theory that reveals how performances—being both theatrical and ritualistic—both provide entertainment and possess efficacy (see Schechner 1988:106–52). Traditional performance forms tend to be efficacious: promulgating a ritual transformation in the spectator-participant. Popular culture performances, on the other hand, are looked at as entertainment, effecting only a temporary "transportation" to another world or state of being in the spectator. In a role-playing game, for example, one can clearly see the entertainment aspect of the game, as players, through their imaginations, transport themselves to Tolkien's world of Middle-earth or the space station *Babylon 5*. But below the surface lie "structures of signification," as Clifford Geertz puts it, which reveal the social significance of cultural events (1973:9). It is through such deep social and cultural structures—"which are at once strange, irregular, and inexplicit" (10)—that one can begin to see transformative moments within the performances comprising the imaginary entertainment environment. To the outsider, these games and Web sites may seem just as strange as would the behaviors observed by someone examining a culture they have never visited. The strength of my analysis comes from the fact that I am an insider, speaking from first-hand experience, as well as a performance studies scholar, trained in analyzing performance forms. Indeed, it as impossible for someone who has not played such games to conduct a proper analysis of a role-playing game, for example, as it would be for a scholar to analyze literature without ever having read a novel.

Some people, however, may feel that such material as that described in this book does not offer much value to society and should not be examined academically. If people play fantasy games, especially if they're adults, then they may be considered escapists, unwilling to face reality. Despite humanity's desire and need to perform, there remains ingrained in mainstream society a social stigma against adult play when it comes to computer games, fantasy role-playing, and other forms of popular culture entertainment. School shootings and satanism are presented by some critics as being outcomes stemming from participation in fantasy games, which create "dangerous" subcultures. People who think that role-playing games or war games project a negative influence on society will most likely continue to hold to those beliefs. But for those who want to consider such issues, this book may help in understanding how these performances work—and perhaps in allowing new conclusions to be drawn. I have written elsewhere on the perceived psychological effects of these games (see Lancaster 1994). Like the antitheatrical prejudice found within Western society—from Plato's treatises to the Puritan ban against street performers in Shakespeare's day—there seems to be an anti–fantasy game prejudice in contemporary society.

This is one reason it is important to analyze thoroughly the performance qualities of fantasy games, and also why I use my own personal experience in explaining how these games function. It is important for people to see how these various forms of popular entertainment function structurally so that they can understand them, rather than just forming an uneducated opinion about the "evil" influence of fantasy games based on surface appearances. This book is not an analysis of science fiction or fantasy subcultures—areas previously examined by such cultural studies scholars as Jenkins (*Textual Poachers*, 1992), Tulloch and Jenkins (*Science Fiction Audiences*, 1995), and Daniel Bernardi (*Star Trek and History*, 1998), to name a few. These scholars tend to examine how subcultural identity relates to the larger power structures within society as fans circulate within the cultures they share and help create. Within the cultural studies paradigm, issues of gender, race, and class are examined in relationship to various cultural and social structures among fans as well as in relationship to the creators of science fiction and fantasy shows. For example, Bernardi, in his *Star Trek and History: Race-ing toward a White Future* (1998), presents a fascinating look at how cultural and social hegemony is institutionalized within the "mega-text"[1] of *Star Trek*—as present in the assumptions of its producers, and transferred to those who imbibe these assumptions within the episodes, and even among the network of fans. These issues, however important—and despite the richness of racial, class, and gender themes within *Babylon 5*—require a culturally political analysis. This approach would take away from my focus on the processes of immersion in fantasy that comprise my thesis. Issues of race, gender, and class can certainly be read into this process, but it is more important for this book that the generic process be described, leaving the cultural studies analysis for a later study. This book describes the various sites of the imaginary entertainment environment and how they can be perceived as sites of performance. It is not an analysis of how race, gender, and class are situated within these sites.

Rather, I feel it is important to examine these various fantasy games—and the performance theories associated with them—in order to show how they create immersion through performance in the minds of their players. This analysis is similar to how a scholar might analyze the theoretical forces shaping the blueprint for a live performance contained within a play: how acting theories associated with bringing a character to life onstage and how the ideas contained within the text help shape a potential performance. This allows me to focus on the structure of the gaming texts and how these texts literally frame the performance. Understanding this will allow the reader to know what is involved within these games, elucidating a process oftentimes mysterious for those who have never played a fantasy game. The cultural studies texts mentioned above do not elucidate the performance structures of the imaginary entertainment environment, and they do not describe the formal performance qualities arising out of the mise-en-scenes of these various sites. This project—which is basically an attempt to examine how these sites can be conceptualized *as* performance—has not been carried out before on such a wide scale, and is the first book to analyze an entire imaginary entertainment environment. Taking a first step in a field permeated by cultural studies analyses of subjects focusing mainly on *Star Trek,* this is also the first scholarly book written by a single author on *Babylon 5*. Furthermore, as it maps out the performance theories revolving around the imaginary entertainment environment of *Babylon 5,* this is the first book to present a performance studies analysis of science fiction.

1. Henry Jenkins in *Textual Poachers* uses the term "meta-text" to examine how *Star Trek* sets an " 'ideal,' . . . against which a film or episode is evaluated" (1992:98).

The Performance Studies Paradigm

The performance studies paradigm as a scholarly field of inquiry had its beginnings in the 1960s theatrical avant-garde. Discontented with conventional European and American drama and proscenium stages where spectators are cut off from the performers, the avant-garde incorporated traditional performances and performance training from indigenous cultures around the world. In some instances these performances even included the spectators as participants. Realizing that conventional institutions of theater in higher education were still examining mostly conventional plays and productions in courses—and were training their students accordingly (these students are *still* led to believe that there are enough jobs in the theater to justify their training in such numbers)—the Department of Graduate Drama at New York University's Tisch School of the Arts said "no" to this approach in the early 1970s. Renaming their drama department the Department of Performance Studies in 1980, the professors at this university decided to train students in intercultural performance forms and unconventional production techniques—the stuff of the avant-garde—and, most important, to give them the tools to examine *all* performance forms—whether occurring on a conventional stage, in cyberspace, or in the wider popular culture. These scholars felt it was time to remold the intellectual ideas of theater into a form of performance analysis that could be applied not just to theater productions and theater history, but to any kind of social, cultural, and political behavior.

Under this logic, a performance on Broadway is neither more nor less important than a performance occurring online in cyberspace or a role-playing game performed in someone's living room. (Indeed, I have been more emotionally moved in some role-playing game performances than at most Broadway plays and musicals I have attended.) Performance studies allows for the analysis of all these different kinds of performances, irrespective of their cultural and social status in society. Rather than inventing its own discipline, performance studies uses already existing methodologies in new ways. It employs theories from linguistics, semiotics, philosophy, sociology, anthropology, and feminism, among others, in order to further understand human behavior *as, in,* and *through* performance. My project is an example of such an approach applied to a popular form of performance-entertainment.

Chapter Overview

The chapters in this book present the various kinds of immersion available in each form of the imaginary entertainment environment. The role-playing game allows players to perform characters other than themselves in *Babylon 5*–like stories; this aspect lessens in the war game and the card game, in which role-playing is more tightly structured. The CD-ROM I describe presents such a limited environment that participants do not really play any kind of role. The chapter on Web pages and fan fiction shows what fans do as they write characters in someone else's imaginary environment, but they do not perform these characters in the conventional sense. On the other hand, in the online role-playing example, participants do, in fact, perform roles as in the conventional role-playing game; I place the online example in this chapter because it is located in cyberspace, thereby thematically linked to the online fan fiction and Web pages. The analyses given in this book can be applied to other games in other imaginary entertainment environments. The environment may be different if one plays in the *Star Wars* universe, but the performance processes are the same, whether in *Babylon 5, Star Trek,* Middle-earth, or elsewhere.

In the introduction, "Performing in Babylon—Performing in Everyday Life: Joe Straczynski's Social Front and the Epic Beginning of an Imaginary Entertainment Environment," I describe how *Babylon 5* came to be aired on television. This includes an examination of the producer of the show, Joe Straczynski, and of the social front (as defined by sociologist Erving Goffman) he projects when talking to fans about the effort it took to put his vision onscreen. In addition, this chapter shows how Straczynski incorporated into his five-year saga an epic form of narrative storytelling, an anti-Aristotelian drama as theorized by playwright Bertolt Brecht in 1927. In *Babylon 5,* the structure of the storytelling involves a montage of *entire episodes*. Most of them stand on their own, but when viewed in their entirety, the juxtaposition of episodes conveys a deeper understanding of the story.

Straczynski had decided to spend time answering fan email and posting comments at online bulletin boards. As a science fiction fan himself, he felt it was his duty to be held accountable for his show. The performance quality of this aspect of "behind-the-scenes" television production is also charted, and here we see his role of producer challenged by fan-critics. Last, the imaginary entertainment environment is located as an evolving historical process. This chapter reveals the fundamental fact that an emerging imaginary entertainment environment does not evolve on its own without the influence of an originating creator. *Babylon 5* originated in one specific person, and was negotiated through a complicated web of social politics in Hollywood before it was presented on television. With its broadcast, a fan base gathered, members of which eventually became the participants in the capitalistic marketing of the fantasy simulacra comprising role-playing games, war games, collectible card games, Web pages, and fan fiction described in this book. Ultimately, the fans are the ones who determine the future history of the universe Straczynski created, for it is the stories they create that keep the imaginary universe of *Babylon 5* alive in the minds of its participants and thus in the wider culture.

In Chapter 1, "Welcome Aboard, Ambassador: Creating a Surrogate Performance in the *Babylon Project,*" I look at how a character is created in a role-playing game. Through rules and oral storytelling, participants become immersed in an imaginary environment where they perform roles, becoming lead characters in an ongoing adventure. Players enact their characters through the verbal utterance of dialogue and action in fulfillment of a story that they essentially improvise. Instead of examining a specific performance, I show the process of character creation in order to show how performances are scripted in this type of game. In addition, I contend that the desire for participation in various imaginary entertainment environments points toward what Joseph Roach calls surrogation. The "process of trying out various candidates in different situations," Roach theorizes, "the doomed search for originals by continuously auditioning stand-ins—is the most important of the many meanings that users intend when they say the word *performance*" (1996:3). In this sense, the imaginary environments explored in this project are surrogates, which attempt to satisfy people's desire for a return to the originating site of fiction, the television episodes of *Babylon 5*, as well as their desire for space exploration. I contend that as manned space exploration ceased by 1975, cultural products and new scientific endeavors filled this vacancy with robotic probes to other planets (including the viewing of images from space probes and the Hubble telescope), written works of science fiction that depict mankind's colonization of space, the visual media of science fiction, such as *Star Trek* and *Babylon 5*, and the immersive performances comprising the imaginary entertainment environment.

In Chapter 2, "'Captain on the Bridge': Six Frames of Performance in the Game *Babylon 5 Wars,*" I examine how war games use rules as a means of simulating military engagements. The military functions of starships are presented through a structure of rules, maps, and ship schematics that determine how participants are reconfigured as starship commanders in space combat. This kind of performance, however, is not that of a conventional drama. Players do not enact an author's text as actors do, with their bodies. Rather, through the technology of rules, players perform a high-tech fantasy where their bodies do not "end at the skin," but become a kind of cyborg, where, through "imagination and in other practice, machines can be prosthetic devices, intimate components, friendly selves" (Haraway 1991:178). The conflict players enact—the performance of the mise-en-scene—takes place on a two-dimensional map. Characters are but cardboard counters, and the psychology and bodies of the characters are schematics on ship control sheets. The heat of the drama pulses through the thoughts and actions of players, fired in the imagination by remembrance of scenes from Straczynski's *Babylon 5* viewed previously on television, but now restored through a war game. I conclude the chapter by examining a set of photographs that depict how this war game takes participants through six frames of performance. Building on Schechner's performance quadrilogue—drama, script, theater, performance—I add to it the frames of fantasy and immersion.

Chapter 3, "Performing the Haptic-Panoptic: The *Babylon 5* Collectible Card Game," is an examination of the history of this kind of game (originating six years before *Pokémon*) and the kind of performance arising from it. The collectible card game combines the desire for collection with the opportunity for putting into play what one has collected. Pictures on the cards evoke a fantasy world. The cards are the interface through which players perform within a rules structure. In the *Babylon 5* game, players perform the part of alien ambassadors who must gain a "sphere of influence" in an attempt to win. Since the script of the story is embedded within the cards, the players have less freedom to choose their own plot, character, and destiny than they find in role-playing games. The random placement of cards may suggest a story, but it is not told through a traditional verbal narrative. Instead, the goals the players attempt to achieve by playing certain cards at particular times engage bits of *Babylon 5* narrative behavior, and, through association with the grand narrative comprising *Babylon 5*, a tale is told through the game structure. This evocation of an associational narrative arises from the pictures on the cards. They represent actual characters, places, and situations that occur on the show. This representation creates the feeling of performing fictive moments from *Babylon 5*. I examine how, between the verbal and the visual, lies a performance of the haptic: players touch the cards, and, by doing so, they touch the characters, locations, and objects from a television show previously viewed only from a distance. Miniature still-shots on the cards—literally cut out and reproduced from a scene—remove the images from their original context, allowing for their reconfiguration in the game. I describe how players lay the cards down scopically in front of them, restoring bits of performance behavior as they attempt to win the game.

In Chapter 4, "Performing at the Interface of the High-Tech and the Bureaucratic: Taking a Tour of the *Official Guide to J. Michael Straczynski's* Babylon 5," I look at an interactive CD-ROM. In this product, participants are supposed to play the part of a visitor touring the *Babylon 5* space station. They engage the environment, exploring where they want to go and activating archived material through an interface. Advertisements for this product state that it is supposed to give consumers the illusion of being on the space station. Through this kind of participation they should be performing as tourists. I examine how this project ultimately fails, for it does not provide the interface for a touristlike performance, but rather a booklike interface by which they experience the CD-ROM as a kind of encyclopedia. In order to mask this failure, the producers of the product engage in the "language games" of bureaucratic and high-tech performances. The bureaucratic branches of advertising, press reviews, and packaging disguise the performance of the actual product (a high-tech book). A bureaucratic performance, Jon McKenzie posits, is related to a high-tech performance, where the bureaucratic qualities of "profitability, flexibility, and optimization" are used to "design and then evaluate and market technologies" as well as to manage bureaucratic workers (1997:39). I also examine this project through Janet Murray's theory of immersive digital environments as given in her book, *Hamlet on the Holodeck* (1997).

Chapter 5, "Webs of Babylon: Textual Poaching Online," offers an examination of fan-created Web pages and fan fiction and how it contrasts with producer-created "sanctioned" material, whether the official Web sites or the originating narrative. Fans participate and perform within the universe of *Babylon 5* by taking their favorite characters and placing them in new stories, in narratives that reflect the fans' own desires. Sometimes these stories go beyond the "canon" of Straczynski's saga. A character who died may be reborn in new stories. Alternate stories allow fans to shape another's characters into their own image. "Fandom here," media scholar Henry Jenkins tells us, "becomes a participatory culture which transforms the experience of media consumption into the production of new texts, indeed of a new culture and a new community" (1992:46). Fans both create new fiction, posting it on the World Wide Web, and form online fan clubs, which usually revolve around particular characters and the actors who perform them. Entire Web sites with multiple pages and links may be devoted to one character or theme. ("The Lurker's Guide to *Babylon 5*" lists over 200 Web pages dedicated to *Babylon 5*.) I show how Web pages and fan fiction allow fans to explore the universe of *Babylon 5* on their own terms outside the original creator's authorial presence. I also take a look at an online role-playing adventure called a MUSH (Multi-User Shared Hallucination).

Chapter 6, "The End of Babylon: From Prelapsarian Fantasies to Post-lapsarian Science Fiction," is a somewhat philosophical examination of the imaginary entertainment environment. I contend that one of the reasons fans see the same film dozens of times, perform in role-playing games, dress up in costumes, play video games, and read novels based on films is to try to recapture—through participation and immersion—the original cathartic moment experienced during the first viewing of the originating material. Rather than seeing these immersive creations as the "toxic excrement of a hyperreal civilization," as Baudrillard believes (1994:13), fans desire to recapture an emotional moment in these other forms in an attempt to relive the emotion experienced in the originating text. These types of performances offer a new kind of mythology, and because of this, popular culture has the potential to bring an efficacious experience to its participants (the essential function of myth). The desire to recapture a cathartic moment speaks also to a failed project of the 1960s: transcendence of humanity through space travel. The policy of expansion into space became sublimated into a nostalgia for space exploration evidenced in science fiction stories and games. Whether the subjectivity of the participants is subsumed into the fantasy project as "conditioned" citizens who vivify the ontological project of another's science fiction and fantasy is open to debate. Like race and gender, the postcolonial project found in *Babylon 5* requires another work, but I do touch upon some of these concerns in this final chapter.

The appendix contains a fan fiction short story and an excerpt from a MUSH. As a side note, this project is not a first-person description, but since I have played these games, I do refer to some of my examples directly in the first person. What follows is an examination of the performance qualities arising out of the imaginary entertainment environment of *Babylon 5*.

Acknowledgments

I thank Daniel Mackay for reading an early draft of this book. His work, *The Fantasy Role-Playing Game: A New Performance Art* (McFarland, 2000), not only pioneered a new field of inquiry into fantasy games, but was seminal to my project and inspired me to map out the performance aesthetics of an entire imaginary entertainment environment. We have had many long discussions and shared ideas on the performance nature of fantasy games. His support and friendship are always appreciated.

Special thanks go to Marshall Blonsky, Henry Jenkins, Brooks McNamara, and Tom Mikotowicz. Each, in his own special way, has supported me over the past few years. Tom encouraged and taught me how to write for publication. Brooks came through just when I needed him. Marshall said just the right things and inspired the opening pages of the preface, as well as giving me a deeper understanding of semiotic analysis. Henry gave some crucial feedback that helped shaped my understanding of the fans' relationship to Straczynski, the show's producer, inspiring me to think about that relationship as a social performance. Not only did Henry agree to write the introduction, but he also gave me the opportunity to teach in the Comparative Media Studies program at MIT after I had completed my doctorate at NYU.

I am so grateful to Jim Burr for accepting my manuscript for the University of Texas Press. He has been kind, gentle, and perceptive in guiding the project through its multifarious stages of production.

I also want to thank Joe Straczynski, not just for giving me permission to cite some of his Internet communications in this book, but for providing me with many pleasurable hours of watching *Babylon 5*—a television masterpiece.

Interacting with *Babylon 5*

Introduction

Performing in Babylon—Performing in Everyday Life

Joe Straczynski's Social Front and the Epic Beginning of an Imaginary Entertainment Environment

> One of the things the show has done is to bring a whole new batch of folks into sf fandom in general, and to give lots of people something they can discuss in common; there is much that tribalizes us and divides us and marginalizes us; it's good to have something that brings us together from time to time.
>
> Joe Straczynski

> For me, it's been a covenant with the fans, to keep my promises when made. I've been on the other end of broken promises by guys promising the moon, the stars and the sky, and don't want to do it to fans in return.
>
> Joe Straczynski (1998d)

Performing a Social Front and the Construction of *Babylon 5*

A discussion of a public figure such as Joe Straczynski must begin with the realization that his persona—as evidenced in interviews, magazine articles, science fiction conventions, books, Web sites, essays, and interactions with fans online—involves a social performance, whether or not he or his fan participants are aware of it. Performance, as defined by sociologist Erving Goffman in his seminal work, *The Presentation of Self in*

Figure 0.1.
Producer John Copeland; executive producer Douglas Netter; and series creator, writer, and executive producer Joe Straczynski received the World Science Fiction Convention's Hugo Award for Straczynski's script "The Coming of Shadows" in 1996. They received the award again in 1997 for his script "Severed Dreams."

Everyday Life (1959), comprises "all the activity of a given participant on a given occasion which serves to influence in any way any of the other participants" (15). Goffman believes that people project a social front—what one could call a personality type—in much the same way as an actor performs a role.

It is important to look at Straczynski's personal history as a kind of performance, as a supplement to the kinds of performances discussed in the other chapters of this book. It needs to be made clear that the performances fans enact are no less and no more important than the performances occurring on *Babylon 5;* neither is the role Straczynski performs when interacting with fans and critics. By examining how a public figure exerts a social performance, we can begin to see how that person, if not to influence people to think and act in a certain way, at least defines the situation so that people will think of him in the way he wants them to. Public figures attempt to force others to act favorably toward them.

Whenever one person tries to impress another—for example, when two people are on a first date, or when a chef is preparing a meal for a patron at a restaurant, or when a television producer interacts with fans online—these people are enacting a social performance. In essence, a person performing in this mode attempts to "control the conduct of others, especially their responsive treatment of him" (Goffman 1959:3). No person on a date wants to make a social blunder, for a misplaced remark or misunderstood gesture could ruin the evening. The chef needs to appear well trained in the culinary arts, and decorates a salmon plate so as to give an appearance that not only has it been prepared by a professional, but that it will taste better than a similar meal cooked at home (thus making the customer feel good about paying the bill). So, as Goffman explains, "This control is achieved largely by influencing the definition of the situation which the others come to formulate, and he can influence this definition by expressing himself in such a way as to give them the kind of impression that will lead them to act voluntarily in accordance with his own plan" (3–4). The chef's purpose is to have people come back to her restaurant, and the guy or girl presumably wants a second date. A television producer wants to please the fans so that they will continue to watch his show.

Joe Straczynski's plan is to be known as the creator of *Babylon 5* and as a producer who cares about his customers, the fans. Straczynski performs a front that includes self-effacing humility (he's just an average "Joe"), while at the same time maintaining roles as educator (he wants to teach people how television is made so viewers can demand better TV—*his* brand of television), "underdog" producer (who had to face challenges to get his vision onscreen), and creative artist (who will not compromise his vision). When it comes to the *Babylon 5* universe, he is the authoritative producer whose very word is canon. All of these roles and attributes comprise Straczynski's social performance, and, as will be seen, when he interacts with fans, "he automatically exerts a moral demand upon the others, obliging them to value and treat him in the manner that persons of his kind have a right to expect" (Goffman 1959:13). Whether at science fiction conventions or online, Straczynski performs a social front that expresses this "moral demand." In his public appearances he will, in Goffman's terms, "mobilize his activity so that it will convey an impression to others which it is in his interests to convey" (4). And it is in his interest to convey an "implicit or explicit claim to be a person of a particular kind" (13)—an innovative Hollywood producer who is also a science fiction fan.

Goffman's project analyzes "non-verbal" communication ("expressions given off" as opposed to "expressions given"), and he refers to the former as a "more theatrical and contextual kind"—"bodily action" (1959:4). I believe this form of communication can be also detected when analyzing a public figure's role as it is performed through magazine and newspaper interviews, as well as through Web sites. The textual expressions within these environments have the effect of being "given off," as I will explain below. In addition, the nonverbal is inextricably tied to the verbal expression and there is also the influence of subtext: it's not what one says, but *how* one says it that evokes another meaning outside and below the textual syntax.

Straczynski, as producer and creator of a science fiction television series—one that has achieved critical success—does not want to come off as an arrogant Hollywood producer who cares more about making money and keeping his job than about his fans, which is the stereotypical nature of the professional role he has taken. So, the "average Joe" social front he performs helps to protect him from this stereotype, and puts him in the position of appearing to care about his fans and his show, which may in fact be accurate. (A social front is not a lie—although it can be.) Straczynski's social performance, however, does contain contradictions, indicating the weakening of his will to maintain the reputable front he has projected in his performances. If we look below the surface of the front he has created for himself, we can see that Straczynski is not just an average person. He has a large amount of power over the fans (he determines the stories and what will happen to the characters within the plot). And he has little humility when he defends himself against professional and fan critics, returning "flame" attacks—the online equivalent of verbal assault and abuse—if he gets burned by someone. It is within these diatribes with fans that we can begin to see cracks appear in the social front persona known professionally as J. Michael Straczynski. What follows is a brief history of Straczynski, his television show, and his relationship to fans, as performed through a social front projected in interviews, books, magazine articles, essays, and Internet postings.

Straczynski's history is as controlled, defined, and random as that of any public figure, for a social front is a mask, and what lies behind it is difficult to determine. The various facets that comprise his social front are, however, clear. Part of this includes growing up in a family that "stayed in one place as little as six months. Never more than a year or two" (1997a:7). Because he didn't stay in one place for long, Straczynski's only constant companions were "television, and the local library," where he read such writers as Asimov, Bradbury, Clarke, Heinlein, and Tolkien (7). After graduating from high school, about twenty years before his initial idea to write *Babylon 5*, Straczynski dedicated himself to writing, averaging ten pages a day, seven days a week. His career has since included playwriting, journalism, and the writing of radio dramas, novels, and short stories. "I was born a writer, it just took me 17 years to learn how to type," he facetiously explains (1997e). The combination of these facts presents Straczynski as a non-Hollywood executive type. He is just another kid who grew up watching television and reading science fiction, got an education, and learned how to write—making the most of a public education system in the midst of a difficult family life and moving from one town to another.

One way that Straczynski is able to come across as an average person is by dressing in jeans when working and attending science fiction conventions (he does not wear a "suit," the typical costume of other producers). He also relates anecdotes to his fans at these conventions, often describing the scene wherein he first conceived the idea of creating *Babylon 5*. In 1986, while taking a shower (he's like everyone else), he received a flash of inspiration for a new kind of science fiction series with a five-year story arc. Straczynski explains: "In the shower at the moment of this revelation, I dashed out and hurriedly scribbled down what would become the main thrust of the series before I could lose the thread of it," recording that revelation in *The Official Babylon 5 Magazine* (1999a:66), "for whatever historical value it may have in showing the thoughts at the very moment that the B5 universe unfurled itself in my head." Straczynski knows that his creation notes have deep historical significance to fans, but he presents this story with such humility it would seem that he does not care about its value. He appears to be just an average guy revealing a deeply held secret: "I've never shown anyone those original notes. Until now." Yet, in this officially sanctioned fan magazine, Straczynski defines his social front not just as an average person, but as creator, the Great Maker, as he is fondly referred to by fans (as well as by his cast and crew). During the lunch hour of Straczynski's directorial debut of the final episode, "Sleeping in Light," the cast and crew came in wearing t-shirts that read on the front: "Shh . . . The Great Maker is Directing," and on the back: "And on the seventh day we wrapped" (1997f).

Despite this nickname, Straczynski continues to present a social front that expresses his role as an "underdog" producer, far from his position as the Great Maker. After writing down the notes for *Babylon 5*, he spent that year writing a pilot movie script, and started making the rounds with it around Hollywood in 1987 (1993a). Even though Straczynski felt that his series could be done on half the budget of *Star Trek: The Next Generation* (1987–1994), many television executives would not believe it. He hooked up with Douglas Netter, who came on board as an executive producer, thereby increasing Straczynski's own status as a little known producer. Since Netter had a reputation around Hollywood for bringing in television series on budget and on time, Warner Bros. threw in their support for the series. In 1991 Warner Bros. organized PTEN, a conglomerate of about 100 local broadcast stations in the United States. Executives would have to be convinced that Netter, producer John Copeland, and Straczynski could *really* do the series as cheaply as they claimed they could. (This same team had worked together on *Captain Power* in 1987.)

Straczynski was also a coproducer on *Murder She Wrote* (1984–1996), where he had begun to realize that part of a series budget was wasted due to poor planning. With proper foresight, he felt, nearly a third of the budget could be saved. Many producers turn in scripts at the last minute, and then in order to make production deadlines workers have to be paid overtime. Special effects were another matter. To do a science fiction series with such optical effects as the *Babylon 5* station, starships, and various planets, if done in the conventional way, would be too expensive. Ron Thornton, of Foundation Imaging in Los Angeles, was hired to come up with a 30-second special effects clip that Straczynski would show Warner Bros. and the PTEN executives. Thornton, using the mid-1980s Amiga home computer with the animation software Lightwave 3D (which can be purchased for $2,200), came up with a CGI (computer graphics image) shot of the *Babylon 5* space station. The pitch, along with the cheaply done special effects, won them over (see Killick 1998).

In November 1991, *Babylon 5* was announced as one of three "flagship" projects for PTEN. The pilot movie, *The Gathering,* was shot during the summer of 1992. On November 7 of that year, Straczynski presented *The Gathering* at a science fiction convention (a tradition Gene Roddenberry began in 1966, when he presented his pilot of *Star Trek* at a convention). The movie was broadcast during the week of February 22, 1993, and earned an Emmy award for visual effects. Because PTEN was not a broadcast company (like ABC, CBS, FOX, and NBC), but a conglomerate of local stations, each one broadcasted *Babylon 5* on a different time and day at each location. The pilot movie received a large enough market share to convince Warner Bros. to go ahead and order the first season of production, which aired beginning the week of January 26, 1994, and would continue with the PTEN market until the fall of 1997.

The series was officially canceled at the end of its fourth season, but not before winning another Emmy for make-up design in 1994, four additional Emmy nominations in 1995 and 1996, and two Hugo Awards in 1996 and 1997 for "The Coming of Shadows" (1995) and "Severed Dreams" (1996). It also earned the *E Pluribis Unum* award for the best dramatic television series to address "fundamental social values in a positive manner," as well as the Space Frontier Foundation Award for Best Vision of the Future ("Lurker's Guide to *Babylon 5*"). The cancellation, however, was not due to low ratings, as was the case with the original *Star Trek* (1966–1969); rather, PTEN, and consequently *Babylon 5*, faced an increasingly tight market as other television companies (such as UPN and the WB) formed their own first-run syndication broadcast conglomerates and competed with station times to present *their* new shows. There simply wasn't any room to squeeze in *Babylon 5* in the shrinking marketplace. The cable station TNT had already picked up the broadcast rights for the first four seasons of *Babylon 5*, and, when it heard about *Babylon 5*'s cancellation, decided to negotiate a purchase for the fifth and final season, which was broadcast in 1998. TNT also purchased four made-for-TV *Babylon 5* films and a spin-off series, *Crusade*, which was broadcast in the summer of 1999. *Babylon 5* completed its fifth season in a genre that rarely makes it past the first year, as evidenced with *Crusade*, which was cancelled after thirteen episodes because of creative differences between Straczynski and studio executives at TNT.

In less than five years Straczynski, the veritable "underdog," broke every Hollywood script-writing record when he wrote 91 episodes out of the entire 110-episode saga (61 of them consecutively), as well as four B5 television movies. However, Straczynski believes that television, and science fiction in particular, is outside the realm of most critics' experience and understanding. "They *always* attack sf. Always have, always will. And always unfairly," Straczynski complained early on in *Babylon 5*'s history. "I'd point to [a] *USA Today* review . . . as emblematic of that approach. [The critic] says that yes, *Babylon 5* might get the ratings, it might succeed, but you should in essence be ashamed if that happens. People have targeted this show with *incredible* vehemence bordering on character assassination" (1994a). Here Straczynski continues to project his role as an underdog producer, one who has to fight and struggle to have critics take his work seriously. These statements become what Goffman calls "corrective practices . . . employed to compensate for discrediting occurrences that have not been successfully avoided" (1959:13). This is done in order to maintain the value and respect he feels he has deserved as a producer, and to maintain emotional ties with his fans.

As part of his corrective practice to maintain his social front as a legitimate producer, Straczynski argues that too many critics spurn television as being a nonliterary medium—a notion he at once agrees with but yet wants to challenge. "Yes, I think that tv storytelling is generally devalued or undervalued by the critical press and by literary critics," he explains, adding: "And for the most part, maybe they've been accurate." He deems himself doubly devalued, however, because much of the mainstream critical press also refuses to take science fiction seriously: "They assume that if the show is sf, then it cannot have any literary or social merit," he points out. "They are, of course, utterly incorrect," he stresses. "Cliché thinking and regurgitative thinking" in writers, he exclaims, "makes for bad TV and movies" (1997e). To counter this kind of "bad television," Straczynski presents himself as a hard worker, claiming that during the week he averages three to four hours of sleep each night: "I'm at the stage in the morning, lunch is usually about 1, I'm there until about 6:30–7:00, I get a bite to eat on the way home in most cases, I get behind the keyboard at about 8–8:30, and I'm there until about 4:30 a.m., and then I crash. On weekends I try to make up for the lost sleep as best I can" (1998c). This statement clearly projects a performance that intends to garner respect from the fans who read the message.

In addition, Straczynski claims that his show is different (therefore superior) from other Hollywood television productions, and by doing so he, as Goffman says, is trying to "control the situation" of how people perceive his own role as the underdog producer creating innovation. "I've never really been part of the Hollywood SYSTEM, and have no desire to do so," Straczynski once said (1994e). In conventional television, audiences are either given plots exploring such issues as whether the heroes "will catch the bad guy" or "cut the wire to the bomb in time (and it's always the blue wire, never the red wire)," Straczynski complains, or they are given stories that deal with "current, trendy issues." It is these kinds of shows, he posits, that breed nonliterary television: "At the end of the hour, the audience has been diverted, even entertained, but not uplifted, ennobled, enriched, or called upon to question, even reconsider their positions on issues of importance." Not only are most shows diversionary, but they are at once "ephemeral and trivial," Straczynski contends. "In the television genre," he adds, writers "generally only think in terms of this week and next week" (1997e). Conventional television series depict a cast of characters thrown into the midst of a one-hour story, and, in the following week, they're placed in a new story. Usually the stories do not connect together and characters rarely change. In contrast, *Babylon 5* is more comparable to Tolkien's multivolume epic *The Lord of the Rings* (1954–1955; revised 1965), wherein each season is one volume of a large saga—"an epic story in the tradition of other epic tales," Straczynski says (1997e). Essentially, he ended up writing a novel for television—a telenovel. In this kind of television, he develops evolving characters who become more than they thought they were within a tightly structured story. And this approach allows him to "set up plot threads that may take years to pay off," he adds.

Despite the claims attributed to Straczynski of being a television innovator, he was not the first to tell stories through this mode. In England the adventuresome but oft-times campy *Dr. Who* (1963–1989) aired in half-hour segments and contained plots that took many episodes to resolve—the series itself lasted twenty-six years. Patrick McGoohan's intelligently written British show *The Prisoner* (1967–1968), though short-lived (seventeen episodes), is considered by many to be one of the finest science fiction series ever made. Terry Nation's *Blake's Seven* (1978–1981), another British production, was a one-hour series that contained a fairly clear beginning, middle, and end over its four-year life. The Brazilian *telenovella* has been around for many years. In the United States, long-running television series are found on daily soap operas that contain plots mapped out months in advance, and these have a certain similarity to the Brazilian form. One of the first successful dramatic one-hour television series to be created within the *telenovella* style in the United States was Steven Bochco's *Hill Street Blues* (1981–1987). In this show, characters grew and changed over the course of the series. At one point in the late 1980s, Straczynski described how he wanted to produce a science fiction series with the same dramatic quality of *Hill Street Blues*. From there, such shows as *L.A. Law, NYPD Blue, Ally McBeal,* and *Sport's Night* (to name a few) began to reveal a new style of television (for the United States) that carried the vision of a single creator. *Sport's Night*'s entire first season (1998–1999), for example, was written by its executive producer Aaron Sorkin, who also wrote the screenplay for the film *A Few Good Men* (1992).

Babylon 5, however, does stand out as one of the first science fiction television series that evokes the depths of classic science fiction novels—Asimov's *Foundation* series being one such example. Most science fiction television, up to this point, tended to pander to an adolescent-minded audience (*Buck Rogers* [1979–1981]and *Battlestar Galactica* [1978–1979], for example), the original *Star Trek* (1966–1969) being mostly an exception. Literary science fiction as found in novels takes its readers seriously and presents issues found in the best of literature. Farah Mendlesohn, a lecturer in American History at the University College of Ripon and York St. John in England, as well as assistant editor for the scholarly journal *Foundation: The International Review of Science Fiction,* presents a similar argument about *Babylon 5:* "The depth of research embedded in this show is fascinating. Season two in particular seemed to be following very closely the break down of the League of Nations in the inter-war years," she explains, "and while Straczynski says that the Yugoslav crisis helped shape his ideas, he clearly also knows his political history of the 1930s" (in Lancaster 1997:13).

This kind of literary achievement contrasts strikingly with the kinds of stories that are "sci-fi," that pejorative term designating what Harlan Ellison (the creative consultant for B5 and the only writer to be honored with the Television Writers' Guild of America Award four times) calls "cheapjack foolishness." Sci-fi is found in the tabloid mentality of UFO abductions, triangular-headed ETs, reinterpreted biblical apocrypha, and just plain bone stick stone gullibility" that the Heaven's Gate cultists got caught up in, he explains (1997). *Independence Day* (1996) is an example of sci-fi. Scholar Mendlesohn agrees that *Babylon 5* is not this brand of sci-fi, but is sf, the acronym associated with literary merit: "B5 is the first piece of television sf to bear any resemblance" to literary science fiction novels, she says. "It has plot depth and more importantly political depth. It does what only sf can do—deal with the major issues without getting too polemical" (1997).

Within these claims, Straczynski's social front is further defined and performed as a producer who creates a literary form of science fiction television, one that deals with issues while at the same time offering an innovative way for pushing the limits of the medium. Just as *Star Trek* became equated with Gene Roddenberry, *Babylon 5* has become Straczynski's social front:

> I created B5 because it was the story I not only wanted to tell, but the story I *needed* to tell. Using sf as a venue would allow me to deal in larger questions and issues of controversy without the political limitations that tend to be applied to other shows. Make the character a minority group member, and lots of complications enter the equation if that character is shown in an unfavorable light; ditto if you show a Caucasian of a particular political stripe (either side, actually) . . . but the moment you substitute *alien* aliens, substitute interstellar affairs for geopolitical struggles, you have a new tool at your disposal: metaphor. And you can tackle issues without the political baggage from either side of the spectrum. (1997e)

Straczynski uses science fiction as a metaphor to comment on today's political and social struggles. One such struggle had its birth in the post–World War II space race, where the desire for empire was extended out into space. As this project failed in the 1970s, these ideals were fictionalized in various television shows, films, and novels. The 1980s and 1990s saw an increased awareness of postcolonial struggles: where nations, left behind in the postimperial wake, had to assert their own individuality and desire in an increasingly shrinking world. Straczynski's *Babylon 5* consistently casts international actors, and key characters are aliens who want to assert their individuality in a diverse galaxy that seems increasingly circled by the upstart humans dominating the political and market economies.

Straczynski set his epic saga on *Babylon 5*, a large cylinder-shaped space station five miles long. Its rotation provides gravity through centrifugal force similar to the mysterious ship found in Arthur C. Clark's novel *Rendezvous with Rama* (1973). Like Rama, *Babylon 5* contains buildings and meadows inside its rotating hull (see figure 5.11, page [144]). Essentially a city of 250,000, *Babylon 5* hosts many different kinds of alien species who live and interact with each other. A cross between a United Nations and Times Square in space, it offers a place of neutrality where aliens and humans communicate their desires and needs in a galaxy of expanding commerce, discovery, and war. Through the Minbari character of Delenn, for example, Straczynski tells the story of a superior alien "race" that had attempted to wipe out the humans. Straczynski hired Yugoslavian film and theater star Mira Furlan to play this character; she had moved to the United States after receiving death threats for refusing to step down from an interracial theater production during the early stages of the Serbian war of ethnic cleansing against Croatians and, later, Bosnians.

Paralleling this, Furlan's character, Delenn, was responsible for carrying on a war not just of ethnic cleansing, but of a species extermination. In the end, however, it was her "humanity" that saved the humans. She goes on to marry one of them, and together they create an alliance that attempts to forge a new peace during the dawn of the Third Age of Mankind—one that is predominantly human-centered and—some might argue—mainly white, a nomenclature representing middle-class values found in the United States at the end of the twentieth century. These issues are present despite the fact that Straczynski claims how his show is able to avoid these issues by using metaphor, allowing one to "tackle issues without the political baggage from either side of the spectrum." In this case, the reality leaks outside the border of the social front Straczynski projects, for within this metaphorical spectrum *are* issues of race, class, and gender.

It is worth just touching upon some of these issues here—to acknowledge their presence. Through the story he controls, Straczynski has placed his characters in situations that eventually lead to the Great War of the Third Age of Mankind, but by the middle of the fourth season the war has ended, and the characters deal with the war's aftermath. The fifth season deals with the political ramifications of reconstruction, led mainly by a white human and a white human-looking Minbari. Bernardi claims, in *Star Trek and History: Race-ing Toward a White Future* (1998), that, similar to "state activity, culture plays a determining role in the hegemonic trajectory—the historical significance—of race" (1998:20). This hegemonic trajectory is the "acceptance of a historical moment as natural or in the best interest of all groups involved" (18). Within the cultural studies paradigm, the issue of race and gender is not about whether one has a certain skin color or sexual organ. It is rather an issue of how a person can be defined and labeled within a hegemonic structure that doesn't allow room for difference on the basis of true equality.[1] So, yes, when John Sheridan and Delenn persuade many of the alien races on board to fight the evil black-colored Shadows on a side representing light—as showcased by the Vorlons, who are made essentially of white light—it does, to some extent, further the cultural code that dark is equated with evil and light with the forces of good. Thus it can be argued that these cultural assumptions are played out as cultural and social codes embedded within the games comprising the imaginary entertainment environment of *Babylon 5*.

Straczynski tries to elide issues of race and class by transcending the debate into the realm of generic humanity, writing stories about the "issues of eternal debate, the Big Questions," such as "who are we, where are we going, why are we here, and what should we as a people be doing to create the future?" Within these kinds of questions he "examines the role of spirituality in a technological culture; the nature and extent of revenge; what is the nature of the soul and how is it formed; the fundamental importance of choice, consequence, and responsibility for those choices in a society that tells you that you have no choices, that consequences don't matter, and that we don't have to act responsibly" (1997e). The explanation of these issues is again part of Straczynski's performance—placing his show within the "eternal debate" of humanity—in an attempt to legitimize his own show in the minds of others. He leaves the main issues of race, class, and gender mainly within the realm of alien metaphor. One could go much deeper into this analysis, but the focus at this point

1. This is clear in today's politics when Democrats and Republicans enact their desire to redraw Congressional districts to favor their constituencies: Republicans try to keep the lines mainly white and middle-class, while Democrats want to make sure the lines reflect an interracial population, so minorities can have a stronger voice within the government.

must return to the performance analysis of the show and of Straczynski. However, for the record, it is only fair to say that Straczynski presents in some of the stories of *Babylon 5* multicultural and multiracial issues and themes, including the depiction of lesbian and bisexual characters (Ivanova), straight relationships (Garibaldi), inter-species-racial relationships (Sheridan and Delenn), homeless elderly characters, impoverished people (lurkers in downbelow), religious diversity, and blue-collar workers.

Holographic Storytelling: From Aristotle to Brecht

One of the most interesting aspects of Straczynski's show is that, in telling his five-year saga, he uses a narrative form rarely used in television storytelling. Fundamentally, there are two major forms of narrative structure writers typically employ. One derives from the writings of Aristotle and the other from playwright Bertolt Brecht, who published an anti-Aristotelian form of drama in 1927. Aristotle explicated his theories on playwriting in the fourth century BCE, defining dramatic tragedy in his *Poetics* as an "imitation of an action that is serious, complete, and of a certain magnitude; . . . through pity and fear effecting the proper purgation of these emotions" (1961:61). He goes on to explain how plot should be constructed as a sequence of actions, linking its beginning, middle, and end together by causality. Aristotle's thoughts on epic drama are somewhat similar to the ideas he lays out for tragic drama, with the exception that an epic has a "multiplicity of plots" (91) and has a "different scale on which it is constructed" (107), by which, "owing to the narrative form, many events simultaneously transacted can be presented" (108). These "varying episodes," he says, "add mass and dignity" and conduce "to grandeur of effect" the story (108).

Over time, the epic has commonly been attributed to the Aristotelian definition, eventually being applied to films that are grand and rather lengthy. Critics refer to such films as *Gone With the Wind* (1939), *Lawrence of Arabia* (1962), and the more recent *Braveheart* (1995) and *Titanic* (1997) as epics. In vernacular parlance "epic" means something grand, heroic, solemn, or, as *Merriam Webster* (1997) describes it, "extending beyond the usual or ordinary especially in size or scope." And yet that most up-to-date dictionary, and even the dated Aristotle, as well as contemporary critics, fail to offer a definition or theory of epic that differentiates it substantially from conventional Aristotelian drama. Describing something that is grand and heroic containing multiple plots does not really capture the essence and structure of the multilayered sagas found in Homer's epics,

Dramatic Theatre	Epic Theatre
plot	narrative
implicates the spectator in a stage situation	turns the spectator into an observer but,
wears down his capacity for action	arouses his capacity for action
provides him with sensations	forces him to take decisions
experience	picture of the world
spectator is involved in something	he is made to face something
suggestion	argument
instinctive feelings are preserved	brought to the point of recognition
the spectator is in the thick of it, shares the experience	the spectator stands outside, studies
the human being is taken for granted	the human being is the object of the inquiry
he is unalterable	he is alterable and able to alter
eyes on the finish	eyes on the course
one scene makes another	each scene for itself
growth	montage
linear development	in curves
evolutionary determinism	jumps
man as a fixed point	man as a process
thought determines being	social being determines thought
feeling	reason

1001 Nights, the plays of Bertolt Brecht, and the science fiction sagas of Asimov (*Foundation*), Bradbury (*The Martian Chronicles*), or Straczynski (*Babylon 5*), to name only a few—all of which are grand in scale and certainly contain variety in their scene structure. These literary forms come closer to a form posited by Brecht in 1927 in a short piece called "The Modern Theatre Is the Epic Theatre." In this brief essay (really program notes to the opera *Aufstieg and Fall der Stadt Mahagonny*), Brecht presents a table that "shows certain changes of emphasis as between the dramatic and epic theatre" (1992:37): The attributes of the dramatic form are almost antithetical to the corresponding attributes in the epic column. The two are not necessarily aesthetic opposites, but when placed alongside each other in a production, their differences become heightened and the spectator receives a form of distanciation—what Brecht called a process of "alienation" (1992:125).

Ultimately, as his theory evolved, Brecht felt that the Aristotelian form "cast a spell" over the audience, transporting them from "normality to 'higher realms'" (1992:122). He wanted, instead, stage productions which, after sucking people into the reality of the stage illusion, distanced the spectators *from* the reality in order to perceive how the *content* spoke to the contemporaneous political, social, and cultural milieu of the audience. The structural aspects of an epic are easier to determine than the social theory Brecht describes. It is rather difficult to see if the social state and awareness of spectators are more altered as a consequence of being exposed to the Aristotelian dramatic form or to the Brechtian epic style. One can easily determine the structural aspects of storytelling and characterization *within* the dramatic text itself by seeing if it adheres to the "dramatic" or the "epic" qualities as spelled out by Brecht. It is more difficult to determine if the subjective view of an audience is altered. What can be seen, however, is whether the production style of a particular play (or television script) adheres more closely to the epic or to the dramatic form.

In the Aristotelian form, "one scene makes another," while in the Brechtian mold "each scene [is] for itself" (1992:37). In *Babylon 5*, the structure of the story is told through what Brecht refers to as the epic quality of montage. In the case of *Babylon 5*, this montage occurs through *entire episodes*. Most of them stand on their own and adhere to the Aristotelian form, but when viewed in their entirety, the juxtaposition of episodes reveals the epic structure of the story. Straczynski calls it holographic storytelling, after one of his crew members told him about it:

> "What it IS," [the crew member] said, "is not side-by-side images, but *overlapping* images, like old fashioned photographic plates stacked up one on top of the other. Each has a piece of the whole picture. When you line them all up, one behind the other, and look through all of them at once, you realize what the picture is. It's three-dimensional storytelling."
>
> I had to think about that one for a long time, but frankly, he's right, and I'm wrong. That *IS* what we're doing, and I've been describing it incorrectly all this time.
>
> Holographic storytelling . . . well, live and learn, I say. (1994h)

This approach focuses on the process of telling the story and is not—like Aristotelian drama—designed to pull the spectator toward a climatic ending. It is the process of watching the story unfold (the "eyes on the course") and not the anticipation of finding out what is going to happen at the end (the "eyes on the finish") that Straczynski, like Brecht, feels is important. This kind of antilinear storytelling evolves through such epic qualities as curves, jumps, and showing characters in the process of development.

One fan complained once about the "well made" (or Aristotelian) television show:

> One of the things that annoys me about some TV shows is the unbalanced timing. The main crisis takes too long to build up to, and the resolution takes place in the last 5 minutes, or in some cases, during the last commercial break.
>
> B5 seems to me to be a lot more balanced in this respect. Do you try to begin the resolution by a certain time to allow time to show the actual resolution before the final break, and use the epilogue for something else? Or just how do you try to do it? Is it in the editing?

Straczynski replies:

> It's generally the same . . . I use a straightforward approach to the stories: teaser sets the tone for the episode, hooks the audience, makes you wonder what the heck's going on. First act introduces the problem in greater detail; here and in act two you get the characters dealing with the problem, with a major problem or complication hitting at the bottom of act 2 . . . act three prepares your characters to deal with the situation, and act four deals with the situation, leaving the tag (and sometimes part of the fourth act) to have some nice character moments. (1998b)

Although many individual episodes of *Babylon 5* tend to adhere to a conventional model of drama, the series taken as a whole has an epic structure. It is not a 90-hour miniseries or movie linked together by Aristotelian causality. Like scenes from Brecht's plays, most episodes of *Babylon 5* stand alone. Scene B does not immediately follow scene A, as in the Aristotelian format. They thematically progress toward an ending—but not in a rising climax (as found in the Aristotelian model), but rather through the depiction of historical moments. Straczynski shows the five-year history of *Babylon 5* as a historical process. This allows him to write episodes that do not end in its given one-hour time frame.

In the pilot film, *The Gathering* (1993), Straczynski foreshadowed events that would not be revealed until the beginning of the second season. For example, the Minbari assassin revealed to commander Sinclair that, "There is a hole in your mind." A typical movie would not have included such a plot point if it was not resolved within its two-hour structure. Even though there was no guarantee that the pilot movie would lead into a full series, Straczynski kept the line, slowly raising the mystery throughout the first season, without answering it, partly, until the beginning of the second, and not wholly until the third season's "War without End."

The difference between Aristotle and Brecht can be seen by comparing the conclusion of *Star Wars: A New Hope* (1977) and the conclusion to the Great War in *Babylon 5*. When Luke Skywalker flew his X-Wing fighter down the trench to destroy the Death Star, he turned off his targeting computer, which was designed to guide proton torpedoes. Instead, he used the Force—a spiritual power more accurate than a computer—to guide the torpedoes into the Death Star's small exhaust port. *Star Wars* followed an Aristotelian structure. The scenes built to a causal climax leading to the destruction of the Death Star. On the other hand, in the fourth-season *Babylon 5* episode "Into the Fire"—the climax to a war that had its genesis in the first season—John Sheridan used reason to ultimately end the war with the Vorlons and Shadows, two paternal First Ones, ancient species evolving in the galaxy for millions of years. They had diametrical views on how to "shepherd" the younger races, such as the humans, Narn, Minbari, and Centauri. The Vorlons believed that the younger races should be guided morally, while the Shadows wanted them to evolve through a form of Darwinian conflict, the weaker dying in favor of the stronger. Sheridan realized that it was time for the younger species to lead themselves without any "parental" influence—whether through moral guidance or evolution through conflict. He talked the First Ones into leaving the galaxy. The war ended not through superior firepower and not even through a military victory, but through one of the most important qualities found in Brecht's list for the epic model: reason. It is clear that Straczynski's approach is closer to the Brechtian method of epic storytelling ("the human being is the object of the inquiry"), as opposed to the more conventional Aristotelian drama ("the human being is taken for granted") that has dominated much of Western storytelling. This kind of writing, Straczynski believes, helps him provide what he calls "guideposts" for humanity.

"As a culture we have come adrift, and are searching for guideposts to the next five years, the next ten years, the next millennium," Straczynski explains. Much of today's literature, he feels, fails to explore large mythic themes that create these guideposts. "The mainstream literary establishment has walked away from the mythmakers, the storytellers' obligation to point to the horizon and tell us where we are going," he states. And he believes that "science fiction is the only genre dealing with the issues of the future and our place in it" (1997e). However, all literature, to a greater or lesser extent, reveals some aspect of the human condition. To say that it is only legitimized through science fiction is an attempt on Straczynski's part to legitimize a genre that is usually referred to pejoratively. Straczynski is a fan/creator and he must dramatize his role as a science fiction producer, for, as Goffman contends, "While in the presence of others, the individual typically infuses his activity with signs which dramatically highlight and portray confirmatory facts that might otherwise remain unapparent or obscure" (1959:30). Straczynski's social front allows him to define himself as a knowledgeable producer, while permitting him the chance to present his own agenda—giving validation to science fiction as a form of television literature.

In an episode from the third season, "Passing through Gethsemane," Straczynski told the story of a Christian monk who was once a serial killer. In Straczynski's universe there is no death penalty. Instead, a criminal's mind is wiped clean and filled with new memories. The murderer in this case was brainwashed into serving mankind. "Is this more or less humane than the death penalty?" Straczynski asks (1997e). His story explores an issue that could conceivably take place in the future and parallels in some ways the current moral debate on the death penalty. His story revolves around the following questions: "What happens when someone like this finds out the truth? Is his soul the soul of a priest, or a killer? Which is the real person? How does he apologize for his sins if he does not remember them? How does he face his god knowing that his soul is the soul of a murderer?" Typical of Straczynski's writing, he doesn't "provide answers to those questions because there *are* no answers," he claims. "But it's important to ask the question. That's the problem with television: too many easy answers and not damned near enough good questions" (1997e). These kinds of philosophical questions and moral issues make his show significant and therefore him significant in the eyes of his fans: "if the individual's activity is to become significant to others, he must mobilize his activity so that it will express *during the interaction* what he wishes to convey" (Goffman 1959:30).

In this way we see another facet of Straczynski's social front—one of educator. He believes that when viewers understand how television shows are made, then "viewers can demand better tv. That's why I've been online every day, for hours a day, since the show went into production. I want those who watch our show to understand why things are done the way they're done in tv, what elements go into the creative and decision-making process. You cannot control what you do not understand" (1997e). But, it must be noted that he also is able to "watch" his own performance online through these postings. He gets feedback on the shows from his fans, who comprise his audience. His responses as well as those of the fans are archived for later viewing on various Web sites. In his role as producer-educator, we see Straczynski come across as a kind of television innovator, creating a series on nearly one-half the budge of *Star Trek:* 1) He saved one-third of his budget by completing scripts well in advance of preproduction (alleviating any need for last-minute overtime by workers to complete set construction, for example); 2) the use of inexpensive, yet aesthetically pleasing computer-generated special effects; 3) writing a science fiction novel for television.

One of his most significant contributions to the television novel is his five-year story arc, for which he had planned a beginning, middle, and end, the story mapped out like a novel. At one point, during a science fiction convention in Seattle, Straczynski pulled out notes containing various plot-points and story-lines for the fifth season. When a fan pointed out this apparent discrepancy between these fresh notes planning the fifth season and the well-known fact that he had written the story out ahead of time as in a novel, Straczynski curtly held to the latter (1997g). Whether he was fleshing out already existing stories or whether he was creating new stories and saying he had the entire five-year story planned out with the detail of novel remained unclear during that convention. He has since made it clear by selling copies of the first season's "Writer's Bible" to *Babylon 5*, indicating how much of the story was mapped out. His major story arc was planned out, and details evolved as the seasons progressed.

This event, like his interactions with fans online, helps Straczynski protect the image of his show and of himself as the innovative producer. It is his kind of show he wants viewers to understand, so that they will continue to watch it. Thousands of pages documenting this process for *Babylon 5* can be found online at the "Lurker's Guide to *Babylon 5*" (www.midwinter.com/lurk/lurker.html). "This is already being used by academicians and other groups to study the medium and learn how better to ask for programs they want, as opposed to the programs they're given,"

Straczynski insists. "And producers of other shows would learn a great deal from this kind of exposure; it's quite bracing, and Hollywood is far, far too insular" (1997e).

From Praise to Criticism: Interacting with the Fans

In an attempt to avoid this trend of Hollywood insularity, Straczynski decided that he would keep an open door to his fans as well as to critics by daily going online to interact with them in order to provide answers to them about the show (except for a three-month hiatus between January and March 1996). In all, he posted over 17,000 replies. This allowed fans not only to participate in the *Babylon 5* universe, but also to interact at a critical level with the creator of that universe. In this way these "spectators stand outside" the drama in order to study it with an almost Brechtian distance. Scholar Henry Jenkins even believes (arguably) that the level of attention fans pay to the "particularity of television narratives . . . puts academic critics to shame" (1992:86). Constance Penley agrees: "there is no better critic than a fan. No one knows the object better than a fan and no one is more critical" (1997:3). During her time "hanging out" with *Star Trek* fanfic writers in the 1980s, Penley believed that these "amateur writers . . . ingeniously subverted and re[wrote] *Star Trek* to make it answerable to their own sexual and social desires" (2–3). (This process, occurring among *Babylon 5* fans, is described in Chapter 5.) Penley even feels that her own "critical stance" as a scholar grew from what she learned from these fan writers: "what I learned most from them was an *attitude* that I later developed into a critical stance" (3).

This kind of attitude challenges the social front Straczynski performs as a television producer. As a science fiction fan he can lurk (observe other postings online without interacting) and post messages on various Web sites, attend science fiction conventions, and talk with other fans as just another person. However, as soon as it became established that he was the creator and head writer—the show runner—of *Babylon 5*, a series many fans love, he could no longer move about with anonymity. In performing the social role of a producer—a business person—Straczynski could never escape the fact that the customer is always right (even when they are wrong). Goffman contends that when a person assumes a professional role in life—whether that of a mail carrier or, as in Straczynski's case, of a television producer—he is not taking on a "material thing, to be possessed and then displayed; it is a pattern of appropriate conduct" that must be "enacted and portrayed, . . . realized" (1959:75).

It is within Straczynski's online social performance that we can begin to see his persona as producer break, and the flippant fan personality—the personality he contends against as embodied by some fan-critics—becomes his own persona, and the "pattern of appropriate conduct" comprising his producer front self-destructs. When one fan asked if he had taken the name for one alien species, the Minbari, from a science fiction novel by C. J. Cherryh, Straczynski "flamed out," his answer revealing his defensiveness when it comes to the perceived unliterary role of his profession:

> No, I did not use "The Faded Sun" [trilogy] as (to quote you) "a source when [I] created the Minbari."
> That's called plagiarism.
>
> And now I'm going to vent for a moment.
>
> Why the fuck is it that every time a TV writer comes up with something, everybody scurries to figure out what book or short story it was swiped from? That standard is virtually never applied to novels that I've seen. But it always comes to us TeeVee types.
>
> I have a brain, you know. I'm perfectly capable of thinking up stuff on my own. I've published novels. I've published short stories. I've written plays. I've never read ANY of Cherryh's work that I can recall.
>
> Instead of suggesting something was cribbed, all you needed to say was, "So, JMS, where did you get the name Minbari?"
>
> And I would've told you that a "minbar" is the name for a pulpit in a Mosque. The first time I heard that, I thought it would be great as a name for an alien or an alien planet. And the people who would live there would be called Minbari.
>
> Not everything that comes out of TV is cribbed, okay?
>
> End of venting.
>
> If I seem a bit pissed, it's not specifically directed at you but at the general sense that TV writers have the creative capacity of blowfish and are incapable of creating *anything* on their own. (And you weren't pointing to just the name but to the whole concept and parts thereof.) I don't mean to flame, but I've heard it enough over the years, and I'm getting a little tired of it.
>
> Every TV writer gets it, and almost no prose writer does, and that's simple discrimination and stereotyping. (1994c)

This example shows Straczynski losing his "expressive coherence," to use Goffman's term, and it is here that we can see what Goffman means when he says that there is a "crucial discrepancy between our all-too-human selves and our socialized selves. As human beings we are presumably creatures of variable impulse with moods and energies that change from one moment to the next. As characters put on for an audience, however, we must not be subject to ups and downs" (1959:56). Straczynski is unable or unwilling to maintain the polite role of producer to his customer, an eager fan, and so an analysis of his online performance reveals his "ups and downs." Part of this expectation placed on Straczynski may derive from the fact that both roles Straczynski and his fans perform—the social front they project—have become, as Goffman would say, "institutionalized in terms of the abstract stereotyped expectations" (1959:27) to which they give rise. Straczynski, whether he likes it or not, is dealing predominantly with a strong *Star Trek* fandom, and these fans were used to the outgoing congenial personality of Gene Roddenberry, which was much different from Straczynski's somewhat introverted, shy personality.

Since Straczynski never is able to get the last word in online, he at one point used his role of producer to convey a message through his television show. Working within this tension between criticizing the medium he writes in—having fought every year to get his show renewed—and the critics who would have loved to see their predictions become the epitaph on yet another failed science fiction series, Straczynski placed the following coda at the end of the concluding fourth-season episode, "The Deconstruction of Falling Stars": "Dedicated to all the people who predicted that the Babylon Project would fail in its mission. . . . Faith manages." This episode was filmed after TNT gave the producers of *Babylon 5* a fifth season. Straczynski had, in fact, previously written and directed what was to be the final episode of *Babylon 5*. After receiving the fifth-season renewal, he pulled the series' closer and placed the segment at the end of the fifth season, writing "Deconstruction" as the replacement for the fourth-season slot. The coda was Straczynski's way of celebrating the fact that they had received their fifth season, despite all the critics who said that *Babylon 5* would not make it. As some fans criticized his show online, the statement was also one way for Straczynski to try to maintain control of the universe he had created. Some fans, however, continue to challenge his authority.

At one point, a fan posted a message online: "Up to ['Into the Fire'] was good, but I can't stand the aftermath, or what I see as JMS' condescending and holier than thou attitude towards fans." Straczynski responded by explaining how some people look to "spoilers" (the release of plot points for a story before it is aired) to determine where a story is heading and usually get it wrong—they "look ahead and write off the shows forthcoming." So, Straczynski said to this fan that "the little gift I dropped into 'Deconstruction' [is] for folks who read spoilers and then dismiss the show as a result" (1997d). This both reveals the playfulness of Straczynski's approach in dealing with his critics, and also renders a recorded performance that locates *Babylon 5* within a history of television production made up of people who have personal feelings, desires, and tastes—all of which determine which shows make it and which fail in the competitive television market. Straczynski knows this all too well, and he must maintain, as much as possible, the role of polite producer for fans, who, in Goffman's words, "grudgingly allow certain symbols of status to establish a performer's right to a given treatment, [. . .] are always ready to pounce on chinks in his symbolic armor in order to discredit his pretensions" (1959:58–59).

The posting of a message online constitutes a performance that does display the type of behavior Goffman defines, despite the fact that the event has already occurred. The posting is not only the record of the event —it *is* the event, the performance between fan and producer displayed on a digital public stage. The original performance between the fan's question, the producer's answer, and then their reading of that answer later is simultaneously the performance and the surface record of the performance. The performance actually occurred within the minds of the fan and Straczynski. Their words—and not gestures or vocal intonations—delineate the physical (or textual) ontology of a virtual performance.

With Internet exchanges, the performance of self is drawn as lines of text. People perform with textual utterances that Austin referred to as a "performative" back in 1955: "The uttering of the words is, indeed, usually a, or even *the,* leading incident in the performance of the act" (1975:8). On the Internet—where there are no verbal utterances—the written text is equivalent to the spoken word. The utterances between Straczynski and fans are not just used to help engage an action—they *are* the action. The "effect upon the referent" in a performative utterance, philosopher Jean-Francois Lyotard explains, "coincides with its enunciation" (1984:9). The reader of such exchanges is reconfigured into the role of spectator in observance of Straczynski's performance of his social front (as defined by Goffman).

Straczynski is unique in Hollywood in that he answers his fans, sometimes defensively. It is this performance between the fans and a producer, however, which immerses them not only in his imaginary universe, but also in his public persona (as a producer). For some fans, to have questions about a producer's show actually answered by the creator and writer of the series is as an honor. When "standing" in the presence of one whom some refer to as "the Great Maker," fans may feel closer to the imaginary universe of *Babylon 5*. Answers to their questions—the performative utterances—place them near the same orbit as the maker of a universe they have watched for five years on television. These fans show the proper obligation of respect to their hero and, in return, receive the same respect. In essence, as Goffman would say, "they commonly seek to acquire information about him or to bring into play information about him already possessed" (1959:1). Many fans perform the role of follower of the Great Maker, asking him specific information about *Babylon 5*. He presumably answers with the authority of one who knows. Straczynski's historical performance of his social front helps shape the exchanges with his fans: "Informed of these ways, the others will know how best to act in order to call forth a desired response from him," Goffman contends (1).

In one recent post, a fan asked Straczynski a perceptive question about a particular plot point after watching the reedited and rebroadcast original pilot movie, *The Gathering* (1993; 1998). Ambassador Kosh, one of the First Ones, sees Commander Sinclair and recognizes him from 1,000 years ago. "So Kosh recognizes that Sinclair is the same person he knew 1000 years in the past as Valen; since Kosh didn't know that this wasn't really Sinclair (else why greet him so?) wouldn't this have given Sinclair a dangerous foreknowledge?" (1998a). This attention to detail and expertise are outside the realm of the observation of most scholars of popular culture, Jenkins argues, giving fans the default status of a "competing education elite, albeit one without official recognition or social power" (1992:86). Most producers are not themselves fans, nor grew out of fandom, and thus they would not even bother to communicate with fans at a critical level about the material they create. So this fan's question, and the thousands like it, would normally circulate within fandom. The competing answers among fans would constitute the only critical discourse on *Babylon 5*. Straczynski, however, apparently answers nearly every question asked by fans. His answer to the above question silences the apparent inconsistency: "Internal dialogue . . . what he was thinking, his reaction" (1998a).

During the first season, Straczynski even incorporated a few ideas from fans into the show, maintaining his role as a producer who cares about his fans. One such instance occurred when he was trying to think of a name for a new kind of mineral; his ideas were repeatedly rejected by the legal department at Warner Bros.:

> When names submitted for a mega corporation and a mineral were rejected for legal reasons, JMS went to the [online service] GEnie B5 Category and asked for suggestions.

The resulting names used are Quantium-40 for the mineral and Universal Terraform for the company. Q-40 is mentioned in "The Parliament of Dreams" and "Mind War." The waiter mentioned in "Parliament" is named for David Strauss, who submitted Q-40. ("Lurker's Guide to *Babylon 5*")

This is the kind of interaction with the fans that Straczynski prefers to perform—it is a logical outcome of the social front he has created for himself (and which is, in some cases, now expected of him—so he becomes defined by his own previous actions and the expectations arising from those actions). If a character in a play, for example, performs an action that does not have any logical grounding in any previous scenes, then the audience knows that something does not ring true—the character seems false.

One time a fan complained about Sheridan's command—in the episode "Endgame" (1997b)—to increase his ship's velocity to ramming speed in an attempt to destroy an orbital weapons platform before it could turn its destructive power against the surface of Earth: "There simply isn't one speed that's better for ramming than other speeds. But just asking for 'ramming speed' is Just Plain Silly. It can be retconned [?], it can be forgiven, but it's Just Plain Silly" (1997f). This kind of criticism gives fans a form of critical empowerment. They, as Jenkins says, have a "moral right to complain about producer actions challenging their own interest in the series property" (1992:87). In this case it was right for that viewer to complain about an action that did not seem logical to him. Thanks to online communication, and Straczynski's desire to read fan questions, he fired back an answer. This time, however, his response, as previously seen in a majority of fan postings, does not have the same tone, and it reflects more irritation than some might expect from an authoritative producer in his position:

(he taps his foot as yet another expert lurches into the field.)

You are in a space ship, in a vacuum, heading toward target X. You understand that it takes time to transfer energy and movement toward another plane, so you go at X-speed toward that object if you want the option of applying thrusters and angling away from the object before you slam into it.

If, on the other hand, you *want* to hit the object, and you have no interest in holding back your thrusters to allow you to diverge from the target in the amount of space remaining between you and it, you proceed at Y speed, with your thrusters putting out their maximum amount of fuel.

Y = ramming speed. (1997g)

Although Straczynski seems to answer the complaint with logical detachment, his opening sentence of impatience is inconsistent with what fans may expect from their hero-producer, and, as Goffman contends, even "sympathetic audiences can be momentarily disturbed, shocked, and weakened in their faith by the discovery of a picayune discrepancy in the impressions presented to them" (1959:51). Many other producers in Hollywood usually avoid such public performances as online interactions.

Straczynski wanted to answer for his show. He did not want to leave fans outside the producer's circle and its knowledge of how a show is made, and he felt that the fans of a television show deserve to be treated well by those who are responsible for making it. He has always felt that "sf media fans are the most exploited group of viewers around. They're expected to watch the show, pony up the dough for merchandise, then shut up and be good little viewers" (1994c). Straczynski says that he doesn't expect the viewers of his show to shut up. He wants to hear their voices. "It's very difficult at times—emotionally, and in terms of time and energy—to stick around (there are currently 1,154 messages in my GEni internet mailbox), but I think that it's important to keep with it. Because it's a way of showing respect to the viewer, to be open and accountable and responsive. Sometimes I get cranky, but I'm human, and that'll happen from time to time. Usually I avoid that" (1994c). Straczynski believes that he has the right to behave in the same manner and tone as his fan-critics, but when he does, he is no longer performing within the producer front many fans expect of him.

At one point, a *Star Trek* fan sent Straczynski an email "bomb" that, when downloaded onto his hard drive, "exploded"—deleting files from storage, including a *Babylon 5* script he was writing. A message popped up on screen: "*Star Trek* Lives." Other virulent fans have flamed Straczynski out of an unmoderated Internet news-group, forcing him into a three-month hiatus, until a moderated site could be set up. (The postings on a moderated site are prescreened.) Partly, these fan attacks originate in the fact that many science fiction shows, placed in an ever tighter market, have to fight to garner their ratings. Jenkins believes that these "fears of competition may be valid, since the emergence of a new fan interest can often be the center of a succession of shifting alliances" (1992:91). Some *Star Trek* fans (and executives) did not want to lose their ratings to *Babylon 5*. In addition, many fans are not able to give input on their favorite shows. In the case of *Babylon 5*, they end up releasing this frustration on the producer. They attack because the anonymous medium allows them to perform their own social fronts in which they themselves attempt to exert legitimacy as individuals with valid opinions, when they otherwise have no voice in the show they want to critique.

Cultural critic Mark Dery believes that "the wraithlike nature of electronic communication accelerates the escalation of hostilities when tempers flare; disembodied, sometimes pseudonymous combatants tend to feel that they can hurl insults with impunity (or at least without bodily harm)" (1994:1). Email bombs and vitriolic attacks sent online are an extreme form of communication that pushes the boundaries of Jenkins' belief that "organized fandom is, perhaps and foremost, an institution of theory and criticism, a semistructured space where competing interpretations and evaluations of common texts are proposed, debated, and negotiated and where readers speculate about the nature of mass media and their own relationship to it" (1992:86).

The fans' relationship with Straczynski is typically performed within the social front—his rules of the situation as he defines it. He is the creator and producer who can log off the Internet at any time. Each fan who realizes this must perhaps interact within the situation as defined by Straczynski. This fan-producer consensus is, as Goffman would say, a kind of "veneer" and it is "facilitated by each participant concealing his own wants behind statements which assert values to which everyone present feels obliged to give lip service" (1959:9). By doing so, "the participants contribute to a single over-all definition of the situation which involves not so much a real agreement as to what exists but rather a real agreement as to whose claims concerning what issues will be temporarily honored" (9–10). Straczynski attempts to fight for this honor—to remain as a respected producer in the eyes of his fans.

However, when this "working consensus" is no longer honored, then any "defensive practices" employed by Straczynski to maintain his social front—"to safeguard the impression fostered by an individual during his presence before others" (1959:14)—cracks, as can be seen in the two examples below. At the close of *Babylon 5*'s first season, as rumors spread that Michael O'Hare was fired at the end of season one and his character, Commander Sinclair, written out of the show, Straczynski answered this concern with his typical logic: "Someone should point out to [the fan-critic] the article appearing this week (out in many newspapers already) for the Tribune Syndicate, in which [the journalist] states that, based on her interviews and sources, it WAS a mutual and amicable parting, that Sinclair is NOT gone, and basically reinforces every single point made here [on the Net]" (1994e). But then he ends this statement more vehemently: "Assuming anyone really cares anymore . . . frankly, I'm getting pretty fucking tired and disgusted with the whole discussion. [This fan] is an idiot, pure and simple" (1994e).

In 1994 he put one fan "on notice," after receiving what he claims was continual harassment:

[Name of fanatic]: you have ended your messages with a "quote" from me stating, "I'm foolin' 'em with these funny footprints!" As with much of what comes out of your and [and that other fanatic's] mouth, this is a lie and a fabrication, I never made that statement.

Just what the hell is your problem, anyway? You put info out that I'm fired, you misquote me, you lie to others on [Internet] systems about me . . . this is stalking behavior on your part, and I'm getting very, very tired of it, and I'm not going to stand for much more of it. You may consider that I am now putting you on formal notice. Henceforth, all further fabrications and downright lies that you post, all harassing messages sent by you, all rumors and deliberate distortions will be forwarded from me to my attorneys, and gathered to be filed with an attorney in your state for potential prosecution under libel laws and anti-stalking laws. Further, I may be forced to take personal legal action against you. Remember that I have your address.

You have deliberately manufactured quotes from me. You have stated, as fact, that I was fired from my job. You have told others that I tracked you down for disagreeing with me, when in fact (as others here can and have agreed to testify), it was incident #1, the firing story, that prompted this action. You (and now, our latest homunculus, [name of another fanatic]) deliberately distort and misrepresent and simply lie about matters injurious to my (and in the latter case, Michael O'Hare's) career.

I would also request the sysop of the system from which you are logging in to be aware of your stalking behavior, and to reconsider your continued access to this forum.

I have had enough of this obsessive behavior from you. You are now under formal notice to stop it and stop it now. I don't know what the reason is for this sick fixation of yours, but get some help for it.

If you don't stop, you, and your family, and your employer will be hearing from my attorneys in very short order.

Enough is enough. (1994e)

Straczynski believes that it is such behavior by obsessive fanatics that deters other producers from logging on to the Internet for discussions:

Y'know . . . [Producers James] Morgan and [Harry] Wong from *X-Files* used to be on the nets a lot, and they got out because they were driven to despair by the casual, callous cruelties of people who judge harshly and without any kind of information . . .

[*Babylon 5* actress] Mira [Furlan] was on for a while, and isn't on anymore, because she says people are just casually cruel, they bitch about things that aren't even true half the time. I know a lot of others, actors and producers, who just don't want to put up with this crap. Some days, I don't blame them. Some days, I think I'd like to join them. (1997f)

In July 1998 Straczynski logged off America Online—his main Internet account—after an irate fan flooded his email box with so many messages that his important mail was shunted aside. (Complaints to AOL did not help.) He has continued to keep his Compuserve account open. Near the end of 1999 he reactivated his AOL account.

However much Straczynski would like to log off, by remaining online he continues to participate in what he calls interactive television. Instead of viewers interacting with the actors and plot onscreen (as with CD-ROMs), however, fans interact with the producer at the level of production process—not fiction. His other front, the one of educator, becomes the reason he claims as to why he stays logged on. Could it not also be the excitement generated from the fact that by logging on Straczynski is able to find out what his viewers actually think about his show? Instead of reading reviews by professional critics, he gets to read the reviews as written by the fans of his show. One time a fan asked Straczynski why he continues to defend his show:

—Oftentimes when people criticize the show, or a character or whatever, you rise to its defense. I could understand you answering questions people have about different aspects of the story—that helps us all. But rebutting people who don't like X or Y or whatever?
—Your work is your work. There is no need to defend it or its quality.
—So, why do you do this?

Straczynski typically weaves in a self-effacing answer in an attempt to come across as someone who is not spiteful when he receives feedback not in line with his expectations:

Usually, I don't . . . if someone doesn't like something, he doesn't like something, that's fine and to be expected. It's when someone deliberately distorts something that I tend to get into it.

Why?

Because I'm an idiot, that's why. (1998b)

Straczynski's apparent contradiction of his social front—his graciousness in answering fan questions and his sarcastic overreaction to a few fan-critics—reveals a complex performance. The social front Straczynski performs is perhaps far different from his private persona. Yet, within the evidence gleaned from his public performance, it can be seen that Straczynski is ethically motivated and rarely suffers fools, or at least those he perceives as fools. But since fans can interact with him only at conventions or online, they will continue to perceive only his public social performance. But within the analysis of this performance his private personality begins to be revealed: Straczynski is not just a producer, and he isn't playing a producer role—he is an intelligent, sometimes impatient artist who desires to answer only to himself.

Immersion in an Imaginary Entertainment Environment

In order to immerse themselves more deeply in the *Babylon 5* universe, fans have to go outside their interactions with Straczynski. Many fans can perform characters in the *Babylon 5* universe. These characters, however, are not performed on television. By touching, playing, and performing with the cultural objects of television, people participate in what Daniel Mackay calls the imaginary entertainment environment: "fictional settings that change over time as if they were real places *and* that are published in a variety of mediums (novels, films, role-playing games, etc.), each of those mediums in communication with the others, and each contributing to the growth, history, and status of the setting" (1998:33). Through the imaginary entertainment environment people can perform in the same fantasy universe as those depicted onscreen in their favorite movies and television shows.

The television series *Babylon 5*, like the multiple *Star Trek* series and the *Star Wars* movies, for example, has become part of a commercial process by which it appears in these other participatory media as if they were real places. By participating in these various sites, people experience the fantasy universe of *Babylon 5* from different perspectives. They perform a character in a role-playing game, a captain on a starship in a war game, an "ambassador" in the collectible card game, or a tourist visiting *Babylon 5* for the first time in a CD-ROM product. They can also write fan fiction and design Web pages. As will be seen in the following chapters, in the imaginary entertainment environment of *Babylon 5*, the ultimate authority of the story lies not in the hands of Straczynski, but in the hands of the fans who promulgate their own desires through the performances they can create. In the end, the fans do have the final word.

The imaginary entertainment environment is a relatively new phenomenon created within late-twentieth-century capitalism. By *fantasy* I mean a genre of fiction set in an imaginary world or universe, such as J. R. R. Tolkien's Middle-earth; George Lucas' galaxy far, far away in his *Star Wars* movies; the Klingon home world in *Star Trek;* or Straczynski's *Babylon 5* space station. An *environment* is the representation of the fantasy world: a conventional role-playing game may have a map that depicts the fantasy world, but the environment is usually described verbally, as in a storyteller's description; a CD-ROM presents its world onscreen through photographic, animated, and cinematic images; a collectible card game enacts its site through pictures on a deck of cards; a war game uses token objects on a map and ship schematics on a sheet of paper to denote battles occurring in deep space. *Immersion* is the process by which participants break the frame of their actual "everyday" world, allowing them to interact in some way within the fantasy environment. An interface provides this immersion. When people engage the interface, the imaginary world or universe represented by the environment envelops the real-world perspective, and, as a consequence, players become immersed in a fantasy universe. My project examines the structure of this interface and the performance qualities evinced through it.

Players of war games designed the first role-playing game, *Dungeons & Dragons* (1974). Instead of enacting a simulation of war, they wanted participants to play in an imaginary world where they could perform as wizards and warriors in a cocreated story, echoing such mythological fantasy motifs as those found in Homer's *Odyssey, Beowulf,* and Tolkien's *The Hobbit* and *The Lord of the Rings*. The popularity of role-playing games spawned a whole generation of text-based computer solo adventure games in the late 1970s and early 1980s, eventually leading to dozens of graphical single-player adventure games. The 1980s evolved textual multiplayer live action computer MUDs (Multi-User Dungeons). Live chats came online in the 1990s, which also saw the development of multiplayer networked computer games. In the 1990s two new entertainment forms appeared: the collectible card game and interactive CD-ROMs. The collectible card game uses a rule structure and pictures on cards to evoke a fantasy environment for players. CD-ROMs are constructed like a movie, but allow players to choose their own adventure path through an onscreen interface.

Each of these sites uniquely structures how people can participate in the *Babylon 5* universe. In the role-playing game, players sit in a room together and verbally cocreate an improvised narrative by playing their own characters (created by following a set of rules) in an imaginary setting controlled by a gamemaster—the instigating storyteller who guides the players on adventures. The collectible card game allows players to take on the role of a *Babylon 5* ambassador depicted as a photograph on a card. The cards are coded with various pictures of characters and sites from the television series that function in a certain way. Players then strategically use a combination of cards in an attempt to gain dominance in the game. The CD-ROM I analyze attempts to transform the user into a tourist who visits the space station *Babylon 5*. Users click on various icon interfaces onscreen to choose where to go and how to behave (within certain preset parameters) in order to explore the station and retrieve archived material about the television series. The war game allows players to simulate military combat in space through the use of ship schematics and a logical rules structure. Fan-created Web sites allow amateur writers to publish their own short stories as well as create *Babylon 5* fan clubs. In all of these immersive fantasy sites, participants interact with the environment through material objects, a kind of interface, such as a character or starship sheet, a deck of cards, or icons on a computer screen. The interface helps participants to experience the fantasy in a certain way.

There are no rehearsals preparing the participants for a performance in these kinds of environments. The designers, on the other hand, have prepared *potentials* for performance within them. In other words, the interface structures how players will participate. Their roles are configured through an interface, which is different for each site. If a person is to play a smuggler in the role-playing game, for example, then her character sheet becomes the tool, the interface, by which she enters the B5 universe and performs this role. It is the launching point for her performance. The interface is a concrete material object that helps open the door to another's imaginary universe. It makes concrete the imaginary.

In these kinds of performances, participants' activities and desires intertwine within the functional characteristics of the environment. This is why people are required to bring a different kind of sensibility to them from what they are used to experiencing when watching television or reading a novel. People in conventional entertainment forms participate vicariously through another's performance. They cannot control the plot or the dramatic action. So-called immersive performances, on the other hand, require a different kind of participatory technique—participants have to actively engage the site as performers. The increased demand for fantasy, coupled with the technological tools allowing for the construction of immersive sites, marks a fundamental shift in people's desire for participation within popular culture. The mainstream performance forms of theater, film, and television no longer satisfy many people's desire for limited participation in performances. Some no longer want to be just spectators.

One place that this is becoming apparent is in mainstream theater. Performance scholar and director Richard Schechner claimed that "it must be clear to all that the theater can exist in this country only with substantial and continuing subsidy" (1969:13). There do not seem to be enough people willing to pay the price to support an unsubsidized theater. Perhaps, due to a lack of a wide theater-going audience in the United States today, new kinds of performances have emerged on the cultural landscape in an attempt to fill in this vacuum. Mainstream theater is being replaced by performances embedded within popular culture. It must be remembered that Shakespeare *was* popular culture in the first half of the nineteenth century in this country, and only became "high culture" when elitists said as much by the late nineteenth century, placing Shakespeare—and other products of "high art"—into a cultural invention wherein spectators were taught the "illusion that the aesthetic products of high culture were originally created to be appreciated . . . with reverent, informed, disciplined seriousness" (Levine 1988:229). The avant-gardists who update the classics with contemporary mise-en-scenes have attempted to bring the popular appeal back to theater. But they have failed to do so. The best theater still remains on the cultural fringe. Avant-garde that goes mainstream is no longer avant-garde. And audiences have been taught too well the illusion that the classics must be produced and observed with reverent awe.

Thus it is within the popular culture performances found in imaginary entertainment environments that one can find exciting new performance forms. These performances are not to be found on the stages of regional theater or on Broadway, nor can you view them on a television or movie screen. People do not purchase tickets and take a seat to watch them. In fact, most of these performances do not even have a conventional audience. The small performances occurring around tables in game stores, at schools, or in the living rooms of people's homes are where human beings are expressing their deepest desires—performing ideas that have burned in the imagination since the terra dawn of humankind.

Chapter 1

Welcome Aboard, Ambassador

Creating a Surrogate Performance with the *Babylon Project*

It was the dawn of the Third Age of Mankind ten years after the Earth-Minbari War. The Babylon Project was a dream given form. Its goal: to prevent another war by creating a place where humans and aliens could work out their differences, peacefully. It's a port of call, home away from home for diplomats, hustlers, entrepreneurs, and wanderers. Humans and aliens wrapped in two million five hundred thousand tons of spinning metal—all alone in the night. It can be a dangerous place, but it's our last best hope for peace. This is the story of the last of the Babylon stations. The year is 2258. The name of the place is Babylon 5.

—Joe Michael Straczynski, 1993

Heard on all twenty-two episodes of *Babylon 5*'s first season, this fifty-second opening monologue, written by Joe Straczynski and performed by actor Michael O'Hare in the role of Commander Jeffrey Sinclair, posits an Earth future of space travel and alien contact. The producers of the show have achieved fictionally what many people desire: the chance to travel and live in space. Companies today, in fact, manufacture the possibilities for such fulfillment.

Stating that travelers on Earth "have run out of places to go," Scott

Fitzsimmons, vice president of Zegrahm Space Voyagers of Seattle, Washington, began booking $98,000 flights on a planned space cruiser to orbit Earth in 2001. Not only is this date the accurate beginning of the new millennium (not 2000), but it also recalls Stanley Kubrick's *2001: A Space Odyssey* (1968)—a definitive milestone of science fiction filmmaking that depicted humanity's early quest into space. It appears that at the beginning of the twentieth-first century, space itself has become, in the minds of many entrepreneurs, "a new destination" for tourists, Fitzsimmons says, "a new challenge, a new frontier" (Salkever 1998:1, 8). Similarly, members of the architectural firm Wimberly, Allison, Tong & Goo, Inc., in Honolulu, Hawaii, are designing a space resort for possible Earth orbit (modeled in some ways on the space station dispicted in *2001*). Howard Wolf, a managing partner of this firm who heads this team, believes that people are "looking for more than a vacation lying on the beach, and they want something to show for it more than a tan. And what could be a more life-transforming experience than seeing our planet from two hundred miles up?" (1, 8). In addition, architects for the famed hotel chain Hilton International have designed a dome-shaped, five-thousand-bed, solar-powered hotel that may one day be built on the Moon ("News in Brief" 1998:2).

Between the science fiction found in films, novels, and television and the reality of the historical Apollo Moon landings, possible orbital tours, and planned space resorts, there lies the genesis of a perceptual shift demarcating a new view where what some people see and experience will no longer be grounded on Earth—but from out among the stars.

Wolfgang Schivelbusch theorizes that the transition from natural horse-drawn transport to the industrialization of travel in the nineteenth century transformed people's impression of time and geographical space. The railroad, he believes, "altered the consciousness of the passengers: they developed a new set of perceptions" (1986:14). Because of changing transportation technology, the travelers' sense of time and space changed as well, for their perception is anchored in the "material base of potentiality" (37). So, Schivelbusch maintains that "if an essential element of a given sociocultural space-time continuum undergoes change, this will affect the entire structure; [and] our perception of space-time will also lose its accustomed orientation" (37). For many people the perceptual shift from Earth-based living to a space-based view has already begun. Some look to the fantastic, yet real, possibility of such companies as Zegrahm's to fulfill their dreams of going out into space. Others read novels, view films, and watch television in an attempt to satisfy similar dreams. And yet others *enact* fantasies to fulfill such desires. Through performed fictions, they in effect realize a romantic fantasy of space travel, reflecting Ray Bradbury's philosophy as expressed on the opening page of *The Martian Chronicles:* "It is good to renew one's wonder. . . . Space travel has again made children of us all" (Bradbury 1979). The role-playing game is one way in which people can "travel" into space.

A Brief History of the Role-Playing Game

The fantasy role-playing game evolved from a confluence of the war gaming industry and mid-1960s fantasy fiction. In 1958 the Avalon-Hill Game Company in Baltimore, Maryland, was founded by Charles Roberts, who had previously, in 1953, designed *Tactics,* "a civilian wargame," which sold about 2,000 copies in five years (Fannon 1996:283 and Fine 1983:9). In 1958, with the introduction of the civil war game *Gettysburg,* the company began to grow in popularity, and by 1962 it had become the fourth largest adult board game publisher (Fine 1983:9). In 1965, as the war game industry burgeoned, the second edition and authorized version of J. R. R. Tolkien's *The Lord of the Rings* was published—a saga that spawned an entire genre of fantasy fiction. Around the same time, hobby war gaming enthusiasts Gary Gygax and Jeff Perren designed a medieval wargame called *Chainmail,* which was published in 1971. Gygax, influenced by Tolkien's novels, infused a fantasy element into the *Chainmail* system, adding such mythological themes and Tolkienesque tropes as wizards, spells, dragons, elves, and dwarves in the second edition, published the following year. Gygax got together with Dave Arneson (who had borrowed elements of this game for the fantasy world he was devising), and they decided to create a new kind of game (see Fannon 1996:122–25).

By 1973, Gygax had partnered with an investor and formed the small company Tactical Studies Rules (TSR) in Lake Geneva, Wisconsin. Later, Gygax and Arneson developed their generic medieval/mythological rulebook, entitled *The Fantasy Game*. Gygax's wife, however, suggested the name of *Dungeons & Dragons,* and TSR subsequently published it in 1974. *D&D* was the world's first role-playing game (Fannon 1996:126; 284). TSR sold about 4,000 copies of *D&D* in 1975. By the end of the decade, the popularity of role-playing games had increased, and in 1980 TSR grossed $8.5 million (Kellman 1983). Throughout the latter half of the 1970s and into the early 1980s, other role-playing companies formed, many of them moving away from generic fantasy settings and publishing games based directly on the preexisting fictional worlds found in novels, film, and television, such as I. C. E.'s *Middle-earth Role-Playing* (1982), based on J.R.R. Tolkien's *The Lord of the Rings* (1954; 1965), FASA's *Star Trek* (1982), and West End Games' *Star Wars* (1987).

Each game uses a different character-creation system, but in general terms the process found in the *Babylon 5* game is similar to those found in other role-playing games. The designers of the *Babylon Project* (1997) follow the tradition pioneered in the 1980s in which designers created games using existing imaginary entertainment environments: a fictional milieu, usually created by one author, which subsequently becomes elaborated by authors working in other media, including novels, film, comics, games, and so forth, and evolves as if it were a real place (Mackay 1998:31).

Transporting to Another Universe

Essentially, in role-playing games, a moderator, called the gamemaster, presents a step-by-step plotted story to players who perform characters. These adventures can take place in many different settings, ranging from a medieval fantasy world to starships in deep space. Players verbally interact with each other as they progress improvisationally through the scenario. Their characters, being individuals in a make-believe world, are unique, possessing qualities, skills, and occupations that may be far different from those of the players themselves. The gamemaster, besides providing narrative description, also performs the parts of other characters the players encounter. The gamemaster allows the players to progress through the plot by using these "nonplayer characters" (NPCs) in much the same way a novelist uses characters the hero meets in a novel. In the role-playing game, the gamemaster gives these nonplayer characters a purpose and adjusts their actions based on what the players do with their own characters. The choices players make are improvised and open-ended, but are influenced by the gamemaster, who tends to guide the overall direction of the narrative. Through this process the players and gamemaster together create a fantasy.

The designers of the *Babylon Project*, a role-playing game based on the television series *Babylon 5*, have created a simulation that transports players into the universe of *Babylon 5*. Players can create and perform in their own stories—enacting plots and character behaviors similar to those found on the television series. The game references an already existing simulation. Fictionally, it simulates life in space. Codes embedded within the game become activated by participants when they play. Through this process, players are transported—not transformed—into the fantasy universe.

Performance theorist and theater director Richard Schechner distinguishes transformation and transportation in this way: in the former, performances "transform people from one status or social identity to another. . . . [They are] the means by which persons achieve their new selves: no performance, no change" (1985:127). A transformative performance changes a person permanently. A transportation performance, on the other hand, renders the transformation *temporarily:* "The performer goes from the 'ordinary world' to the 'performative world,' " Schechner contends, "from one time/space reference to another, from one personality to one or more others. He plays a character, battles demons, goes into trance, travels to the sky or under the sea or earth: he is transformed, enabled to do things 'in performance' he cannot do ordinarily. But when the performance is over . . . he returns to where he started" (126). Like actors, players in the *Babylon Project* game perform roles, but they never become their characters permanently, and neither are they transformed into a new social state—as, for example, are the bride and groom during the performance of a wedding ceremony.

During the performance itself, however, players do perform as someone other than themselves. This transportation evolves through several steps. First, players buy a rulebook, which describes how participants play the game. Without the rules there can be no performance. Theorist Johan Huizinga defines the activity of play as a "voluntary activity or occupation executed within certain fixed limits of time and place, according to rules freely accepted but absolutely binding, having its aim in itself and accompanied by a feeling of tension, joy, and the consciousness that it is 'different' from 'ordinary life' " (1955:28). Rules for role-playing games situate players in prescribed roles and demarcate what kind of fantasy they will play.

Second, players, by following guidelines in the rulebook, create characters. Unlike conventional actors, who rely on a playwright to create characters from the text of a play, in a role-playing game there is no script or story determining the kinds of characters players perform. Instead, the rules provide the relevant material for players to create physical and psychological profiles of characters: their history, physical attributes, phobias, skills, education, and so forth. Players choose and write down all the relevant information on a character record sheet. This data forms the basis from which the player will draw inspiration while performing her character during the game.

Embedded within this sheet are coded behavioral bits, potentials for performance. These embedded behaviors indicate how a player should perform his character. Schechner classifies these behaviors as "organized sequences of events, scripted actions, known texts, scored movements" (35–36). Data on the role-player's character sheet contains, in an organized layout, the potential score or script from which players perform certain actions or behaviors during the game. "The performers get in touch with, recover, remember, or even invent these strips of behavior," Schechner contends, "and then rebehave according to these strips, either by being absorbed into them (playing a role, going into trance) or by existing side by side with them (Brecht's *Verfremdungseffekt*)" (36). The character sheet provides the interface for entering the fantasy world. It lays out for players the limits and possibilities in the performance of their characters.

The final stage of transportation occurs when the player performs her character within a story cocreated with other players and guided by a gamemaster, the person who controls the other characters the players meet within a typically Aristotelian-structured narrative (which is often created by the gamemaster). This is not necessarily an aesthetic performance in the conventional sense. Role-players are not actors. They do not train their bodies and voices to create a polished performance. They do not rehearse. As they perform their actions, however, the players' sense of the ordinary does become altered. Because they lay out the history, attributes, looks, and skills of their characters, they possess an emotional attachment to them, becoming a part of them, and the players' sense of time and space is altered—their imagination transports them to the "Dawn of the Third Age of Mankind . . . in the tense period just prior to and concurrent with the television show's first season," as the back of the rulebook states.

Babylon 5 (1993–1998) depicted the story of a politically neutral space station where various humans and aliens communicated their desires and needs in a galaxy of expanding commerce, discovery, and war. Like the fictional space station, the *Babylon Project* is a "dream given form." Here, players can enter the universe of *Babylon 5*. The designers of the game, Joseph Cochran and Charles Ryan, have embedded in the rules tropes from the television series in order to ensure that players become transported to the same imaginary environment conceived by Straczynski for his television series.

Creating a Character in the *Babylon Project*

The 196-page rulebook provides the blueprint for this transportation into Straczynski's universe. Pages 1–18 give background information about the game and describe the history and setting of the *Babylon 5* universe. Chapter 1, "Characters," first describes the process of creating a character (19–37). The rules also provide a brief background for four of the major species in *Babylon 5*, summarizing the history, government, military, colonies, diplomatic relations, society, and telepaths of those species: humans, Narns, Centauri, and Minbari (37–51). This provides a quick overview for players trying to decide what species they want to play. The skills and characteristics are described between pages 51 and 66. The second chapter, "Game System" (67–118), provides gamemasters with the tools needed to create adventures and tells them how to use the empirical data of the character record sheet to determine whether players have been successful in resolving tasks—including the simulation of armed combat in the game. The third chapter, "The Environment" (119–68), describes the political, social, cultural, and technological milieu occupied by all the major species in the *Babylon 5* universe. It also provides a map of the nearby star systems, listing colonies and different species present in this section of the galaxy. The last chapter, "The Campaign" (169–92), gives the gamemaster a prepared adventure to use with his players. It provides a premise, plot, scene descriptions, and nonplayer characters. The last few pages contain a character work sheet, character record sheet, and a gamemaster reference sheet for players to photocopy.

By following along in the *Babylon Project*'s rulebook, players create characters who live in the future-Earth universe of *Babylon 5*. This step-by-step process of character creation expresses both a quantitative and a qualitative performance. In a quantitative performance, a player assigns numerical schema as the means of depicting what her character looks like, what she can do, and who she is. In a qualitative performance players use a written nomenclature to give their characters a background history, personality characteristics, and desires.

The designers of the game recommend a three-part process in creating the "initial concept" of the character: determining the "character identity" (species and profession choice), the "archetype," and the "basic history" (Cochran 1997:22). Character identity "describes the facet of the character most central to its concept" such as a " 'dedicated EarthForce space jock' or 'itinerant construction worker' [or a] 'passionate Mars separatist' " (22). Let's say I choose a human deep space surveyor. This initial concept references a character appearing in a couple of episodes from the first season of *Babylon 5*, and also marks a desire on my part to travel in the depths of space and look on the colorful glow of nebulae. This is the kind of desire Zegrahm Space Voyagers caters to. Although I will probably never take this trip, my creation of such a character in this role-playing game provides the potential quality for simulating such a trip. The character I create will allow me to perform the role of a galactic explorer simulacrum.

In the nineteenth century, the American railroad "served to open up, for the first time, vast regions of previously unsettled wilderness" (Schivelbusch 1986:89). This spirit of exploration (and colonization) played a part in the United States space program as well. Scholar Howard McCurdy describes how, from its inception, the space program promised the realization of the "romantic dream" of human exploration and colonization of our solar system by the dawn of the twenty-first century, "just as their ancestors had crossed oceans to investigate foreign lands. Space stations would ring the earth; humans would colonize the Moon and Mars" (1997:1). If not the dawn of the twenty-first century, the *Babylon Project* game places players in the dawn of the Third Age of Mankind in the twenty-third century, making it, as Baudrillard contends, "a desperate re-hallucination of the past" (1994:123), which once promised such goals.

Straczynski, the creator, executive producer, and writer for *Babylon 5*, laments the fact that we have not yet colonized space:

> The space program is currently log-jammed, and if it doesn't get cleared up soon, we're going to be left in the dust, literally as well as figuratively. We have to get NASA off its image of two guys standing on a Martian hill planting a flag to communities of people working and living in space. The space shuttle was primarily designed as part of a link; space shuttle builds space station; space station is hub for mars mission and lunar colony; lunar colony is hub for more mars missions and mars colony. But we lost that thread, and now it's been relegated to being a high-tech ferry service. (1995a)

People lack a feasible means of space travel today, and so they are unable to explore and settle the vast regions of the final frontier, despite the fact that they desire to achieve this goal. It is not enough for some people to find fulfillment for this desire in the vicarious experience of science fiction stories. It seems the only way they can get out into space is through immersive simulations. The role-playing game allows players to enact, through surrogation, unfulfilled romantic dreams of space colonization. (I describe this surrogate process in more detail near the end of this chapter.)

The second step in character creation is determining the character's archetype: "a short descriptor that conveys a bit about the impression the character makes on others," the rules say (Cochran 1997:23). This includes the gender, age, "and a couple of adjectives that reveal a little bit of personality or conjure a visual image" such as " 'a cocky young woman, in a sharp, crisply-ironed EarthForce fighter pilot's uniform' " (23). The reference to a female character in a role-playing game raises several interpretive possibilities: the desire on the part of game companies 1) to encourage more women to participate in a predominately male-centered hobby; to provide a politically correct example (expressing the fact that there are women who do participate in hobby gaming); and to satisfy an adolescent male's prurient interest in a "cocky young" woman character. The archetype for my character will be a "jaded fifty-two-year-old loner who wears an old crumpled EarthForce uniform."

The archetype is supposed to describe a character's impression on other characters as much it is supposed to determine the impression the player makes on other players. "Instead of an abstract icon," Cochran writes, "you control the life of a realistic person" (1997:19). The archetype is the psychological and physical description of a nondescript character: a human deep space explorer. The character is created and performed by the player, and the archetype—the descriptor embedded in the rule system and enacted by the player—is supposed to create the seed leading to the "birth" of a "realistic person," performed later during an adventure scenario in front of other players. The embedded archetype performs on the player during the process of character creation—it stimulates the kind of history the character may have, what kind of events shaped his life, and perhaps where he grew up.

The archetype, however, is also a performance of memory, stirring up latent bits of amalgamated images from popular culture, including the television show *Babylon 5*. In particular, the "cocky young woman" archetype for the human fighter pilot identity given in the rulebook conjures up the personality tropes of Lt. Commander Susan Ivanova (Claudia Christian) from *Babylon 5* and Princess Leia Organa (Carrie Fisher) from *Star Wars* (1977). Role-playing scholar Daniel Mackay, borrowing the term *lexia* from literary theorist Roland Barthes, calls the recuperation of popular culture "performance lexias" (Mackay 1998:89–90). A performance lexia is similar to a strip of behavior: a bit of behavior that connotes meaning derived from other performances. A player who says, "Use the Force," during a role-playing game performance reiterates a science fiction trope found in the *Star Wars* movies and connotes a certain mystical behavior that other players understand from watching those films.

Barthes defines a lexia as a "unit of reading," a "segment within which we observe the distribution of meaning" (1985:85). Within these arbitrary units of meaning, lexias allow the analyzer of texts to " 'skim off' the meanings, the connotations" in slow motion, as Barthes puts it (85). Mackay, by applying this idea to role-playing games, attempts to explicate the process by which players utilize connotations of popular culture in performance (1998:84). He contends that "a shared experience of popular culture interpenetrates both the process of character creation and the performance of character" (87). Players "recontextualize" these elements into a "score of product art that composes a common reference point for the players' many allusions and creative choices in role-playing" (87).

Mackay explains that "the role-played performance appears to establish an *alternate* reality, derived from patterns established in the artifacts of popular culture" (1998:92). This, he adds, is "really nothing more than the cut-and-pasted, re-mixed, and sampled recapitulation of . . . popular culture" (92). He concludes, however, by noting that the participants in role-playing games "recoup the popular culture consumed by many because the form of the game encourages the players to bring their affective selves, their subjective selves, to the table and to winnow the concepts and images of our environment thick with these things through that subjectivity" (93). On the surface, Mackay contends, it seems as if players are "recapitulating" generic fantasy motifs—the ontogeny of a performance summarizes a phylogenetic order of popular culture. Even though elements of the game evolved within popular culture, the fact remains that role-playing games allow players to *recuperate* popular culture ideas into a form that suits the particular desires of players, as Mackay later posits. In a *recapitulation* performance players merely summarize or rehash previous bits of stored popular culture behaviors: the images control the players. In a *recuperative* performance, on the other hand, the players are inspired by those images. They crystallize them in a process of diagenesis caused by the compound pressure of desire and performance.

A recuperative performance occurs during both the playing and the creation of a character. Embedded within this character creation process are *potentials* for performance. Players reference these when performing the character in a role-playing adventure. (An adventure in a role-playing game refers to the story players participate in as their characters.) If I were to create a "cocky young smuggler" character, for example, my immediate connotation would be to think about the personality traits of Han Solo (Harrison Ford) from *Star Wars,* Michael Garibaldi (Jerry Doyle), and, perhaps, Captain Sheridan (Bruce Boxleitner), these last two both from *Babylon 5*. My character would be an amalgam of behavioral bits from these characters—to be "restored" by me during the construction of my character and later while playing him in an actual role-playing adventure. But, it must be remembered, these "strips of restored behavior" are not simply the recuperation of amalgamated bits of a character, but the recuperation of them by an actor. "Restored behavior is 'out there,' distant from 'me,'" Schechner asserts. "It is separate and therefore can be 'worked on,' changed, even though it has 'already happened'" (1985:36). The actors Harrison Ford, Bruce Boxleitner, and Jerry Doyle have already performed characters with similar bits of archetypal descriptors that a role-player's "cocky young smuggler" character "restores" (in his own way) during the role-playing game.

This procedure of creating my brief character identity and archetype (identity: human deep space explorer; archetype: jaded fifty-two-year-old loner who wears a crumpled EarthForce uniform) not only restores bits of popular culture behavior from *Babylon 5*, it also expresses a kind of Austinian performative: "both an *action* and an *utterance*" (1971:15). A performed event will then "characteristically 'take effect,'" Austin believes —meaning that "in consequence of the performance of this act, such-and-such a future event, *if* it happens, will be *in order*" (14). The statement "My character is a jaded fifty-two-year-old loner who wears a crumpled EarthForce uniform and surveys deep space objects" allows for the rest of the character creation process to take effect, and later, after the character is completed, the archetypal image allows me to perform that character in a role-playing adventure. After the character has been empirically recorded on a character record sheet, I can then perform the character, which contains, embedded within it, the potential for performative actions within the game.

This analysis of the performance of an archetype leads to the question of whether the archetype is an amalgamated *stereotype* allowing players to easily perform a character embedded with familiar references or whether it is an attempt to reference a Jungian archetype—an idea or model that is "derived from the experience of the race and is present in the unconscious of the individual" (*Merriam Webster's* 1997). If the latter, then the game designers are hoping the archetype descriptor may perhaps impel players to create "heroes" who, according to myth scholar Joseph Campbell, "retreat from the world scene of secondary effects to those causal zones of the psyche where the difficulties really reside, and there to clarify the difficulties, eradicate them in his own case . . . and break through to the undistorted, direct experience and assimilation of what C. G. Jung has called 'the archetypal images'" (1968:17–18).

The *Babylon Project* role-playing game seems to promote the mythical "hero's journey" as mapped out by Campbell in *The Hero with a Thousand Faces* (1968), a form used in *Star Wars:* George Lucas has said that he attempted "to take mythological principles and apply them to a story" (Henderson 1997:10). And Straczynski created *Babylon 5* to set an example of the "storyteller's obligation" to be a "mythmaker"—"to point to the horizon and tell us where we are going" as a culture (1997e). Turning to this mythical theme of the hero in science fiction, the designers of the *Babylon 5* role-playing game indicate that the players' characters have a "destiny" to fulfill: "the fact that your characters play lead roles in their adventures makes them special. Fate tends to be on their side" (Cochran 1997:21).

Despite this connection to mythology, the description of the player's character—since it is designed to convey a familiar archetype to others—becomes a stereotype. The character tropes borrowed from popular culture performances, when rendered into a role-playing game performance, cause characters to be stereotypical. Therefore we may get another Han Solo–type character, or a Garibaldi-like character. Myth, Barthes asserts, "transforms history into nature"—the process by which culture becomes familiar (1972:129). Rather than supporting the almost utopian view of myth shared by Campbell and his followers, postmodern literary philosophers such as Barthes and Umberto Eco take an opposite view of myth. Terms such as "archetype," Eco says, "serve only to indicate a preestablished and frequently reappearing narrative situation" (1986:200).

But stereotypes are not necessarily a negative influence in gaming, for it is exactly these evocations that players may desire. The recycling of archetypes ends up creating an "intense emotion accompanied by the vague feeling of a déjà vu that everybody yearns to see again," Eco contends (1986:200). The performance of these mythical characters becomes second nature—embedded as they are in Baudrillard's semiosphere: a culture so filled with media images that people live and breathe it like the air. The siren of mythical tropes as promulgated by Lucas and Straczynski is eclipsed by the fact that viewers never become the heroes they watch.

These tropes may be recuperated in performance, allowing the players to *relive* what they have already experienced from watching episodes of *Babylon 5*, *Star Trek*, and *Star Wars*, but that performance rarely, if ever, is translated into real "mythical" journeys—which, in today's world, seems as mythical as the myth itself. And this is why Baudrillard claims that in a world of simulation, the "real cannot surpass the model" (1994:122). For "fragments" of this simulation "have become for us the so-called real world," which "contrive to give [simulation] the feeling of the real, of the banal, of lived experience, to reinvent the real as fiction, precisely because it has disappeared from our life" (124).

I have analyzed the first two steps in creating a character for the *Babylon Project*. The next step in the character creation performance helps players give their characters more originality, to increase the possibilities of simulation. The player is directed to sketch out a character history in three phases: childhood (where the character was born and raised and "anything particularly noteworthy"); development (education and coming of age); and adulthood (career and "any major events of his or her adult life to date") (Cochran 1997:24). The rules also suggest naming the character at this stage. My character, Devin Smith, was born at the Sirius III Mining Outpost in 2205. When he was twelve, an explosion ripped through the habitat ring of the station where he was living. His parents were killed. He was shipped to Earth and placed into military foster care when it was learned he had a high aptitude for math. He served in the Earth-Dilgar War. He was dishonorably discharged after he accidentally caused the death of half his crew members. Now he explores star routes and surveys planets for mining companies. The gamemaster, during an adventure, may take aspects of this character's background history (which I created through prodding from the rules) and weave it into the story. Up through this stage, players enact a qualitative performance in order to provide a general background for their characters. From these qualities they are then directed to derive quantitative "attributes" for their characters.

Attributes are divided into four categories, which are listed on the character record sheet (included below are the numbers for a "typical" human character). These numerical values, found in nearly every role-playing game, help the players and gamemaster determine their characters' abilities to perform skills and tasks in the game (figure 1.1). In the rules, Cochran says that they "define some of your character's specific capabilities in game terms" (1997:25–26), representing "the natural, inherent aptitudes that characters have for certain different types of interaction with the world around them" (25).

Cultural Attributes	Mental Attributes	Physical Attributes	Derived Attributes
Charm: 6	Intelligence: 5	Strength: 4	Toughness: 0
Finesse: 6	Insight: 5	Agility: 5	Initiative: 4
Presence: 4	Wits: 4	Endurance: 4	Resolve: 5
Xenorelation: 5	Perception: 4	Coordination: 5	

Figure 1.1.
Character attributes chart for the *Babylon Project* role-playing game. © 1997 Warner Bros.

A numerical value, ranging from one through nine, assigned to each attribute, empirically determines the character's capability in each category. For example, one means "very inept," a five, "average," a nine, "incredibly apt." Each category includes different attributes. For example, Cultural Attributes represent a character's ability to interact and get along with "other sentient beings": Charm—the ability to "engender a friendly response"; Finesse—the ability to "manipulate" others; Presence—"force of personality"; Xenorelation—how well the character "relates to other" species. So, a "four" assigned to the attribute "Xenorelation" would mean that my character has an "adequate" ability in relating to alien species. Each major species has its own "Typical Attribute Values" laid out on a chart. Narns, the humanoid reptilian species, for example, have a typical value of "six" for their strength—twenty percent higher than an average adult human.

After the attributes are filled out, the rules require that the player furnish more details of the character's history in three phases: childhood, development, and adulthood (as discussed above). The rules list a series of questions the player is directed to answer for each phase. For the childhood stage the questions help the player to describe where the character was born, where he lived (in an urban, rural, space station, or domed colony city), family class, the kind of relationship with parents and their occupation, any siblings, childhood interests, and so forth. The questions for the development period specify the kind of schooling the character had, his favorite subject, whether he was a good or bad student, his interests outside school, whether he developed any important relationships during this time, and so forth. For the final phase, adulthood, the player must describe what the character does for a living, the responsibility of that position, peer recognition, kind of lifestyle, where he lives, any romantic interests, kinds of friends and where they hang out, and so forth. The answers to these questions help the player choose several "Learned Skills" (including any specialties) and "Characteristics" for each of the three growth phases.

The Skills category includes such things as anthropology, athletics, biology, business, combat, diplomacy, survival, military tactics, and so forth. Characteristics include: contentious, curious, dedicated, fanatical, heartless, impulsive, proud, and so on. The rules provide a description of each skill (with a list of specialties) and of each characteristic that spans fifteen pages (Cochran 1997:51–66). Other games, such as *GURPS* (*Generic Universal Role-Playing System*, 1986) from Steve Jackson Games, list hundreds of skills and personality traits. What is interesting about the *Babylon Project* is the fact that most of the skills and characteristics on this list come from episodes of *Babylon 5*. When players design their characters, and later when they play an adventure, they activate strips of stored behavior—performance potentials—embedded within these skills and characteristics. The designers have cited a line of dialogue for each characteristic in the rules. In other words, the characteristics they have placed in the rules of the game are embedded within the show itself.

For example, under the characteristic "Fanatical," which the rules use for a being who "firmly believes that his or her most passionate viewpoints are the only possible correct ones," there is the following quotation from an episode of B5: "It says in the book of G'Quan . . ." (Cochran 1997:58). The rest of the quotation is not given. What it elicits in the player, however, is the remembrance of the Narn character Ambassador G'Kar (Andreas Katsulas), who continually reads and searches the book of G'Quan to find answers to some of the challenges facing him over the course of the show. A player may be inspired by G'Kar from the show and create a similar character, perhaps becoming a follower of G'Quan. He would use the bits of stored behavioral information from Andreas Katsulas' performance in the show and restore it in his own performance while creating the character and during game-play. In addition, the gamemaster may take Straczynski's ideas about the book of G'Quan and his followers as described in the show and elaborate them further within a role-playing adventure. The reference to this book in the game rules under this heading is clearly a reference to a scene from the series (figure 1.2), a trope players will use (restore in performance) if they choose the "Fanatical" characteristic in the creation of their character.

Let us look at how I developed my character, Devin Smith. Because he had flown around the Sirius system with his father, who mined asteroids, I chose the geography (star system) and geology skills. In addition, he

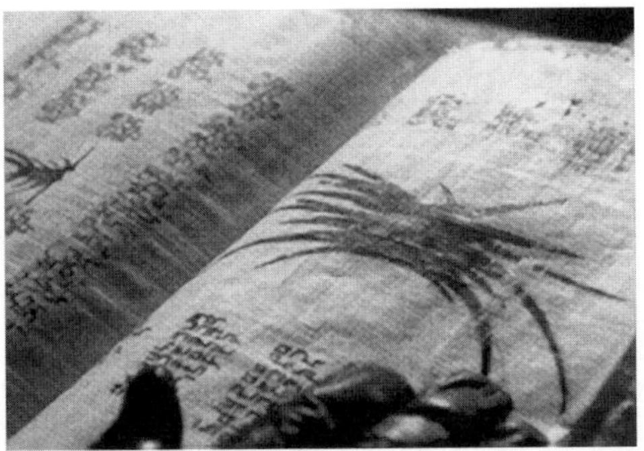

Figure 1.2.
A page from G'Kar's holy book, the book of G'Quan, as seen in "Matters of Honor." A reference to this book is listed in the rules under the characteristic "Fanatical." © 1995 Warner Bros.

speaks the Vreetan and Ch'lon languages, since these neighboring aliens frequented his home system. Mathematics is a natural aptitude that marks him for military use later. I feel the contentious and haunted characteristics best define his childhood attitude since his parents were killed in the station explosion when he was twelve. I determine that during the development stage, when he was conscripted by the military, Devin was trained in aerospatial navigation, hyperspatial navigation, and starship piloting, including space combat tactics. His characteristics at this stage include dedication and stubbornness. His adult phase includes the gaining of enemies as the result of a mistake that caused his ship to explode, killing half the crew, followed by a dishonorable discharge from EarthForce. I transfer all of this information onto the Character Record sheet provided with the game (figure 1.3). The data on this sheet represents, in an empirical way, my character. It provides numerical guideposts used in determining his capabilities of performing certain skills and tasks within the game.

Enacting the Performance and Immersion in the Imaginary

As a starship pilot, Devin's skills include weapon systems, ship handling, mechanical engineering, and philosophy (from reading during his long flights in space). Skills are assigned a numerical value, which will be used later during game-play to determine whether a character succeeds in completing a particular task. For example, if my character was surveying a new planet and looking for certain minerals, the gamemaster, as the referee, would determine the difficulty of the task. I would achieve suc-

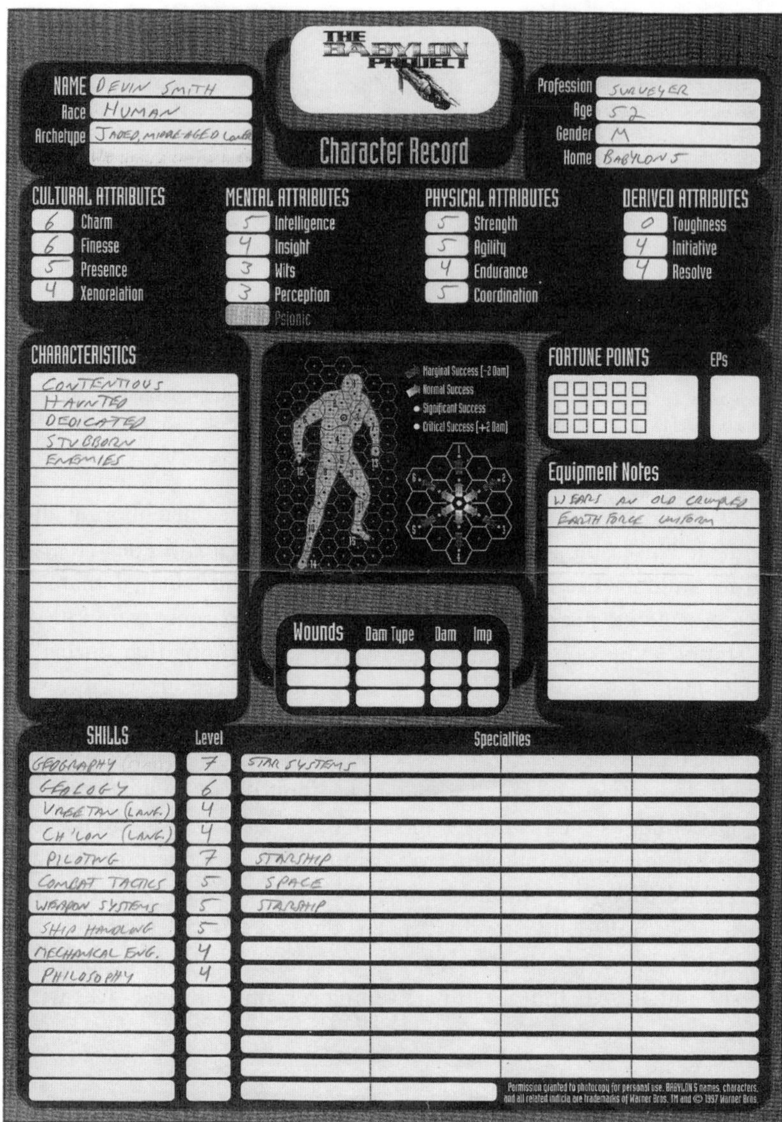

THE BABYLON PROJECT

Character Record

NAME: DEVIN SMITH
Race: HUMAN
Archetype: JADED, MIDDLE-AGED Lo[illegible]

Profession: SURVEYER
Age: 52
Gender: M
Home: BABYLON 5

CULTURAL ATTRIBUTES
6 Charm
6 Finesse
5 Presence
4 Xenorelation

MENTAL ATTRIBUTES
5 Intelligence
4 Insight
3 Wits
3 Perception
Psionic

PHYSICAL ATTRIBUTES
5 Strength
5 Agility
4 Endurance
5 Coordination

DERIVED ATTRIBUTES
0 Toughness
4 Initiative
4 Resolve

CHARACTERISTICS
CONTENTIOUS
HAUNTED
DEDICATED
STUBBORN
ENEMIES

FORTUNE POINTS

EPs

Equipment Notes
WEARS AN OLD CRUMPLED
EARTH FORCE UNIFORM

Wounds	Dam Type	Dam	Imp

SKILLS	Level	Specialties
GEOGRAPHY	7	STAR SYSTEMS
GEOLOGY	6	
VREETAN (LANG.)	4	
CH'LON (LANG.)	4	
PILOTING	7	STARSHIP
COMBAT TACTICS	5	SPACE
WEAPON SYSTEMS	5	STARSHIP
SHIP HANDLING	5	
MECHANICAL ENG.	4	
PHILOSOPHY	4	

Permission granted to photocopy for personal use. BABYLON 5 names, characters, and all related indicia are trademarks of Warner Bros. TM and © 1997 Warner Bros.

Figure 1.3.
The character sheet for my character, Devin Smith. The empirical data allows me to restore behavior from the universe of *Babylon 5.* © 1997 Warner Bros.

cess if the intelligence and skill factor were determined to be within the character's means.

Let us say that during an adventure, my character takes his survey ship into hyperspace. The gamemaster, using a plot device, decides that the engines of my ship malfunction, knocking it off course. My character uses his mechanical engineering skill in an attempt to repair the engines. Typically a die roll is made, computed as a function of the skill rating versus a difficulty factor. The gamemaster—who has predetermined where my ship will go (not in my intended direction)—places a high difficulty rating on completing the repair. My character fails to repair the engine (as computed by the die roll), and my ship, out of control, arrives at an unknown star system. There I discover the ruins of an ancient alien civilization on one of the planets. The gamemaster has set up a situation where an engine failure is the means for causing my character to explore a mysterious world. The gamemaster could have assigned a different rating for the mechanical failure, a number that would have made it easier for my character to make a temporary repair. This may then have led me to dock at the space station *Babylon 5*, where I could conduct the needed repairs. While there, my character could meet other aliens and have an "adventure" on the station.

The gamemaster, guiding the overall narrative of the adventure, throws in certain obstacles that allow the story to unfold in certain directions. Role-playing chronicler Sean Patrick Fannon says, rather flamboyantly, that a "gamemaster must have the Heart of a Bard, the Soul of an Artist, the Intellect of a Scientist, the Insight of a Philosopher, the Foresight of a General, the Memory of a Historian, the Will of an Umpire, the Compassion of a Priest, the Flexibility of a Diplomat, the Ego of an Auteur, and the Instincts of a Gambler" (1996:39). Scholar Gary Alan Fine calls the gamemaster, more simply, a referee who "maintains ultimate interpretive authority" (1983:72). This interpretation, however, remains on a descriptive level. The gamemaster may have ultimate authority in describing a character's particular action, but the interpretation is still *by* the player and remains relatively *internal*. Since a player has invested a lot of time and emotion in creating a character, she begins to identify with that character. During the creation of a character, the history, characteristics, and skills become a part of the player. She is forced to think about the universe of *Babylon 5* through the eyes of that character. This is how players become immersed in that universe.

In the episode "Messages from Earth" we see a mysterious Shadow vessel over the surface of Mars (figure 1.4). I use just such an image as a

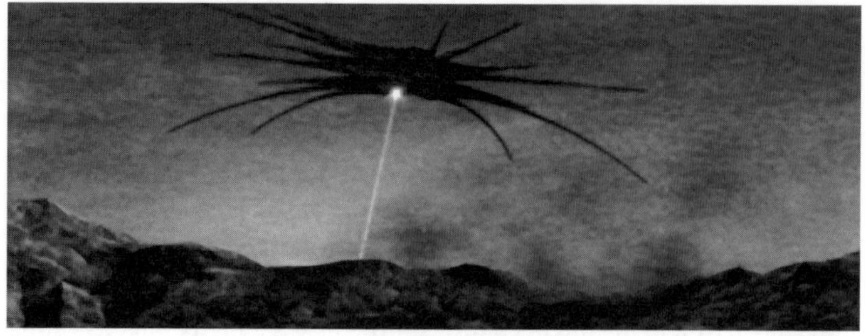

Figure 1.4.
A mysterious ship over the surface of Mars in "Messages from Earth." © 1996 Warner Bros.

reference in my desire to explore unknown worlds and mysterious alien civilizations. The idea for my character (a deep space surveyor) was inspired partly from this strip of behavior, allowing me to restore—to relive and perform the memories attributed to this scene—the behavior I have already experienced from watching *Babylon 5*. During the game, my character could meet such a ship. The gamemaster may set up such an encounter in order to fulfill this expectation. Through this process of immersion I enter into the *Babylon 5* universe.

Because of my experience in role-playing games, however, and my understanding of the *Babylon 5* universe, as well as my knowledge of how character, fiction, and performance function practically, I can draw on certain fictive and performance tropes in order to perform a character in an adventure without any of the attendant empirical attributes found on a character sheet. The data is ultimately designed to help somewhat inexperienced players perform. A character's history, for example, may be improvised during play, rather than being laid out during the character creation stage. In this case, players rely on a free association of what Mackay calls fictive blocks: "self-contained, de-contextualized tropes" (1998:88). These are "memorable images culled from the player's experience with film, in famous lines, quotable postures, and in . . . literary passages" formerly "embodied in the real, non-diegetic environment of the player" (88). The statistical information found on a character record sheet helps players perform these fictive blocks garnered from popular culture—wherein the stored data embedded in the character sheet, like a script, becomes restored during game-play. This same information, as stored in the rule book, becomes restored during the process of creating a character. The character creation process and the recording of that information onto a sheet of paper collect the memories of *Babylon 5* into a form that allows for easy recuperation during game play. Thus players immerse themselves in the universe of *Babylon 5*.

The player, within a boundary delimited by play, is given the freedom to be "born" in a world that she formerly visited only vicariously when watching the television series. Now, through a mechanized, empirically centered rules system, she is "transported" into that universe as a character. The designers of the game use tropes from the series to help immerse participants in the fictional universe of *Babylon 5*. One hundred and ten episodes and four movies provide players of this game a ninety-hour database of material. Players and the gamemaster draw upon these images and memories when both creating and playing characters.

The imaginary world engendered by game-play references the memory of images players see in their own minds. Players describe an action or event their characters perform, but the action is only heard verbally and seen through gesture. Players, however, see, in their imagination, the characters in the fantasy world. They reference a set of memories, images, and tropes previously derived from watching *Babylon 5* and other material from popular culture. They see them played in a "movie of the mind." Instead of their creating a visual play or movie, the performance of a role-playing game occurs only in the individual minds of players. Each player sees a different performance. This process of referencing tropic images is called strips of imaginary behavior by Mackay. The fictive blocks, he contends, "are stored by the potential role-player as *strips of imaginary behavior*—non-real behavior that takes place in an imaginary environment. As strips of imaginary behavior . . . such *lexia* are the very substance of play" (1998:90). The performance comes about, Mackay contends, "through a process that consists of assembling strips of imaginary behavior from that player's personal and cultural score of such strips" (91). The creation of the character is the preparation for a later performance with a group of players.

The entire process of creating a character is in some ways similar to the rehearsal process of a play production. A rehearsal of a play leads to a formal aesthetic performance, of course. This is not the case in a role-playing game, where players perform through verbal and physical gestures, improvisationally. However, during conventional rehearsals actors begin to identify with their characters. They must "get to know them" if they are to perform that character in a realistic drama—a form invented at the end of the nineteenth century and sharpened into theoretical and practical focus by the Russian performer and director Konstantin Stanislavsky in the early twentieth century. Most acting schools in Europe and the United States derive their teachings from Stanislavsky's formulation of psychological and physical realism. In this form of acting, Stanislavsky contends, "the main cause of any feeling [derived from physical actions] is the thought process by which an actor finds the inner vision of the actions which his character in the play has performed or is about to perform in the given circumstances of the play" (Gorchakov 1994:84). An actor finds this "inner vision" by asking himself, " 'How would I behave if it happened to me in real life?' " (85). As part of this process of creating realistic emotions onstage, "the character's biography must be as familiar as his own, and he must constantly fill that biography with new facts" (96). Like actors, players of role-playing games create characters nearly as familiar as themselves. Through the character creation process, players become reconfigured into their characters who live in the *Babylon 5* universe.

Participants in role-playing games are not actors, however. They do not train their bodies and voices in order to create an aesthetically pleasing performance. Players do not block out action within a physical mise-en-scene. In some ways, an action occurring during a role-playing game performance is not a theatrical act, but a speech act, what J. L. Austin calls a "performative utterance" used in "performing an action" (1975:6). The verbalization of a statement (such as "I do" at a wedding ceremony; or "I," as my character Devin Smith, "draw my gun," in a role-playing game), comprises the action of what *is* done. A performative [utterance] "is not to *describe* my doing . . . it is to do it," Austin contends (6). In a role-playing game performance, players do not just improvisationally describe what their characters will do in a given scene: what they say is the action itself.

In the example I gave earlier about my character, Devin Smith, journeying through hyperspace, the gamemaster said that the ship engines malfunctioned. During this moment, the gamemaster is speaking a performative utterance. Her verbal utterance not only conveys the act, it is the act. In a role-playing game, players sit around a table as the gamemaster conveys the narrative through scene descriptions and improvisationally performs the parts of the various characters the players meet within the adventure. The character sheet contains the framework, the blueprint, the script, for the player's performative utterances. Knowing that my character has some engineering ability, I respond with my own performative: "I attempt to repair the engines." During a role-playing game, in Austin's parlance, "I am not reporting" an act: "I am indulging in it" (1975:6). In a role-playing game performance, this indulging "induces engrossment," as sociologist Gary Alan Fine explains, "and promotes identification with the [characters]" among the players (1983:3).

A performative, Jean-François Lyotard contends, "is not subject to discussion or verification" (1984:9). In a role-playing game, the "addressee" is placed (or engrossed) "within the new context created by the utterance" (9) when the statement occurs. The performative takes them out of a "real world" frame into a "fantasy world" frame of mind. This is not open to "verification." It happens as a consequence of the performative. During various moments of the game, however, players may step outside the fantasy frame in order to clarify the scene they are in or to discuss a point from the rules, such as when I roll some dice to see if my character repairs the damage to the engines, for example. These other kinds of statements or a discussion about rules do not provide engrossment, therefore they are not performatives.

A performative utterance induces fantasy. In the minds of players, the performative statements they utter are the actions of their characters. As Austin says, a performative is "both an *action* and an *utterance*" (1971:15). In this way Schechner's theory of restored behaviors is complimented by Austin's concept of the performative. The utterance restores behavior, engrossing players in the fantasy. In my example, the fantasy was evoked through statements that have embedded within them tropes from *Babylon 5:* hyperspace, jump engines, alien beings, and so forth. The players, familiar with Straczynski's work, restore these behavioral tropes in the game. Players can "see"—restore—in their minds various strips of behavior found in episodes of *Babylon 5*.

A character allows participants in the *Babylon 5* universe to perform, as Schechner would say, in "a field of limitless potential, free as it is from both the person (not) and the person impersonated (not not)" (1985:123). An actor playing the role of Hamlet "is between a denial of being another (= I am me) and a denial of not being another (= I am Hamlet)" (123). In a role-playing game this field of limitless potential is delineated by a set of rules that allows a performance to take place through a player's identification with a character, initiated through the creation of that character by following the rules step-by-step and modeled on existing images, tropes, and fictive blocks from popular culture. I may be me, but in gameplay, I am Devin Smith in the universe of *Babylon 5*, and this simulacrum is the closest that I will likely get to achieving a desire to live in space. NASA may provide images from the Hubble Space Telescope and robotic probes cast out into the depth of our solar system, Zegrahm Space Voyagers of Seattle may book $98,000 flights into Earth orbit, but with a $20 rulebook a group of players cannot just simulate the imaginary performance of traveling into space, they can simulate this performance through immersion in the universe of *Babylon 5*. Not only is the simulation more feasible than the real, but it may in fact be more desirable than the real.

So, when enacting characters in a role-playing game, players—instead of identifying with the "inner vision" of the playwright and preparing to perform a script—tap into the ninety-hour database of *Babylon 5*, as well as other popular culture materials. By identifying with these images, players, *as they create* their characters, become immersed in *Babylon 5*. The character sheet is an interface that taps into their memories and provides a kind of hypertext link into strips of behavior within the imaginary universe of *Babylon 5*. As players commit to their role, dedicating a certain amount of time to creating their characters' history, skills, and personality characteristics, they link their thoughts and memories to the preexisting fictional universe of *Babylon 5*.

The process of writing a character profile on a sheet of paper creates for the player a living interface to Straczynski's previously authored universe of *Babylon 5*. It is a performative utterance. Players commit themselves to defining who they are within a former history in the *Babylon 5* universe, and the process commits them to performing further actions in the future during game-play. "I name this ship *Liberte*," Austin says about a performative action (1971:13). The procedure of naming it is a performance in action. It commits the name in performance—despite the fact that the firm hiring the architect to design the ship and an attendant legal process had previously named it. In a similar way, players use the rules from the *Babylon Project* and the images from *Babylon 5*, which itself is inspired by the classic works of science fiction, to create a structure that will allow them to perform in a fictional universe previously experienced only vicariously. And this is the performance, the restoration of previously stored strips of behavior that the players "get in touch with, recover, remember, or even invent" (Schechner 1985:36).

For example, as I create my character, Devin Smith, I remember a scene from the *Babylon 5* episode "Mind War" (1994f) by Straczynski. One of the characters in the episode, Catherine Sakai (Julia Nickson), is a surveyor hired to explore a planet. She was warned by the Narn ambassador, G'Kar (Andreas Katsulas), to stay away from Sigma 957. Ignoring the warning, Sakai arrives in orbit above the alien world. While she is surveying it, a mysterious alien ship full of flashing colors arrives and flies near her ship before entering hyperspace. Because of this fly-by her ship loses power and nearly crashes into the planet. G'Kar had known that Sakai would ignore her warning, and so he sent out a couple of ships to rescue her. Back at *Babylon 5*, the rescued Sakai asks G'Kar what she had seen out there. The two of them are standing in the Zocalo, a bazaar of various shops. They stand next to a bouquet of flowers.

Sakai: Ambassador, while I was out there I saw something. What was it?

G'Kar turns and points to an ant walking on a flower.

G'Kar: What is this?

Sakai: An ant.

G'Kar: Ant.

Sakai: So much gets shipped up from Earth on commercial transports it's hard to keep them out.

G'Kar: Yeah. I have just picked it up on the tip of my glove. If I put it down again and it asks another ant, "What was that?"—how would it explain? There are things in the universe billions of years older than either of our races. And they are vast . . . timeless. And if they are aware of us at all it is as little more than ants. And we have as much chance of communicating with them as an ant has with us. We know. We've tried. And we've learned that we can either stay out from underfoot or be stepped on.

Sakai: That's it? That's all you know?

G'Kar: Yes. They are a mystery. And I am both terrified and reassured to know that there are still wonders in the universe—that we have not yet explained everything. Whatever they are, Miss Sakai, they walk near Sigma nine-five-seven, and they must walk there alone.

The quotation: "There are things in the universe billions of years older than either of our races. And they are vast . . . timeless," as well as the attendant image of a mysterious First One ship flying near Sigma 957 in that episode (figure 1.5), inspires me to create a character who can explore the depths of space and discover such aliens. By doing so, I restore this image, recuperating it from popular culture into a role-playing game performance. During the course of game play, I, like other players, hope to try, as G'Kar did, to communicate with mysterious aliens such as the one described here. The dynamic of such images can be restored through performance when I create and play my character. Players desire immersion in such wonder—that is why many play these games, and that is how the designers have structured the game: to recuperate some semblance of a "dream given form." Players will not enact—in Mackay's term, recapitulate—the same scene as the one described above, but the idea, the images drawn from such scenes, is restored and recuperated during a character's creation and subsequent performance.

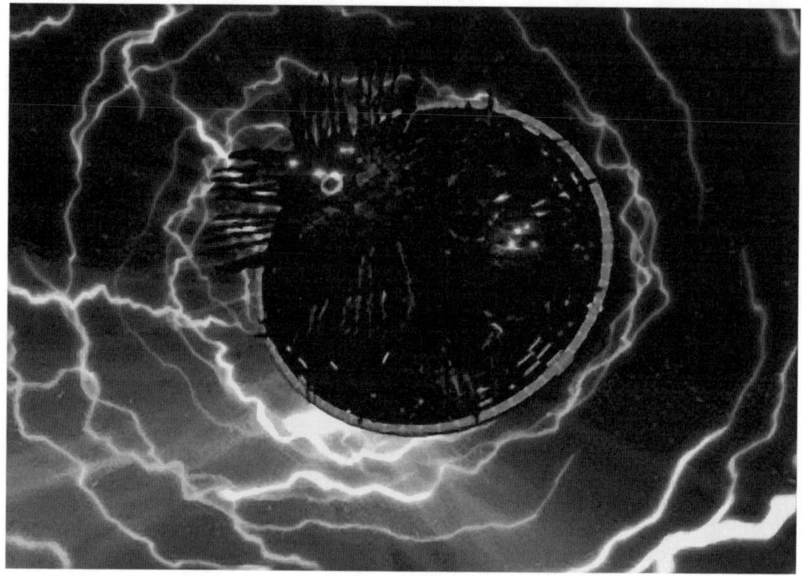

Figure 1.5.
Image of a mysterious First One ship flying near Sigma 957 from "Mind War." Photograph © 1994 Warner Bros.

From NASA to *Babylon 5:* A Surrogate Longing for Wonder

The writer of "Mind War," Straczynski, remarked that one of the reasons he created *Babylon 5* was to bring back a sense of wonder to a genre he had been exposed to as a child. "The one thing that to me always typified SF was the sense of *wonder.* Of something mysterious out there," he explains:

> And that is the one thing that I feel is so missing from much of TV SF; not to pick on S[tar] T[rek], but the reality is that going from world to world [in *Star Trek*] seems like going from [the convenience store] 7–11 to 7–11. It's all established, there's not much mystery. (Not in all cases, I'm sure that one or two could be found, but in general.) There should be *differences,* and things we don't understand and will *never* fully understand. (For me, one of the best episodes in this regard is "Mind War," specifically the tag of the episode [described above], which still gives me a shiver even though I've now seen it over a dozen times. (1994g)

It is this "wonder," the "element most emblematic of science fiction at its very best," that Straczynski received when reading science fiction. He facetiously blames his love for science fiction on Ray Bradbury, one of the "grandmasters" of science fiction: "It's all that damned Bradbury's fault" (1997:7). It was the sense of wonder he gained while reading the works of classic science fiction earlier in his life that inspired him to create that feeling in a television series: "Ancient monuments that towered thousands of feet above you, mysterious secrets revealed at terrible price; great fleets of starships riding fire, passing overhead en route to distant suns; aliens whose thoughts are akin to our own as the spider. *The sense of wonder*" (9). Players want to immerse themselves in this same kind of wonder as found in *Babylon 5* and in written works of science fiction. This fictional recuperation of popular culture images through performance in the *Babylon Project*—itself a technological construct of postmodernity (structured as it is from modernism's mechanized rules structure coupled with a popular culture's circulation through capitalistic commodities)—configures players in an empirical data arrangement culled from a culture where, through simulation, they attempt to live in that semiosphere.

This simulation is what performance theorist Joseph Roach would call a surrogate performance: "how [a] culture reproduces and re-creates itself" through performance (1996:2). This kind of performance, Roach explains, "continues as actual or perceived vacancies occur in the network of relations that constitutes the social fabric. Into the cavities created by loss through death or *other forms of departures*, I hypothesize, survivors attempt to fit satisfactory alternatives" (2; emphasis added). The perceived loss of a manned space program, ending in the mid-1970s, did not foreclose the desire, dream, and hopes for humanity's reach into space. Instead, it was repressed beneath the surface of national consciousness and political policy, the pressure causing it to surface in various performances.

Unmanned probes to the outer planets—the Pioneers, the Voyagers, and Galileo—all brought back images of stark wonder: the probes became humanity's eye that plucked images from the depths of space and beamed them back to Earth. These robotic probes performed high-tech wonders in the imagination of many. These projects were part of a process by which some people's desire for manned space exploration was assuaged. The "process of trying out various candidates in different situations," Roach theorizes, "the doomed search for originals by continuously auditioning stand-ins—is the most important of the many meanings that users intend when they say the word *performance*" (1996:3). In this sense, planetary probes act as a surrogate attempting to fulfill people's desire for manned space exploration.

Fiction provides another avenue for surrogation. Some writers, such as Straczynski, even used NASA's high-tech surrogate performance—an image of Voyager's fly-by image depicting a volcanic eruption on Io, one of Jupiter's moons (figure 1.6). Jupiter and its moons appeared as important tropes in *2001: A Space Odyssey* and in *Babylon 5*. Within these performances, theorist Roach contends, "blossom the most florid nostalgias for authenticity and origin" (1996:3–4). Players of science fiction role-playing games draw upon such images in an attempt to fulfill romantic notions of manned space travel. In a scene described in the script of "The Coming of Shadows" (a scene ultimately not broadcast) Straczynski wrote: "And where the beam [from an enemy warship] struck, the planet ERUPTS in a blast that is similar in appearance to the volcanoes on Io: seen in silhouette, a geyser against space" (1996a:397). This is evidence of how science fiction writers recuperate NASA images to help depict their fantasies.

Role-playing games provide yet another form of surrogation. These substitutions, however, were and are not the "real" thing. They are a performance that, Roach contends, "stands in for an elusive entity that it is not but that it must vainly aspire both to embody and to replace" (1996:3). The *Babylon Project* is not only a surrogate performance of play-

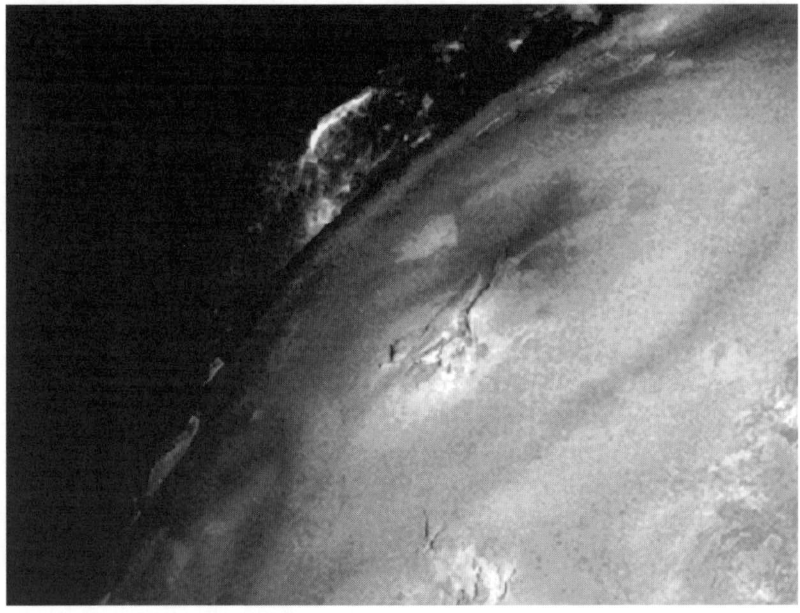

Figure 1.6.
Voyager's hi-tech surrogate performance: a fly-by image depicting a volcanic eruption on Io, one of Jupiter's moons. Photograph courtesy of NASA.

ers' desire to participate in the universe of *Babylon 5*, it is an attempt to fulfill many people's romantic desire to travel and explore the stars and alien worlds. In Schivelbusch's parlance, like the railroad before it, space probes serve to open up vast regions of unexplored and unsettled space in the imaginations of many. Yet without the possibility for actual space travel, people can only explore and settle space through a performance of simulation. Within their characters, participants travel virtually to distant planets and star systems depicted on *Babylon 5*.

In other words, a player's role-playing game performance is a substitution that replaces an older form of popular culture with a new one. The character sheet is comprised of sedimentary layers storing *Babylon 5* memories as a kind of surrogate. Players become diagenetically transformed by restoring these behaviors during the pressure of performance. "Human agents draw on these resources of memory stored up (but also reinvented) in what" Roach calls "the kinesthetic imagination"—a site that "inhabits the realm of the virtual" (1996:26–27). Roach may be talking about Circum-Atlantic performance, but his theory is just as applicable to role-playing games. Players recuperate popular culture through performance. Instead of lines in a play that actors perform when enacting a script, or movements restored through a dancer's body, the character sheet provides a text of potential surrogate behaviors players activate verbally during game play.

There are three layers of recuperative performance operating within the *Babylon Project* game. They point toward what Roach calls the "truth of simulation, of fantasy, of daydreams, . . . its effect on human action may have material consequences of the most tangible sort and of the widest scope" (1996:27). These interlaced layers are the desire to explore space (including its attendant images from space probes and the Hubble Telescope); written works of science fiction depicting humanity's colonization of space; and the visual media of science fiction, such as *Star Trek* and *Babylon 5*. The cross-fertilization of desire between science and fiction began before the United States government created NASA, whose function was to take us out into space, in 1958. The "so-called fathers of modern rocketry," as McCurdy explains, were inspired by science fiction (1997:18).

Rocket scientist Konstantin Tsiolkovskii himself wrote works of fiction that were intended to take readers out into space. Robert Goddard, who in 1926 became the first person to launch a rocket propelled by liquid fuel, was inspired by Jules Verne and H. G. Wells. "Goddard remembers climbing a backyard cherry tree and dreaming of a voyage to Mars," McCurdy tells us (1997:18). In addition, a group of science fiction writers, led by *New York Herald Tribune* reporter Edward Pendray, formed the American Interplanetary Society in 1930 (19). Events such as these helped inspire the dream of manned space exploration. Arthur C. Clark, a prolific science fiction writer, who cowrote the script for *2001: A Space Odyssey* (along with director Stanley Kubrick), was the scientist who proposed the idea of a network of orbital communication satellites in 1945. After the success of the Apollo Moon landings in the late 1960s and early 1970s, which were spurred on by Cold War competition, further interest in space exploration seemed to wane, and the Apollo program was closed down. "In the decade following the 1969 landing on the Moon, many Americans turned inward and scaled back their expectations. The public lost interest in space exploration," McCurdy contends (1997:147). Citing the popular arguments against space travel, McCurdy provides a familiar list of the reasons for this loss: "Environmentalists talked about limits to growth and learning to live with fewer resources. Opinion leaders warned about the dangers of technology, and President Jimmy Carter delivered a nationally televised address on the national sense of malaise" (147). Whether Carter's malaise speech was a reaction to the Iranian hostage crisis, the United States coming out of the Vietnam War, and an oil shortage crisis, which caused a lack of desire for further space exploration, is not made clear. McCurdy feels, however, that it was this attitude of "national despondency that those pushing space frontiers wanted to sweep away" (147).

The space program was reduced to space shuttle flights into Earth's orbit, and the Moon, Mars, and the outer planets are reserved now only for space probes. It took the ideas of science fiction writers to galvanize the rocket scientists who gave us space flight, and it took Cold War funding to create an actual race to space. Science fiction writers (of novels, films, and television), even more prolific than before, still create visions of humans colonizing space. And because that idealistic goal is not attainable in reality today, it is through such simulated performances as role-playing games that many take a surrogate trip to the stars. This performance is a form of "kinesthetic imagination," to use Roach's term. It "is not only an impetus and method for the restoration of behavior," he tells us, "but also a means of its imaginative expansion through those extensions of the range of bodily movements and puissances that technological invention and specialized social organization can provide" (Roach 1996:27). Into this "technological invention" comes the role-playing game, which attempts to create "vortices of behavior" that "canalize specified needs, desires, and habits in order to reproduce them" in performance (28).

Figure 1.7.
Crystal city of Minbar. Photograph © 1996 Warner Bros.

The image of the city of Minbar, with its blue crystal buildings that spire into the air (figure 1.7), is reminiscent of Ray Bradbury's *The Martian Chronicles,* where he describes "a house of crystal pillars on the planet Mars by the edge of an empty sea" (1979:2). Straczynski received inspiration from classic works of science fiction and translated it to television, restoring an image from another text. As writers like Bradbury helped inspire rocket scientists and romanticized manned space exploration, so is Straczynski today providing the same inspiration. (*Babylon 5* became a favorite of NASA and his cancelled spin-off series, *Crusade,* had received the scientific advice of NASA's Jet Propulsion Laboratory.)

The *Babylon Project* gives players the mechanism to immerse themselves in the universe of *Babylon 5*. The character record sheet becomes the site, the interface, for transforming this fantasy into performed reality. However much the images of outer space and science fiction are disseminated through popular culture, they do not galvanize public sentiment for a new push into space. Instead, the rest of the solar system remains silent, untouched by our footsteps. And it is only through a surrogate performance, as found in such immersive sites as role-playing games, that participants are reconfigured and transported out among the stars.

Chapter 2

"Captain on the Bridge"

Six Frames of Immersion in the Game *Babylon 5 Wars*

Battlefield Tourism

Battlefields are some of the most popular tourist attractions. Elizabeth Diller and Ricardo Scofidio, architects concerned with theorizing on the connection between war and tourism, contend that battlefields fulfill "a desire for the extreme, which is bound together with a fascination for heroism" (1994:25). If not in actuality, then through virtual images evoked by historical memory, war films, and news footage, the "battlefield is a site of high drama, encoded with ideology and consecrated by bloodshed. Battlefields are strong attractions insofar as they directly feed the tourist's desire for 'aura,' a quality deemed absent in the mediated world but considered retrievable in sites of the cultural past" (25). The authenticity, the "aura" Diller and Scofidio mention is as much mediated, however, as the rest of the "mediated world." The typical tourist, not a former soldier or witness to an actual battle, views the battlefield through mediated images: in her mind the tourist overlies the battlefield with tropic images from war movies, photographs, novels, film, history books, and news footage. However much the site is "mute without the paper that is needed to name it, explain it, and validate it for the tourist—the elaborate system of texts and artifacts which help to authenticate the 'authenticate' " (28), it still conjures no "picture" for the tourist without these mediated images. The authentic artifacts of the battlefield help prompt the narrative memories. Battlefields are not the only places where this occurs, for war games elicit these mediated images of battles as well.

Games of strategy, such as chess, have existed for centuries. But war games that simulate actual combat are relatively new. Most simulation war games grew out of a post–World War II growth in hobby wargaming, which began in 1953 when Charles Roberts published *Tactics;* in 1958 he founded the Avalon-Hill Game Company, a leading publisher of war games through the 1990s. Before that, around the time of World War I, H. G. Wells wrote the rules to the game *Little Wars* (1913), in which players used miniature figures and a sand table to simulate a battlefield environment. Fletcher Pratt published his naval war game around this time as well. War games, as sites of simulation for training, were developed by the Prussians in the nineteenth century (Fannon 1996:283).

Simulation war games provide the participant with a different kind of impression of war than what tourists receive when visiting sites of war memorials; such tourists "devote their leisure time to come and see, remember, or conjure up, something they may know little or nothing about" (Zavatta 1994:11). In war tourism, Sylvie Zavatta contends, sites of history become remanaged into "the (re)creation of places of memory" which have the "aura of patriotic and historical significance"—the past becomes "perfect(ed)" as it is "constituted in the present" (12–13). Within this "perfect(ed) past" the tourist "tries to grasp the impalpable—and back home, with an ostentatious gesture (backed up by photos), he can endlessly proclaim, just like the soldier whose heroism he could have admired: I was there" (13).

Tourists visit battlefields and see over them images of war deriving from mediated memory (through books, film, and television). They take photographs of an empty battlefield so they can later look at them and relive the memories they had when they visited the real site. War games, on the other hand, provide a "safe" way for tourists of war to *participate* in a battle. Players are neither tourists nor soldiers, however: through a structure of rules, they can participate in a simulation of a war they never experienced. Photographs may give tourists a record of being at a historical monument, but a war game gives players a sense of participating in the battle itself. Without the fear of injury or death, the war gamer experiences the "fun and glory" of a battle, whether in World War II games or in the futuristic combat of science fiction war games. In the former, players simulate historical wars; in the latter, they perform battles occurring in science fiction stories.

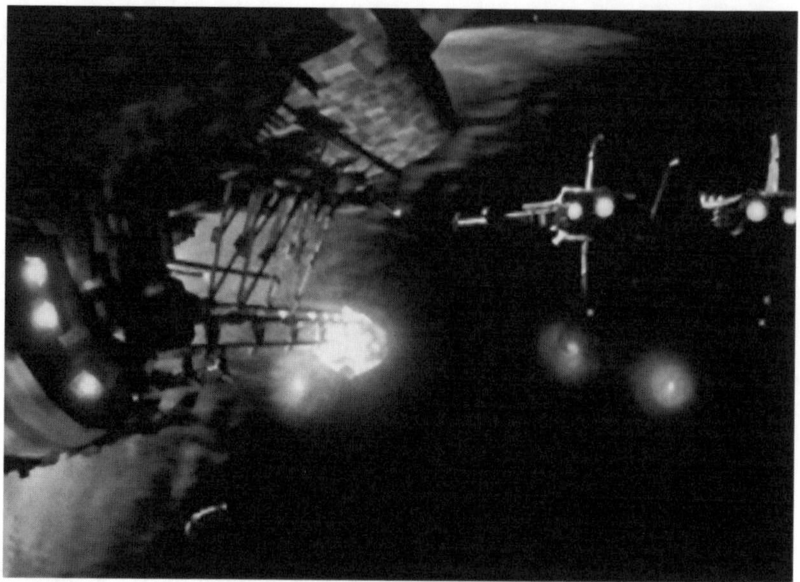

Figure 2.1.
Using mass-drivers, Centauri war cruisers propel asteroids onto the surface of the Narn home world in "The Long, Twilight Struggle." Photograph © 1995 Warner Bros.

One of the "wonders" Straczynski lists as being "emblematic of science fiction at its very best" is the image of "great fleets of starships riding fire, passing overhead en route to distant suns" (1997:9). Designers of the game *Babylon 5 Wars* transported Straczynski's stories of starships riding fire from his television show to a board game. The game reconfigures players into the role of starship captains who determine what actions their ships will enact. A system of rules defines the function and abilities of ships and describes what players can do with them. Players manipulate either cardboard pieces with pictures of ships on them or lead miniatures that they can paint, moving them on a two-dimensional hexagonal surface. Each ship also has an accompanying reference chart listing such key functions as the location of weapons, engines, hanger bays, bridge, and thrusters, and hull structure. Each of these structures contains a finite amount of graph paper–like squares indicating how much damage it can take before it is destroyed. The sensors, for example, are represented by a grid containing twenty squares, indicating that the sensor can take twenty points of damage before it is destroyed. Through a low-tech device (rules, sheets of paper, and cardboard counters on a map), players enact a high-tech performance—the simulation of starship combat in the *Babylon 5* universe.

Low-tech simulations are modeled on such high-tech images as the one shown on the opening page of this chapter—which in itself is a simulacra based on Straczynski's script. Cardboard and paper are virtual images of an object created from the imagination. The starships appearing on television are created from computer code. Actors who perform as captains of these ships perform Schechnerian "strips of behavior" from Straczynski's television script. The performances by these actors are not the actions of someone who has actually experienced starship combat, and players of this war game do not actually perform combat either. Rather, they restore the behaviors of a simulacrum. "To simulate," philosopher Jean Baudrillard writes, "is to feign to have what one doesn't have" (1994:3). Players simulate a type of combat that does not exist.

The pieces on the map, the ship display sheets, weapon systems, and movement—the rules structure—all reference starship combat from episodes of *Babylon 5* previously viewed by players. Like battlefield tourists, players "visit" and perform simulated battles from episodes of *Babylon 5*. When they play this war game, participants immerse themselves in this universe. Through a set of rules they reenact events that have already taken place in fiction. The rules set up the capabilities of the starships participants control—and like captains, players know the limits of the ships they "command." Although players may not see themselves literally as Captain Sheridan (Bruce Boxleitner) on *Babylon 5*, they do perform actions similar to this character. Causal actions in a war game have simulated consequences. Each ship in *Babylon 5 Wars,* as are the characters in the *Babylon Project* role-playing game, is represented in an empirical way, almost as if the ships themselves are characters. Players perform as great fleets high among the stars battling each other in an agon from a *Babylon 5* episode.

This combat is not scripted by dialogue or a writer's scene description, however. Instead, the architecture of starship "characters" is delineated empirically as a schematic of energy, movement, and weapons—translating and reducing the possibilities and potentials for action of these ships into data on sheets of paper. Players maneuver their ships in a dance around a map as they look for the best opportunity to unleash laser cannons, particle beams, and so forth against their enemy in an attempt to claim victory. This application of energy, movement, and combat occurring at each turn is modeled on classical drama, with an Aristotelian beginning, middle, and end.

In *Babylon 5 Wars* the Aristotelian structure (given in parentheses) can be seen in the "Combat Sequence of Play": 1. Start of Turn Actions (= instigating elements), 2. Movement (= action and conflict), 3. Combat (= climax), and 4. End of Turn Actions (= denouement). Within the symbolic timeframe of the game, this sequence represents ten seconds—each turn is like an act taking about thirty minutes to play in actual time. First, players determine the amount of power their ships have, who has initiative, and the electronic warfare status, and then announce how much their ships are accelerating or decelerating this turn. During the movement phase, players maneuver their ships on a hexagonal map—the distance they travel is determined by the speed of their ship. After movement, players secretly determine which ships will fire at targets and then announce this action. Weapon hits are determined as a function of distance for each weapon. Players resolve any damage received and the location of that damage on each ship's corresponding schematic sheet. These determinations are based on random rolls of dice cross-referenced on a damage table. During the final phase, players land or launch any small fighter craft and adjust the power levels of their ships to account for any damage received (see Graw and Glass 1997:7). The rather dry rules structure is rife with dramatic conflict. It contains the script of potential actions for combat behavior. Data on sheets of paper represents arcing laser beams and pulse cannons that can, for example, shear off sections of an Omega Class destroyer that has a (fictional) crew of two hundred and fifty people.

Although the game simulates, even glorifies, the crippling and destruction of starships, it does not depict the death of the crews who are on board these cruisers. Like any simulation, the game does not have consequences outside the fact that a damaged ship does not perform as well as an undamaged one. For the player, who performs the role of the ship itself, damage does not mean the death of her crew but the crippling of the ship's empirical capability to function, to perform, at its peak potential. It lessens her possibility to "win." War games, unlike real wars, simulate only the high-tech performance of hardware. The consequences are the removal of data that represents the ship's potential as a piece of hardware. In a real war this translates into the death of crews who perform the tasks that give a ship combat its capability in the first place. In the simulated world, damage translates into loss of face. Unlike real military simulations, however, players are not training for war. They are instead reliving a story of a fictional war as told through a television series. Instead of just watching the story of alien civilizations at war many fans want to *play* the battles from this fictional war—they want to simulate the simulated and perform within the virtual, making it concrete, something they can touch.

The designers of the game have embedded within the rules bits of behavior from *Babylon 5,* allowing players to simulate actions already performed in episodes of the show. For example, in the episode "Severed Dreams," Straczynski's second scene reveals a civil war battle between an Earth Alliance ship, the *Clarkstown,* and a rebel Earth ship, the *Alexander.* On board the *Alexander,* Lt. Trainor turns to the commanding officer, Major Ryan, and argues for conflict against the loyalists:

Trainor: . . . You've got to let me open fire with the aft batteries.
Ryan: I don't want to kill any more of our own ships!
Trainor: We have no choice! Forward interceptors on the *Clarkstown* are down. We can punch through the hull. Major, please. Let me take the gloves off the firing team.
Ryan: Tell the aft batteries to open fire. (Straczynski 1996b)

Lt. Trainor orders the weapons to fire, and the viewer sees red laser beams reach from out the rear of the ship into the *Clarkstown,* destroying it, and chunks of metal debris float off into space.

Looking at the "Earth Alliance Omega Destroyer" control sheet provided with the game (similar to the Hyperion shown in figure 2.7), one can see how the designers took elements from "Severed Dreams" and translated them into game rules. "Forward interceptors on the *Clarkstown* are down," Trainor says. In the rules, Bruce Graw and Robert Glass, both designers of the game, describe the "interceptor" weapon as being "highly effective at deflecting some or all of an incoming shot," adding that such weapons "also generate an energy web which surrounds the ship," reducing "the effectiveness of incoming lasers" (1997:43). This description, in game rule terms, restores the performance trope of the scene from "Severed Dreams." Take out the interceptors on an enemy ship, and the player, too, could reenact the *potential* for such a destructive moment as the one found in this scene. If the player fires the correct weapons and scores a hit, and the defending ship is unable to perform an appropriate defense, then it could be destroyed like the *Clarkstown.*

In the game, the "bulk of hits on most ships is *structure,* representing the actual hull of the vessel. . . . *If a structure block is completely destroyed, that side of the ship breaks apart at the end of the turn*" (Graw and Glass 1997:23). The authors emphasize the climatic moment of the game as if to say that players, too, can play the part of Major Ryan and Lt. Trainor ("Major, please. Let me take the gloves off the firing team") and destroy the enemy ship in a restored behavior of fiery destruction. The flames and pieces of debris provided by computer special effects, however, are not included with the game. Pencil marks on a black and white sheet of paper provide the only visual in witnessing a weapon strike, for the performance of destruction is indicated in the game as squares that players mark off on ship control sheets. This is the only indication that damage occurs. The rules also do not provide a narrative comment about this destruction.

Indeed, the game is formatted in the "play" of a "hunt." According to performance scholar Richard Schechner, play evolved as a form of hunting: a lot of "play behavior is adapted from hunting, [and] that hunting is a kind of playing" (1988:102). From this hunting play, Schechner contends, drama developed. The "circumpolar hunting cultures," he writes, "translated strategic, future-oriented hunting behavior into strategic language: story-telling" (103). The drama in a war game is not, however, what we are used to seeing in our popular stage productions, where an author's words are performed onstage by actors. It is a cyborg drama, composed of elements of machine and animal. The players are cyborglike (part machine, part human flesh), pursuing the destruction of their opponents' ships. Their perceptions are reconfigured by the rules, and, in the game, players align their ship-bodies in the best position to unleash an orgasmic fury of laser-red destruction, hoping to reach the primary structure of the ship, for if this "is completely destroyed, the ship blows up immediately . . . and is removed from play" (Graw and Glass 1997:23). From the players' point of view, part of the pleasure of the game, ironically, comes from receiving damage.

Schechner perceives only the pleasure of the hunt in play: it "belongs to species that depend on other species for life, who stalk, attack, and kill prey" (1988:98). The "playing at killing emphasizes individual or small-group action and teamwork" (102). He makes no mention, however, of the pleasure of being the hunted. Usually the hunted is a weak herbivore that has no chance to defend itself, but only to hide and escape. In a simulated war game, both sides are carnivorous, and this stems partly from an ancestral form of play intended as training to keep predators in peak performance: "play keeps in practice, on call, a regular, crisis-oriented expenditure of kinetic energy. In play, energy is spent in behavior that is not only harmless but fun. *Decisively, play allows kinetic potential to be maintained not by being stored but by being spent*" (99). If a player loses a ship, he gets to reperform a virtual image from scenes of destruction in *Babylon 5:* a special effects destruction stored in his imagination activated in the game from his own performance. Unlike the captain of the *Clarkstown,* however, players get to play again, so a loser in one game can become a winner in another. The pleasure comes from the hunt as well as from being the hunted, for the prey, if skilled, can turn and become the hunter. In real military training (called war games), as well as among animals and humans that hunt, Schechner's theory about maintaining one's kinetic potential is plausible. However, in a simulation of a television show depicting science fiction warfare as a form of leisure, that thesis does not hold up, because both sides are the hunter and have the potential to win the next round. This game is an entertainment for cyborgs.

Within the architectural space of *Babylon 5 Wars*—itself a cultural artifact—the map and starship control sheets represent the schema from a fictional story. This schema, explicated by rules, temporarily transforms the perceptual field of the players: players perceive those starships (and their representative data) as potential actions of both machine selves and human selves. The conflict of this drama is not performed by the bodies of trained actors on a stage who are enacting an author's words. Through a combination of rules, counters on a map, and ship control sheets, players become reconfigured and subsequently immersed in the universe of *Babylon 5*. The players do not literally perform the part of starship captains, and neither do they interact with any kind of crew. Instead, they are transformed into cyborg characters—rules and empirical ship display sheets comprise the geometry and trajectory of their performance in and as *machine*.

This machine, embedded with images from the television show, absorbs and then reconstitutes the subject within a combat simulator where there are no people, no families lost in the battle—no need to acknowledge the wives (and husbands) of dead soldiers floating invisibly between the phosphorous memory of a fictional scene on television and the cold marked graphs of paper representing the deaths this game avoids. It fulfills Baudrillard's notion that an age of simulation is marked by a "transition from signs that dissimulate something to signs that dissimulate that there is nothing" (1994:6). Each strategic thought about energy application in the game, tactical movements of starships on the map board, or the decision to fire destructive tendrils from laser cannons "stands," in the words of postmodern scholar Fredric Jameson, "like an imperative to grow new organs, to expand our sensorium and our body to some new, yet unimaginable, perhaps ultimately impossible, dimensions" (1991:39). In effect, the players are reconfigured into the universe of *Babylon 5* as bodies of starships. Players perform a high-tech fantasy where their bodies do not "end at the skin," but become part of a Harawayian cyborg, where, through "imagination and in other practice, machines can be prosthetic devices, intimate components, friendly selves" (Haraway 1991:178). The story players perform, the conflicts they enact, the mise-en-scene they lay out take place on a two-dimensional map. Characters are but cardboard counters. Their psychology and bodies are schematics on ship control sheets.

If, as Haraway maintains, in the cyborg age we use machines as intimate prosthetic devices—where we do not distinguish between the machine and ourselves—it is really only "as a fiction" that we find the cyborg "mapping our social and bodily reality" (1991:150). Haraway's cyborg is supposed to "contribute to socialist-feminist culture and theory" (150), but, in the world of simulated war games, the cyborg has been translated into a perverse machine where literally "the boundary between science fiction and social reality is an optical illusion" (149). The science fiction of *Babylon 5*—itself a metaphor for our contemporary world, explaining as it does where we are going and what "we as a people should be doing to create the future," as Straczynski claims (1997e)—is translated into a war game where humanity is subsumed in a machianic social reality. The players are placed in a game, which, because it is a reference to *Babylon 5*, seems to express something of Straczynski's vision. But this is only an optical illusion. In the reality of the game, the players are immersed in a "clean" simulation of war without any of the side effects occurring within the stories of *Babylon 5* itself.

The players are reconfigured as machine. The cyborg, being a "condensed image of both imagination and material reality" (Haraway 1991: 150), reconfigures the identity of the players into imaginary starships performing acts of war without the side effects of a "material reality"—the direct consequences of real war that Straczynski at times depicts in his fictional series. In "Severed Dreams," described above, Straczynski attempts to weave this element of real consequences into his story. After they destroy the *Clarkstown,* Major Ryan turns to Lt. Trainor and talks about the loss of her captain as well as their own commanding officer, General Hague (who was killed in an earlier battle):

Ryan: Bill, did you ever meet the captain of the *Clarkstown*?
Trainor: No, sir.
Ryan: He and the general were at the academy together. Hague introduced me to him

last summer. He has a wife back home, three small children, an Abyssinian cat named Max. That's what makes this war different from anything we have ever gone through before. This time we know everyone we kill. I'll try to find something to say to both of their wives—God knows what. (Straczynski 1996b)

As a simulation of ship-to-ship space combat, *Babylon 5 Wars* does not attempt to depict the lives of the personnel of the ships within the game. Instead, players determine such actions as how fast their ships will go, where to move on the map, and when to fire. The game stays at the level of many simulation war games: there is a winner and a loser. The performance of simulated war, of space combat, may signify that there is nothing behind it but another simulation (the television show), but despite this *Babylon 5 Wars* is competitive and "hot." And the heat of the drama pulses through the thoughts and actions of players, fired by the imagination of scenes from Straczynski's *Babylon 5*, formerly viewed on television but now restored through a war game.

Deconstructing a Scenario: Units of Connotation

An example scenario provided in the game depicts the "civil war" scene described in "Severed Dreams" (see figure 2.5 below). Breaking it into Barthesian lexias (arbitrary units of connotation) allows me to explicate the various layers of meaning in its structure. Each lexia is numbered, and will be so referenced below.

(1) Scenario Two: Former Friends (Earth vs. Earth).

(2) Earth Force Player #1: 1 Rebel Omega Destroyer, 24 Standard Starfuries [fighter craft].
Earth Force Player #2: 2 Loyalist Hyperion Heavy Cruisers, 12 Standard Starfuries.

(3) Set up 10 hexes apart in a pursuit format, with the Omega Destroyer and its fighters facing away from the Heavy Cruisers. All units are moving at speed 10 at the start of the game.

(4) Player #1 wins if the Omega Destroyer can disengage from the scenario, regardless of any damage he has inflicted (or how many fighters he has lost). Otherwise, Player #2 wins.

(5) Special rules: Due to fuel limitations, none of the capital ships may accelerate or decelerate by more than 10 per turn. Ramming by ships is not allowed; ramming by fighters is permitted.

(6) *Comments: The fighters are really the key to this battle, as they are the only things which can get close enough to hurt the fleeing Omega. The pursuer should ignore the Omega (except to keep on its tail) until the attacking Furies are dealt with.*

(7) *Despite how it may appear, this is a tough scenario for the pursuit forces unless the rebels make a key mistake.* (Graw and Glass 1997:72)

(1) *Scenario Two: Former Friends (Earth vs. Earth).* First, this scenario represents the "drama" of the scene in the Schechnerian sense: it provides the written outline for hot, intense action. On the one side are the fleeing rebels reminiscent of Major Ryan and his forces who support *Babylon 5*'s position in working with alien civilizations. The pursuing forces represent the forces of the *Clarkstown,* the loyalists who are "pro-Earth" and want to cleanse Earth of "subversive" alien influences. The title, "Former Friends," indicates that these two enemies were once friendly—a friendship that went beyond race, gender, or nationality, as indicated by the subheading, "Earth vs. Earth." The conflict revolves around a political policy that questions whether Earth, as the pure homeland of humans, should continue to have contact with the other *species* of alien civilizations. The writer gives just the minimum facts needed to allow players to engage in the game. There is no attempt to describe any particular political ontology comprising the scenario's own existence, yet, without a reference to the story that provides this link, the scenario has no life outside its own field of simulation. Without its specific reference to the *Babylon 5* scene, this scenario would be empty of any meaning.

(2) *Earth Force Player #1: 1 Rebel Omega Destroyer, 24 Standard Starfuries [fighter craft]. Earth Force Player #2: 2 Loyalist Hyperion Heavy Cruisers, 12 Standard Starfuries.* Here we are given two sides: rebels versus loyalists. The rebels are perceived as the underdog (there are two loyalist capital ships against one rebel ship). Omega is the last letter of the Greek alphabet; the Omega Class destroyer is the newest or latest ship class in Earth Force. Hyperion is the Titan of light and the father of the sun. The titanic pro-Earth forces can accept no light, no other influence but the purity of humanity—they can tolerate no alien influence. The pro-alien side is therefore impure. Hyperion was also the name of the original online domain for a fan-created Web page, "The Lurker's Guide to Babylon 5." Straczynski chose to name this ship the Hyperion in honor of the Web site. The squadrons of fighters are like World War II fighter planes launched from an aircraft carrier. The weapons and ships of outer

space are modeled on a future projection of present military capabilities. Fighters have the ability to destroy large ships, while capital ships provide support as well as firepower to the fleet. Around this dance of meaning, players manipulate the machinations of intense weaponry and the graceful movements of two hundred-and-thirty-meter-long ships represented by cardboard pieces one inch in size.

(3) *Set up 10 hexes apart in a pursuit format, with the Omega Destroyer and its fighters facing away from the Heavy Cruisers. All units are moving at speed 10 at the start of the game.* The number ten is a base metric unit that is used mainly in the sciences to measure phenomena with precision. In the game, the unit may be arbitrary but, as a reference to a unit of space, it connotes the authority of science within the science fiction universe of *Babylon 5*—showing that this scenario, too, follows the laws of Newtonian mechanics, that force does indeed equal mass times acceleration (F = ma), creating intense vectors of pursuit. The game has to break movement and velocity down into discrete units in order to override the fact that there really is no movement other than that derived from the players' desire to maneuver their pieces on the map board to a location where the rules say one can deliver the most destruction from high-tech laser beam weapons (as interpreted by data charts). The drama is delineated in terms of vectors of scientific authority—the science fiction of weapons arcs across the map space in the minds of players, and this only recalled from the database images stored while watching *Babylon 5*. These weapons, however, are no longer only within the realm of science fiction. In 1997 the United States Army test-fired a laser at one of their own older military satellites orbiting two hundred and sixty miles above Earth. This program evolved from President Reagan's Strategic Defense Initiative (Landay 1997:4).

The black mapboard, its surface shaped by hexagonal grids, becomes the space where cardboard starships evoke immense battles. The battle is seen only in the imagination of the players, and its only visible manifestation is the players moving cardboard pieces on this map. The ship control sheets become the visible record of what the players have done in the scene. This performance is, like all performances, ephemeral—the whole of it can never be captured or recorded, since it is never seen. The mise-en-scene appears only in the minds of the players. The sheets of paper are the interface to the history of the imaginary battle. The scenario lays out the drama, but the script—the performance text or "basic code of the events," as Schechner puts it (1988:72)—is found within the structure of the rulebook embedded by tropes from *Babylon 5*.

(4) *Player #1 wins if the Omega Destroyer can disengage from the scenario, regardless of any damage he has inflicted (or how many fighters he has lost). Otherwise, Player #2 wins.* Victory conditions determine who wins and who loses. As in war, one side is the victor, the other the vanquished. In simulated war games loss brings about damaged ships on a display sheet and destruction brings about the removal of a cardboard piece from the map. In "Severed Dreams" Major Ryan escaped with his ship and crew to *Babylon 5*. The *Clarkstown* was destroyed. In war games, part of the pleasure comes from the fact that one can reenact—simulate—a fictional or historical battle that has already taken place. Fantasy battles are restored through games in order for participants to *relive* the moment of pleasure experienced when viewing them once (or many times) before on television. The act of making the fictional real creates a "precession of simulacra," as Baudrillard contends: the models "no longer constitute the imaginary in relation to the real, they are themselves an anticipation of the real" (1994:122), which "contrive[s] to give them the feeling of the real" (124). To enter the simulation of *Babylon 5* is to enter a virtual universe—which does not exist outside the fictional delineation and enactment of memory.

(5) *Special rules: Due to fuel limitations, none of the capital ships may accelerate or decelerate by more than 10 per turn. Ramming by ships is not allowed; ramming by fighters is permitted.* Even in space, ships can run out of fuel. This is an arbitrary decision limiting how fast the ships can go. If the Omega Destroyer could accelerate in units greater than ten, it could escape more easily and victory could be achieved without any combat. In "Severed Dreams," Major Ryan chose not to escape quickly, because he did not want to leave any of his fighter crews behind. He would have to slow down the ship to let the Starfuries land, giving the *Clarkstown* the opportunity to destroy them. By not choosing to run, he was forced to fire and destroy the ship. In the game, however, the player could sacrifice the fighters, because the victory conditions allow for their abandonment. Within the scenario it is easy to make this decision, for the simulation does not include the representations of actual pilots, but counters, each representing certain units of firepower. This is seen also in fighters being allowed to ram a capital ship, like kamikaze pilots did in World War II. The evocation of a World War II tactic connotes a war in which good and evil were clearly defined. It gives players a historical context, making the simulacrum appear more real.

(6) *Comments: The fighters are really the key to this battle, as they are the only things which can get close enough to hurt the fleeing Omega. The pur-*

suer should ignore the Omega (except to keep on its tail) until the attacking Furies are dealt with. The comments, offset by italics from the rest of the scenario, seem to suggest the presence of a general, or rather, a historical record. This battle has already taken place, it seems to be implied, and all the players need do is follow the historical progression and they too could win (or lose). What's interesting in *Babylon 5 Wars* and other science fiction and fantasy war games in general is the fact that these games simulate battles that have never taken place or have taken place only in works of fiction. A traditional war game, on the other hand, attempts to simulate actual battles from World War II, for example, or places contemporary military forces into plausible simulated engagements. The players themselves may have never experienced real combat, but the simulation is a model of an actual historical event or plausible scenario. In science fiction combat simulations, the scenarios allow players to recreate fictional events. They become immersed in the fictional world of this simulation and experience it by reliving images from *Babylon 5* or *Star Wars*, or whatever the particular imaginary environment they use to simulate the battle.

The battle drive is replaced by a virtual scopic drive—participants want to *see*, to *live*, in the fictional universe constructed out of another's imagination. This battle simulation is a way of participating in a universe formerly experienced vicariously through the performance of actors (and special effects) onscreen. War games seem to proffer what war theorist Paul Virilio calls the "technicians' version of an all-seeing Divinity, ever ruling out accident and surprise" (1989:4). The contemporary war machine is searching for "a general system of illumination that will allow everything to be seen and known, at every moment and in every place" (4). The commentary for this scenario is the designers' attempt to provide players with an all-knowing, all-seeing "intelligence" needed to win the battle. The pieces on the map are laid out for all to see. The scopic drive of a war game evinces itself through the mind of players as they apply vectors of intelligence to trap their opponent along laser lines of force leading to a performance of destruction. The rules help players visibly manifest a desire to captain a starship in a futuristic battlefield of high-tech special effects—the black and white board filled with rainbows of fiery beams. Spinning metal chunks break apart from enemy ships in a display of destruction imaged in the imagination from a database of special effects recuperated from science fiction media.

(7) *Despite how it may appear, this is a tough scenario for the pursuit forces unless the rebels make a key mistake.* This observation provides artificial tension. The scenario may look easy for the loyalist (who has two capital

ships compared to one for the rebels), but it is trickier to win than it at first seems. This implied air of authority is presented in a tone of a war veteran who helps a new recruit in the field of battle. To make a mistake in the theater of war is to invite death. To make a similar error during the performance of a war game simulation leads to the possibility of losing a game. "Winning," play theorist Johan Huizinga tells us, "means showing oneself superior in the outcome of the game. . . . to excel others, to be the first and to be honoured for that" (1955:50).

Huizinga believes that the real reason war is enacted is not "economic expansion," but "pride and vainglory, the desire for prestige and the pomps of superiority" (1955:90). Echoing this desire, players at one level feel the inner adrenaline rush of victory—all the time and energy in plotting a move and executing firepower at the right moment will either pay off with the defeat of the opponent or lead to another turn, in which the player must apply new tactics in order to reposition himself for the possibility of victory. The movement of cardboard pieces on a paper map becomes the movement of a desire to pursue and/or escape the performance of an opponent, which is the *only* reality of the simulation. This desire for the simulation, for victory in war, is a longing for something that cannot be attained: space flight, the pleasure of living in the universe of *Babylon 5*, an escape from present-day Earth. "We have," Baudrillard argues in speaking about the Gulf War, "neither need of nor the taste for real drama or real war. What we require is the aphrodisiac spice of the multiplication of fakes and the hallucination of violence" (1995:75). So tourists take pictures of a battlefield in order to relive memories of a war they never experienced—or have seen only in the simulacra of films and news media. Others play war games in order to experience combat by means of an illusion. In *Babylon 5 Wars*, participants simulate what-they-are-not in order to relive an experience previously viewed on a television show. This process occurs by immersing the game's players in *Babylon 5* battles through several frames of performance.

Frames of Performance and the Process of Immersion

Schechner distinguishes four concentric layers occurring during a performance (1988:72): the frames of drama, script, theater, and performance. The drama is placed in the innermost frame. It is what the writer writes—comprised of a "written text, score, scenario, instruction, plan, or map." It is "intense (heated up)." This frame lies within the "domain of the author," and it is detached from the actual "doing" of the text or scenario. The script is the performance text—all the elements going into the interpretation and enactment of what the author has written, the drama; it is "the basic code of events" or "patterns of doing"[1] (70) inscribed in the performers' bodies as modes of behavior, delineating and explaining what performers do and how they perform. The script is the interior map of the production that occurs in the theatrical frame. The script frame lies in the domain of the teacher, master, or director. The theater frame is the "manifestation or representation of the drama and/or script." It is what the performers do onstage—the exterior, visual performance: the mise-en-scene the spectators observe. It is essentially the physical manifestation of what is written down in the play, enacted onstage. The outermost performance frame represents the "whole constellation of events, most of them passing unnoticed, that take place in/among both performers and audience" (72). The performance is more than just the events occurring on the stage; it includes the spectators' presence in the auditorium, the purchasing of their tickets, conversations among them, a couple on a date, a critic's review of the performance. Although Schechner is talking about theatrical performance in its many manifestations, these frames of performance can be applied to all the performances that make up the imaginary entertainment environment, including the *Babylon 5* war game.

Drawing on Erving Goffman's *Frame Analysis* (1974), Gary Alan Fine's *Shared Fantasy* (1983), and the work of Schechner, Daniel Mackay expands this frame analysis for role-playing games in *The Dolorous Role* (1998:60–67; 83–150), in which he examines how players reiterate and then recuperate popular culture allusions during the performance of a game. I extend this analysis to the war game in order to show the process of immersion. The performance of war game simulations is predicated on Schechner's four frames of performance—each layer reconstitutes the subject, altering the perceptual field of participants in the game. The theater of war through simulation is an event that is internal, private, and shared only among the participants, as Mackay says about role-playing games. Within these games there are no outside spectators. The participants are at once the performers and the spectators. An analysis of these frames shows how players become immersed in *Babylon 5*.

1. With the rise of the written word and literacy in the West, Schechner theorizes, "the active sense of script was forgotten, almost entirely displaced by drama; and the doings of a particular production became the way to present drama in a new way" (1988:71). What is said—the performance of the written word—became more important than *how* it was performed. So, in the West the "script no longer functioned as a code for transmitting action through time. . . . Maintaining the words intact grew in importance; how they were said, and what gestures accompanied them, was a matter of individual choice, and of lesser importance" (71).

The simulation of a performance of war translates Schechner's four areas of performance into: scenario (drama); rules (script); pieces on a map board the players manipulate (theater); and the entire space where the participants play, as well as any reference in their minds to *Babylon 5* episodes, or any other spaces of memory that locate their game in a fictional universe (performance). These layers frame the subjective experience of the participant; each helps to ultimately reconfigure the participant into a starship captain performing in a military simulation. The outermost frame, performance, comprises the whole event: the room the players are in, the pieces on the board, the images of *Babylon 5* starship combat in their minds. If this is the realm of the audience, as Schechner says, then the spectator in a simulated battle must also be the participant. Spectators who are not taking part in the action become quickly bored since they do not see the *entire* mise-en-scene comprising the theater of war the players are creating. Nonparticipatory spectators may see the pieces on the hexagonal mapboard and the player's ship control sheets, which reveal the effective firepower and relative strengths of combatants' starships, yet without a reconfiguration through the two innermost frames (the rules and the scenario), they will not know what is going on. They will remain at the level of noninterpretation. In addition, the outermost frame also lies within the realm of the virtual. In moving from inside to outside—from scenario (drama), rules (script), mise-en-scene (theater), to performances—one can see how the innermost layers provide the *interface,* the visible representation, that, like a hypertext button, keys up the entire performance within the player's imagination.

For us, Schechner's frames begin to break down at the level of subjective experience. His innermost frame is the "drama," the written text or scenario this drama expresses, allowing it to be interpreted by the script. It is then performed (the theater) for spectators (what is seen in the entire performance space). What Schechner leaves out, however, is the subjective frame—the imaginary world of the fiction. The event onstage (the theatrical presentation) is one interpretation of the dramatic text. It is, in essence, a selection of restored behaviors found within the drama that the teacher, master, or director interprets through the mise-en-scene. All the gestures, costumes, movement, physical actions of the performers, and their placement within an environment onstage are a physicalization of the drama.

In a novel, readers create a different mise-en-scene as they interpret descriptions in an author's text. A novel is not a performance, but the act of reading a novel causes the reader to act as the interpreter of the text as she translates that drama into a set of codes (the script) that becomes performed in her imagination. Words on a page provide the physical presence (the theater) in her mind. Characters and scenes and voices become virtually "visible" within the mindscape. She is at once the spectator and a participant in the novel. The words are the interface to the author's imaginary mise-en-scene. Thus a person who walks into a room and views a person reading a book is watching a performance of reading. Even if that person picks up the same book and turns to the same page as the reader, he will not be able to see the exact same theatricalization of that drama, even though they share the same words, since each person interprets what they read somewhat differently. The spectator in a conventional theater production may view a production of *Othello,* but the images onstage will not be the same ones the spectator envisioned if she read the play before seeing any kind of production of it. Once she does see one production, however, the basis of comparison may shift from her original theatrical reading of the drama to this first production, and any subsequent interpretations of the production by other directors and performers the spectator views will be based on a combination of memories retained from "viewing" the original reading and perhaps having them replaced by the viewing of an actual production.

Schechner's innermost frame, the drama, does not come to life just in the theatrical frame. Rather, the world from which it is created—the universe the author has constructed of which this story is but a part—exists in a fifth frame, the inner fantasy layer, the site of the imaginary world of the author's creation. Here exists the universe of *Babylon 5,* Tolkien's Middle-earth, Lucas's *Star Wars* universe, Shakespeare's world of *Othello,* and so forth. This central layer also folds outward, spreading its tendrils through the other frames and encompassing their very existence in a feedback loop. Without the fictional world created from the imagination, there is no frame of reference to which these other layers connect and relate. The drama is not just the scenario or play the author has written—but the fictional world or universe wherein the story takes place.

In *Babylon 5 Wars* the players become immersed through these five frames. The performance: players sit at a table in a room with the map board and playing pieces before them. A spectator can view this exterior mise-en-scene. The theater: players move pieces on the map, manipulate ship control sheets (record energy levels), choose what weapons to fire, roll dice to determine if the weapons hit and where, and allocate any damage on the ship sheet. The script: the rules arbitrate what actions players are allowed to enact within the limits of the game. The drama: the sce-

Fantasy: Universe of B5. Scene from "Severed Dreams."
Drama: Written scenario "Former Friends."
Script: The rules determine what behaviors players can restore.
Theater: The exterior, visible mise-en-scene of the script and drama. The players' behavior among themselves, as well as the actions and manipulation of the pieces on the map, ship control sheets, and rolling of dice. The virtual image, or physicalization, of the fantasy world.
Performance: The indicative world surrounding and comprising the environment of the game. Players sitting around a table in a room. Where the game is played.
Immersion: The performance subjunctive surrounds the indicative world so that now the fantasy world seems real. The players are *as if* virtual starship commanders riding fire.

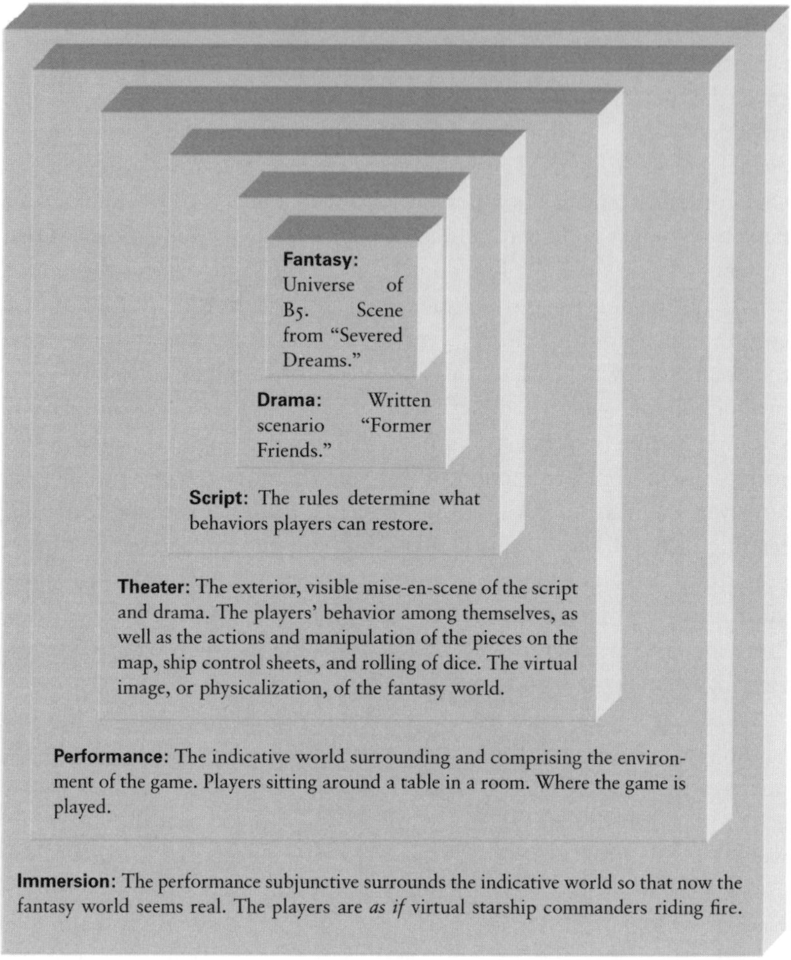

Figure 2.2.
Six Frames of an Immersive Performance, by Kurt Lancaster.

nario the players choose to play determines what ships they use and what their victory conditions are. The fifth, most central, layer I call the fantasy frame: it is the imaginary universe of *Babylon 5* created by Straczynski. A sixth all-encompassing layer is what I call the frame of immersion. As the result of the other five frames being activated, the participants of *Babylon 5 Wars* are immersed in the universe of *Babylon 5*. They are transported into the central fantasy frame, which surrounds their perceptual world. Figure 2.2 depicts the six frames of performance occurring in the game *Babylon 5 Wars*.

Actions occurring in Schechner's four frames trigger memories and images from episodes of *Babylon 5* (the fantasy frame). Players essentially rebehave, or perform, these tropic images as if they were there. They relive memories of *Babylon 5* in and as performance. The ship pieces on the map and the ship control sheets are the interfaces that activate this fantasy performance. By themselves they do not hold much meaning, but in combination with all the other frames they activate a world of fantasy for the players. Like photographs of a World War II memorial, the pieces performed *in action* put the players onto a battlefield so that they can say—holding up the marked-off ship control sheets—that they were there, too: in the battles they have viewed on television.

Fantasy immersion, however, is a special consequence of simulation, not necessarily attained in the same way if a spectator only read a novel, watched television, or visited a battlefield. These other forms are laid out for the spectator, who follows a pattern of words in a novel, observes the action onstage or onscreen, or experiences mediated images of war. These people can become immersed in the theater unfolding before them, but they do not participate as performers in that action. In immersive performances, on the other hand, participants perform the actions, and, because of this, the fantasy seems more real—it is *as if* it is happening to them. As they pass through the frames, participating in the simulation, the fantasy is enacted, performed. Schechner, in his essay "Restoration of Behavior," would say that the fantasy is a "performance subjunctive"—the simultaneous placement of the participant in the indicative world as it exists and the subjunctive world as if it exists, creating "the subjunctive mood of restored behavior" (1985:92–93). This is what happens to actors onstage and this is what happens to participants in immersive fantasy performances.

Immersion occurs as the fantasy frame expands around all the other frames, causing it to seem *as if* it were a real environment. The other frames reconfigure the participants, and immerse them in the fantasy. The pieces on the board are virtual images, the concrete physicalization of a fantasy world that has no existence except the imaginary. To experience the "performance subjunctive" means that a participant has become immersed in a fantasy. Immersion is a virtual state. It is not a virtual reality, but a virtual fantasy. The players are not starship captains in the indicative world as it exists around them, but while they play the game, they are virtually commanders riding their ships into fire. For the time being, their actions and consequences comprise a world *as if* real. The players imagine themselves as starship captains fighting a battle in Straczynski's *Baby-*

lon 5 universe. This same process occurs in fantasy role-playing games and other sites of fantasy immersion.

Immersion in Fantasy

This process of immersion can be laid out visually through photographs. One of the most popular episodes, "Severed Dreams," written by Straczynski, won the Hugo Award in 1997, and presented here are two shots from its second scene.

Players who have watched episodes of *Babylon 5* vividly remember scenes such as those shown in figures 2.3 and 2.4. The scenes from which these two shots come provide the game designers with an example to emulate, and the players themselves are inspired by these fantasy images derived from their own memory. During the game there are no special effects. Players rely on previously stored "strips" of images to help them "see" the internal performance of the exterior performance on the map board and ship display sheets.

As discussed above, game designers, most likely inspired by the above episode, wrote a dramatic scenario (figure 2.5) recreating the scene in *Babylon 5 Wars*. It provides the players with the agon for play. On the one

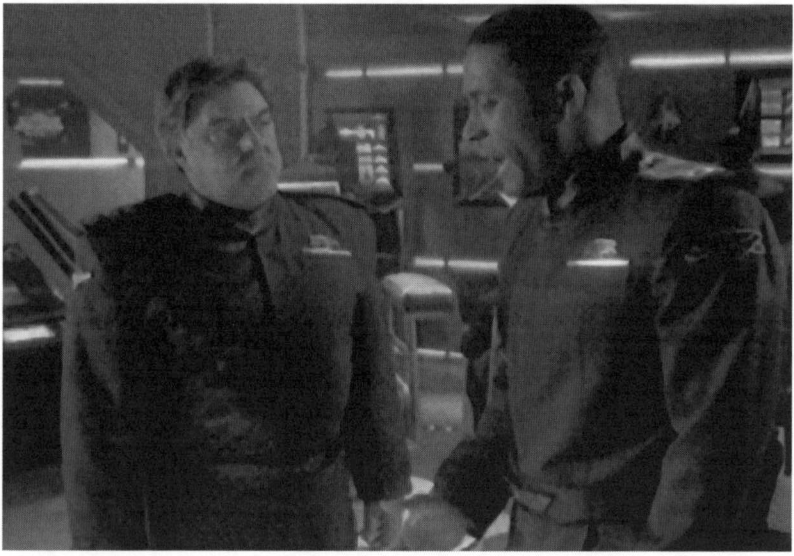

Figure 2.3.
Fantasy (universe of *Babylon 5*): Lt. Trainor asks Major Ryan to let him "take the gloves off the firing team" in "Severed Dreams." Photograph © 1996 Warner Bros.

Figure 2.4.
Fantasy: *Clarkstown* fires at the *Alexander.* Photograph © 1996 Warner Bros.

Scenario Two: Former Friends (Earth vs. Earth)

Earth Force Player #1: 1 Rebel Omega Destroyer, 24 Standard Starfuries.

Earth Force Player #2: 2 Loyalist Hyperion Heavy Cruisers, 12 Standard Starfuries.

Set up 10 hexes apart in a pursuit format, with the Omega Destroyer and its fighters facing away from the Heavy Cruisers. All units are moving speed 10 at the start of the game.

Player #1 wins if the Omega Destroyer can disengage from the scenario, regardless of any damage he has inflicted (or how many fighters he has lost). Otherwise, Player #2 wins.

Special rules: Due to fuel limitations, none of the capital ships may accelerate or decelerate by more than 10 per turn. Ramming by ships is not allowed; ramming by fighters is permitted.

Comments: The fighters are really the key to this battle, as they are the only things which can get close enough to hurt the fleeing Omega. The pursuer should ignore the Omega (except to keep on its tail) until the attacking Furies are dealt with. Despite how it may appear, this is a tough scenario for the pursuit force unless the rebels make a key mistake.

Figure 2.5.
Drama: the scenario provides the drama. From *Babylon 5 Wars,* Agents of Gaming, Dayton, OH. © 1997 Warner Bros.

side there will be a victor, on the other the vanquished. The game does not reenact the scene from "Severed Dreams" precisely. Instead, it represents the potential actions of it. The players, through the use of the rules (the set of scripted possible actions), will determine how the scene plays out in their performance of the game.

In the script shown in figure 2.6, the players are told how to move their

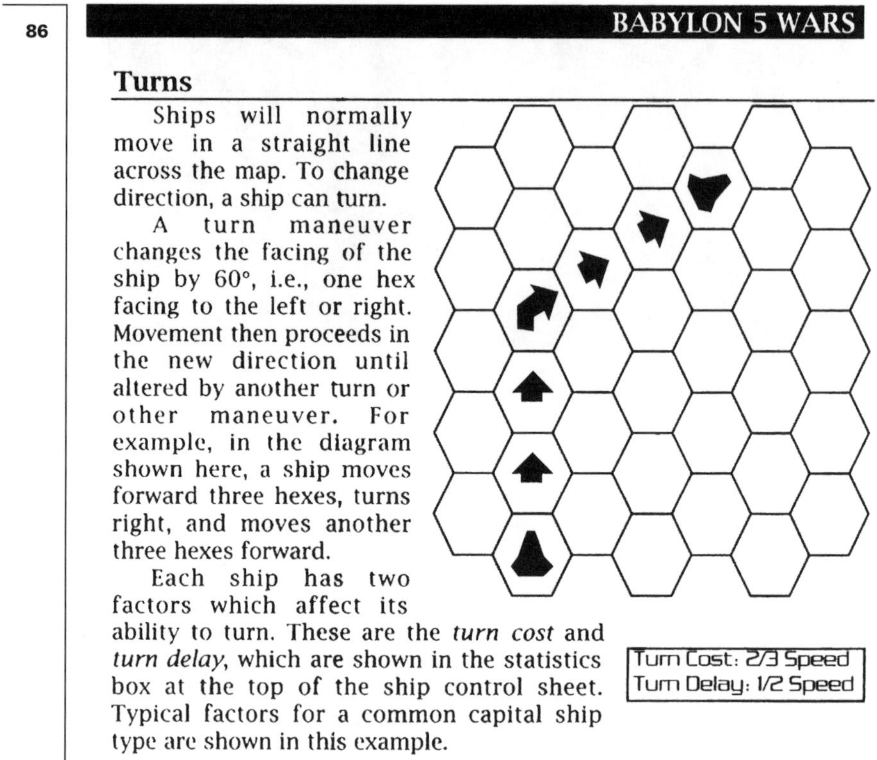

BABYLON 5 WARS

Turns

Ships will normally move in a straight line across the map. To change direction, a ship can turn.

A turn maneuver changes the facing of the ship by 60°, i.e., one hex facing to the left or right. Movement then proceeds in the new direction until altered by another turn or other maneuver. For example, in the diagram shown here, a ship moves forward three hexes, turns right, and moves another three hexes forward.

Each ship has two factors which affect its ability to turn. These are the *turn cost* and *turn delay*, which are shown in the statistics box at the top of the ship control sheet. Typical factors for a common capital ship type are shown in this example.

Turn Cost: 2/3 Speed
Turn Delay: 1/2 Speed

Figure 2.6.
Script: the rules provide the code of potential actions. From *Babylon 5 Wars,* Agents of Gaming, Dayton, OH. © 1997 Warner Bros.

ships on the map—one example of possible allowed actions. According to Schechner, it takes a teacher, master, or director to interpret a given scenario comprising a drama. In a simulation war game, the rules provide both the interpretation and the *what* of possible actions. If a player breaks the rule, then there is no script and the performance of the game falls apart. On the record sheet shown (figure 2.7), players check off various boxes as the ship becomes progressively more damaged, and they thereby enact the theater of war.

Players perform their roles as starship captains by manipulating the game pieces as they simulate starship combat (figure 2.8). The cardboard counters and schematic sheets with ship data on them are not the whole of the performance. Players must invest themselves in the action of the game by referring to the script (rules). All of these elements are the physicaliza-

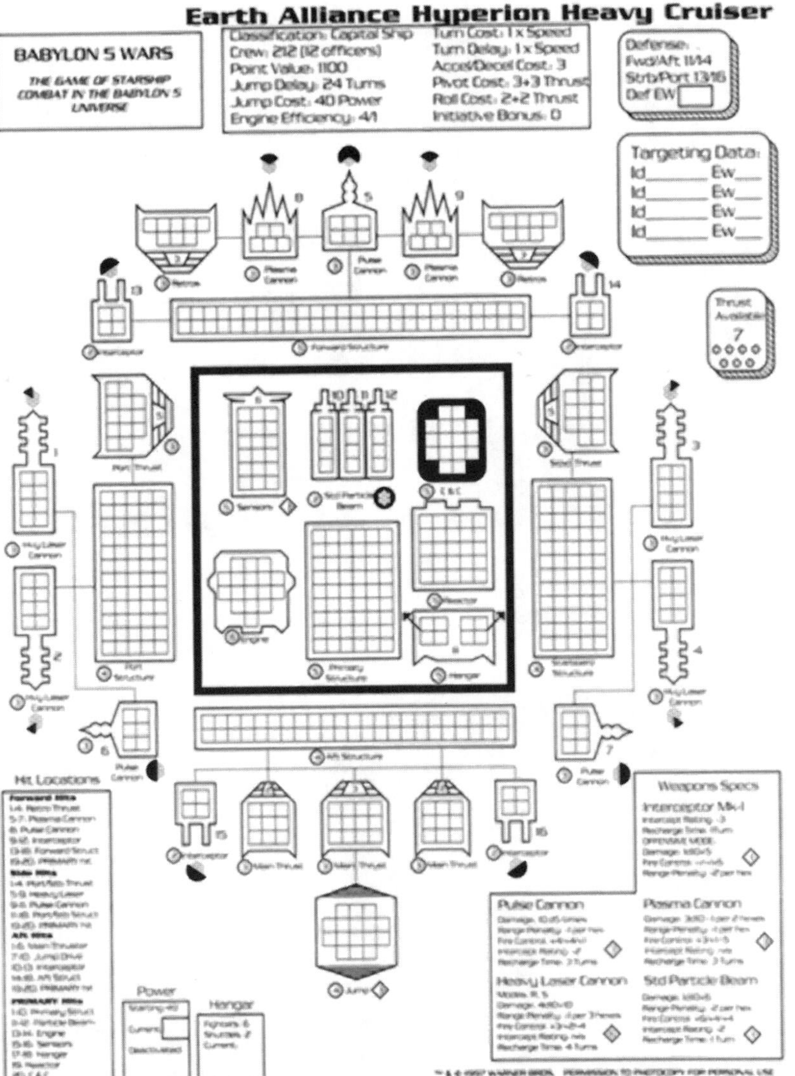

Figure 2.7.

Theater: Hyperion heavy cruiser record sheet. From *Babylon 5 Wars,* Agents of Gaming, Dayton, OH. © 1997 Warner Bros.

Figure 2.8.
Theater: players performing in *Babylon 5 Wars,* Agents of Gaming, Dayton, OH. © 1997 Warner Bros. Location: Wizards of the Coast Game Center, Seattle, WA. Photograph © 1998 Kurt Lancaster.

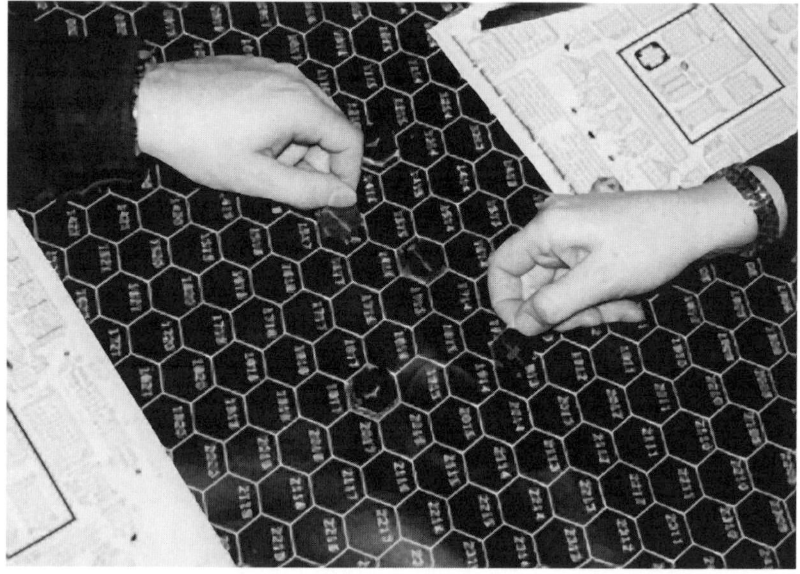

Figure 2.9.
Theater: players moving pieces. *Babylon 5 Wars,* Agents of Gaming, Dayton, OH. © 1997 Warner Bros. Location: Wizards of the Coast Game Center, Seattle, WA. Photograph © 1998 Kurt Lancaster.

Figure 2.10.
Performance: players sitting around a table as they play *Babylon 5 Wars,* Agents of Gaming, Dayton, OH. © 1997 Warner Bros. Location: Wizards of the Coast Game Center, Seattle, WA. Photograph © 1998 Kurt Lancaster.

tion, or virtual images, of the fantasy frame. This concrete physicalization is the interface to the imaginary universe of *Babylon 5*. During the performance, the spectators see players sitting at a table with game pieces (figures 2.8, 2.9, and 2.10). They see the space where the game is played and they see the players and the pieces on the board, but they do not see the *entire* performance.

When they play the scenario "Former Friends" (figures 2.11 and 2.12), players recuperate a fictive moment from the episode, and they become immersed in the *Babylon 5* universe. Spectators cannot see the full internal performance, so they do not become immersed in the game unless they participate. Players become reconfigured *as if* they are starship commanders riding ships into fire. They conjure up images from memory of a scene from the episode as they play this scenario. For the players, immersion creates a virtual fantasy.

As part of the imaginary entertainment environment, the war game fulfills the desire for immersion in battles that participants have already experienced vicariously in a book or on-screen. They now become the leaders of the battle. They are given the responsibility for command decisions that will lead to either their opponent's (simulated) destruction or their

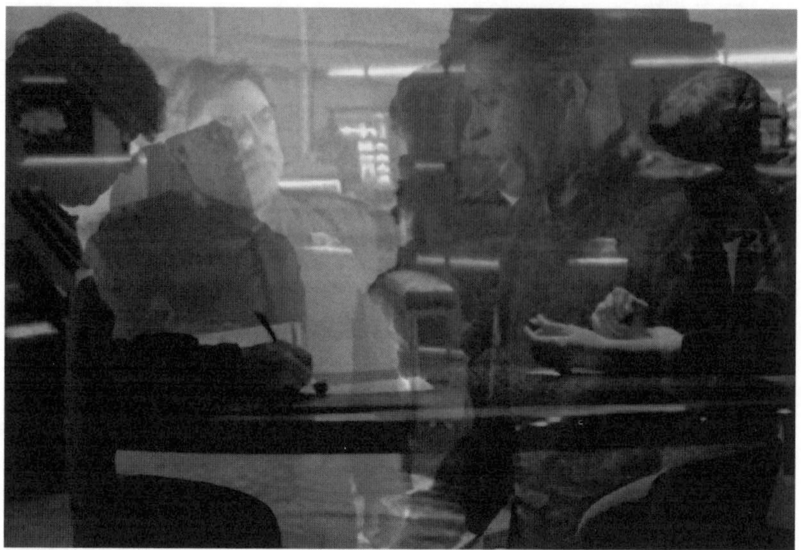

Figure 2.11.
Immersion: players "reenacting" a fictive moment from *Babylon 5* as they play the scenario. *Babylon 5 Wars,* Agents of Gaming, Dayton, OH. © 1997 Warner Bros. Location: Wizards of the Coast Game Center, Seattle, WA.

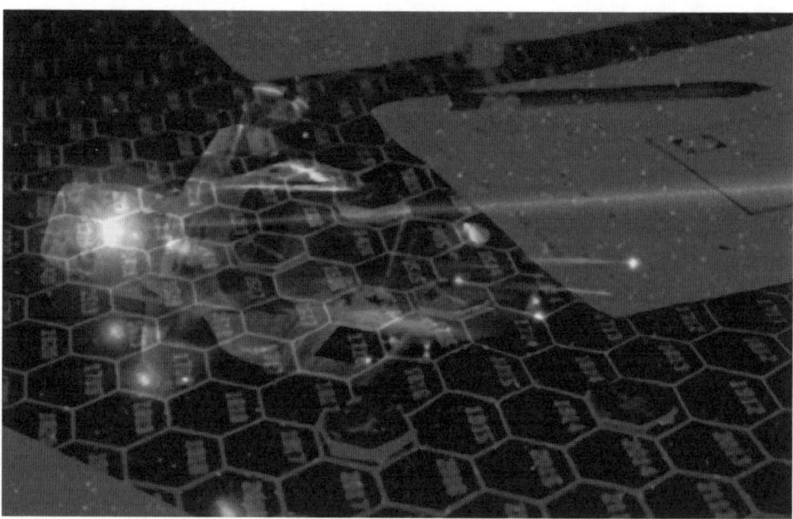

Figure 2.12.
Immersion: the game pieces represent battles that occur on episodes of *Babylon 5. Babylon 5 Wars,* Agents of Gaming, Dayton, OH. © 1997 Warner Bros.

own. The rules script the environment of the simulation, delineating the possible actions within the fantasy. Because players are no longer satisfied with just reading about science fiction battles, the fiction has now become a virtual history and the players of these games can visit such sites through a performance of simulation. Episodes of *Babylon 5* have created this history in the imaginations of the players. These images viewed in the past (depicting a fictional future) become a source for their own mediated performance of war.

This simulation is another form of Roach's surrogation through which players restore strips of *Babylon 5* battle behavior. No longer able to view new science fiction battles on-screen, the players substitute a desire to recreate—restore—those battles in simulation. If the role-playing game attempts to fill the vacuum left by the loss of the manned space program, the war game *Babylon 5 Wars* attempts to satiate a desire for something players can never experience: combat with high-tech starships. Computer-generated special effects are replaced by a schematic code that quantifies these battles, slowing them down for players to experience. This allows them to restore bits of arcing laser blasts and fiery explosions not as a special effect they watch but as a surrogate they perform.

Chapter 3

Performing the Haptic-Panoptic

The *Babylon 5* Collectible Card Game

The collectible card game had its beginning in the 1990s. *Magic: The Gathering*, designed by Richard Garfield, was the first design of this type (a medieval-style fantasy card game reminiscent of *Dungeons & Dragons*). *Magic* became a multimillion dollar business and put the small West Coast game publisher Wizards of the Coast in a position of dominance within the fantasy game industry. When Garfield's collectible card game was published in 1993, he could not foresee the $40 million Wizards of the Coast would earn in the following year. *Babylon 5* was in the second season of its five-year story, and those first two seasons cost about the same amount of money as the gross take on Garfield's game. As much money was spent on the sale of *Magic: The Gathering* as advertisers were willing to spend on two seasons of *Babylon 5*. Soon other companies would design collectible card games based on already existing fantasy worlds such as Middle-earth, *Star Wars, Star Trek, X-Files, Highlander, Dune,* and so on. In 1997 Wizards of the Coast received patent rights to their game and purchased the bankrupt TSR, Inc.—the publisher that had led the fantasy renaissance of the 1970s and 1980s with the first role-playing game, *Dungeon & Dragons* (1974).

The *Babylon 5* collectible card game permits players to perform, in a highly structured manner, the part of an ambassador of an interstellar civilization. As this character, a player may "build a Faction, then set an

Agenda for your Faction to pursue. By fulfilling your Faction's Agenda and accumulating Power, you will lead your race to a position of dominance and win the game" (Ackels et al. 1997:4). Straczynski's *Babylon 5* space station functions as a "United Nations" in space—a site of diplomacy where humans and aliens attempt to work out their differences as they expand their respective spheres of influence in the galaxy. A recurring scene in *Babylon 5* is a group of ambassadors sitting at a table arguing about matters of state. Beneath the diplomatic surface, however, lie acts of intrigue and military campaigns. In this card game the designers have attempted to capture the flavor of the intrigues, diplomatic actions, and military strikes found in the series.

Sequence of Play

A game-turn is comprised of the following sequence: ready, conflict, action, aftermath, and draw. In each turn, players struggle to gain dominance in the game using a pool of cards they own. During the ready round, players prepare their hand for a new turn. The conflict phase allows players to initiate a military, diplomatic, or intrigue action. During the action round, they choose from among a dozen different kinds of activities in an attempt to gain the upper hand. These activities can include, for example, using different cards to support or oppose an attack or to lead a fleet of ships into battle, playing certain cards to enhance others, and so forth. This is followed by an aftermath, in which players resolve any conflicts initiated in the action round. They then lay down aftermath cards, which can either enhance their position or weaken their opponent. The turn concludes with players discarding cards and drawing a new one from their individually built decks. Each player has his own deck of cards suited to the particular species he is playing. The rules describe what players can do and when.

A deck is comprised of several different types of cards, each having a special function. In the *Babylon 5* game, players compose a deck of at least forty-five cards (chosen from a pool of over four hundred). Some cards have more value than others, rated on a value scale ranging from "common," to "uncommon," to "rare." Like baseball cards, they are collectible and tradable—the rarer cards have greater monetary value than the common and uncommon ones. There are nine different types of cards: character, group, fleet, location, enhancement, event, agenda, conflict, and aftermath. Each is layered with information, letting players know how particular cards are used in the game. This information includes the name of the card, the type of card, any special function the card has, and the "cost" to bring the card into play. As an ambassador, a player has a certain amount of "influence"—translated in game terms as empirical points that determine the kind of power or sway he has among the people he represents. The player uses these points to bring other cards into play, whether characters, fleets of warships, or an agenda; these cards in turn have a different number of influence or score points. When a player attains twenty points of influence he wins the game. The cards visually represent tropic elements of intrigue, war, and diplomacy found on episodes of *Babylon 5*.

The cards in a player's hands are hidden from other players' view. At the proper moment, the player will lay out certain cards from her hand, setting up a mise-en-scene called the "playing field" around one of the four main ambassadors she plays: Human (Jeffrey Sinclair), Centauri (Londo Mollari), Minbari (Delenn), and Narn (G'Kar). Around the ambassador are placed other cards—a row of support—including characters, institutions (such as the Psi Corp), fleets of ships, and location cards (such as a homeworld or colony). The player can also promote character cards from this supporting row of cards to an "Inner Circle." The player uses an Inner Circle to promote other supporting characters into the Inner Circle; support or oppose a fleet during military action; increase influence in the game; or use any of the special abilities described on the card, such as diplomacy or intrigue, for instance. With these cards players attempt to create intrigues or battles, or conduct acts of diplomacy against other players. As they win various conflicts, their influence increases. As conflicts increase, tensions between the various civilizations rise, and may lead to war.

Character cards have certain abilities, which are indicated by a number. These abilities include the various skills the character possesses, including diplomacy, intrigue, leadership, and psionic ratings (the mind powers of the psi corps). The character card for Jeffrey Sinclair (the commander of the *Babylon 5* during the show's first season), for example, lists a diplomacy skill of four and a leadership ability of three. If the card is a military fleet or a homeworld it has a military strength ability representing its capability in combat. Every card also has a description indicating any special functions it has beyond the four generic abilities. The special function for the Sinclair character card, for example, states: "Rotate Jeffrey Sinclair to prevent the Minbari tension towards the Humans from increasing for the rest of the turn" (figure 3.1). High tensions lead to war. Sinclair, strong in diplomatic skill, has the ability to ease tensions, lessening the chance of war.

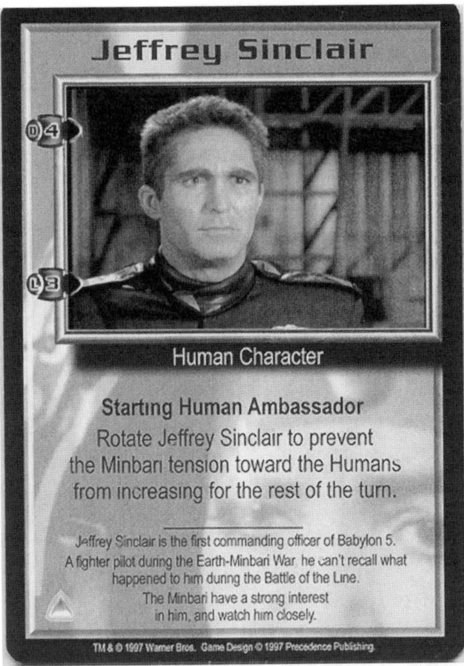

Figure 3.1.
The character card for Jeffrey Sinclair (Michael O'Hare). Notice the several pieces of information scattered around the card. From *Babylon 5 Collectible Card Game,* Precedence Publishing, Tempe, AZ. © 1997 Warner Bros.

Rotating the card on the table from a vertical to a horizontal position indicates that the player has used an ability on that card or performed some other action during the turn. The card cannot be used again until the next turn. The numerical values represent the relative strengths of characters in determining who wins a diplomatic, military, psionic, or intrigue conflict.

After a conflict is resolved, when those with the highest ability total win, and those with the lowest lose, players "may play any number of valid aftermath cards. Aftermath cards reflect the change and growth of characters, resulting from their choices and experiences. They are used to tell a character's story, showing how their life has been affected as a consequence of their actions" (Ackels et al. 1997:30). The aftermath cards, containing narrative tropes from the show, are an attempt on the part of the game designers to translate *Babylon 5*'s story arc into an essentially nonnarrative and nonlinear form and to build character development in the structure of the game. One of Straczynski's thematic purposes for

Figure 3.2.
The character Susan Ivanova has a diplomacy rating of "1" and a leadership ability of "3." From *Babylon 5 Collectible Card Game,* Precedence Publishing, Tempe, AZ. © 1997 Warner Bros.

Babylon 5 was to examine "the fundamental importance of choice, consequence, and responsibility for those choices in a society that tells you that you have no choices, that consequences don't matter, and that we don't have to act responsibly" (1997e). Aftermath cards represent the consequences for any actions players may take with their characters.

For example, a player (performing the role of Jeffrey Sinclair, the human Ambassador) has lost a diplomatic conflict with the Centauri. One of Sinclair's inner-circle characters, Susan Ivanova, the first officer of *Babylon 5* (figure 3.2), helped support the conflict (the card was rotated, indicating that the character cannot be used again until it is "readied"—rotated back to a perpendicular position at the beginning of the next turn). Her diplomatic skill is a "one," rather low. This empirical data represents the character's impatience and lack of desire for diplomacy as portrayed on episodes of *Babylon 5*. The Centauri player, during the aftermath phase of the conflict, decides to play the aftermath card "Disenchantment" on the Ivanova character. According to this card, the human player's character Ivanova must be demoted from her inner-circle position to a lower level "supporting character" position within the game's mise-en-scene. In addition, the character cannot be used again during the next turn, as she normally would if the aftermath card were not played on her.

Character and Narrative

The designers have incorporated, or translated, Straczynski's desire for character development by placing a "caption" on the bottom of the cards in an attempt to support this narrative act within the game. The caption for the "Disenchantment" aftermath card, for example, states: "Powerful events beyond the control of *Babylon 5*'s command staff threaten to undermine the station's status. The military officers in charge must follow orders from Earth or face disciplinary action. The only other option is treason" (figure 3.3). As the rules say, the captions have no effect on

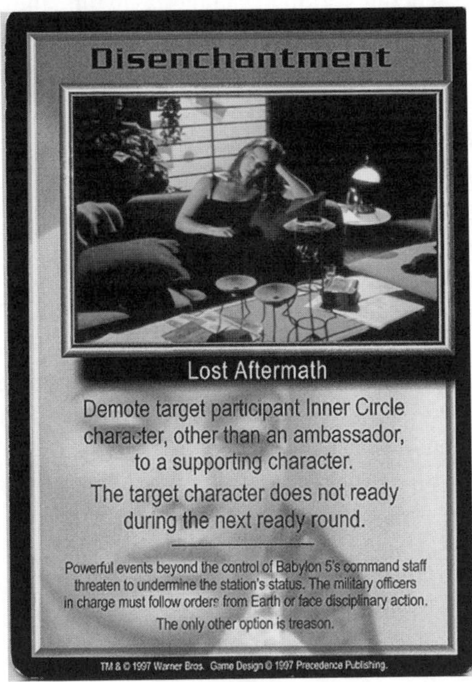

Figure 3.3.
An opponent can play this "Disenchantment" card against a player who initiated a conflict and who subsequently lost. From *Babylon 5 Collectible Card Game,* Precedence Publishing, Tempe, AZ. © 1997 Warner Bros.

game-play, yet however much these descriptions do not directly influence the players through the rules, these evocative statements may, in fact, help them perform the *memory* of the caption's origin. In essence, the card is embedded with a narrative trope that references a scene from *Babylon 5*. As players perform the actions on these cards they activate these embedded strips of behavior in their imagination. This process immerses players in the universe of *Babylon 5*.

The scene embedded in the "Disenchantment" card may not even reflect what happens in the "story" of the game. The scene is removed from its original context, and, by the nature of the game, it has the potential, through montage, to express new meaning. The Russian film theorist and director Sergei Eisenstein contends that montage is created when "two film pieces of any kind, placed together, inevitably combine into a new concept, a new quality, arising out of that juxtaposition" (1975:4). The players end up "telling" a "story" by juxtaposing the different cards within play. Instead of two or more images being placed alongside each other in order to generate certain meanings, as in film, the cards are placed within the context of a rules structure. In other words, the rules themselves help determine the meaning of the cards' juxtaposition with each other. The text on the cards is an interpretation of a scene from the show, while the image on the card may either support this idea or not—and so distill new associations that may not necessarily relate to the picture. In any case, players reenact scenes previously viewed on *Babylon 5*. The scenes on television become the generic representations of new scenes the players perform in their game. For example, in the episode "The Coming of Shadows," Ambassador G'Kar declared war on the Centauri (figure 3.4). G'Kar's picture and the quotation in the caption of the card—"They have crossed the line we cannot allow them to cross. As a result, two hours ago my government officially declared war. . . . Our hope for peace is over. We are now at war. We are now at war" (Straczynski 1995)—become the generic recuperation of that scene within the game. If the human player declares war on the Narn, this is the card that she would use, despite the fact that the image on the card does not match the actual event occurring in the game. However it is depicted, an illusion of a story is created. Players are already familiar with the declaration of war trope from the episode, and by playing that card in the game they restore the original performance of it through memory. By performing such mnemonic juxtapositions, players create their own game narrative. Like the other games of the imaginary entertainment environment, this is an "in-group" game.

Furthermore, the game evokes the *atmosphere* of a narrative in two

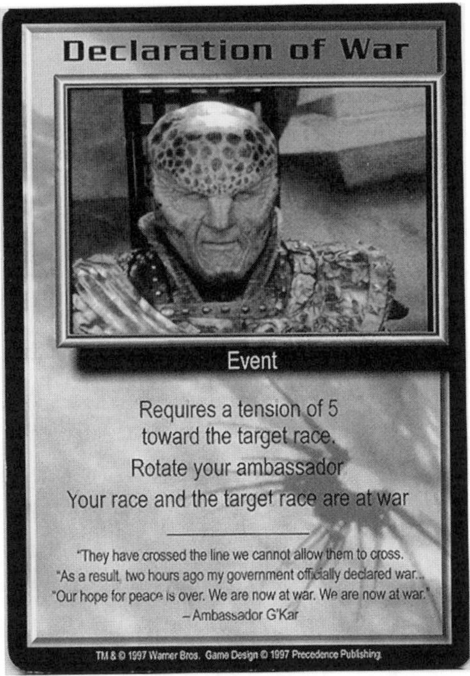

Figure 3.4.
Ambassador G'Kar declares war on the Centauri in "The Coming of Shadows" (1995). From *Babylon 5 Collectible Card Game,* Precedence Publishing, Tempe, AZ. © 1997 Warner Bros.

ways. Through the rules it attempts to persuade players to say lines similar to those the ambassadors used in the show. "Players are strongly encouraged to narrate the actions of their characters," the rules suggest. "As you play cards from your hand, you should briefly explain how your card play affects the story . . . or explain how your characters feel about the card play of your opponents" (Ackels et al. 1997:17). G'Kar's declaration of war, described in the previous paragraph, becomes the basis for a player to say similar lines (in a way similar to the actor's). However, the designers know that players are not actors performing roles. For example, the rules say: "The Centauri plays [the card] 'Test Their Mettle' and targets the Narn. He says (in a bad imitation of Londo's accent [as performed by Peter Jurassic]): 'Now it is time for the Centauri Republic to rise up and reclaim its rightful place in the galaxy. For too long have we suffered the unjust advances of the Narn Regime. No more!' " (17). The game designers have attempted to make the game a nexus between the story of *Babylon 5* and the actors' performance of this story through a structure that allows game players to recuperate both of these elements within an amateur performance. No other collectible card game that I am aware of suggests that players verbalize their roles, which were formerly performed by actors. Instead, and more practically, the "story" is usually "told" through the playing of cards. By juxtaposing the cards, recuperating an actor's performance, and restoring narrative tropes from episodes of *Babylon 5*, players create a new kind of narrative—one structured by rules and a random assortment of cards.

Haptic-Panoptic Performance

The cards may suggest a story, but this story is not told through a traditional verbal narrative. Instead, the goals the players attempt to achieve by playing certain cards at a particular time engage bits of *Babylon 5* narrative behavior, and, through association with the grand narrative comprising one hundred and ten episodes of *Babylon 5*, a tale is told. If a player had never watched any of the episodes, the game would lack narrative association for him, and would fail to generate the meanings experienced by fans of the show. This evocation of an associational narrative arises from the pictures on the cards. These depict actual characters, places, and situations that occur on the show. They allow players to perform fictive moments from *Babylon 5*.

Between the verbal and the visual lies a haptic performance: players touch the cards, locations, characters, and narrative situations from a television show they have only previously viewed from a distance. Miniature still-shots on the cards—literally cut out and reproduced from an episodic scene—remove the shot from its original context, allowing players to slow down and stop a scene previously viewed at 30 frames per second, the point where one can now touch and reconfigure it (figure 3.5). Players lay the cards down in front of them. Each move becomes a strategy, bringing the player closer to winning. The original strip of behavior comprising the scene from which the still-shot was taken is physically embedded on the card. This embedded behavior is restructured by the game designers, who placed it within a set of rules giving players the tools, the means, for applying these behaviors in different patterns as they attempt to win the game. During this process, a story is told.

In the collectible card game based on *Star Trek: The Next Generation*, players place crew cards beneath starship cards and then move these ships to different planet cards on the table. Crews then "beam" down to the planets and explore them, discovering the new life forms depicted in the series. Crews may encounter such hazards as booby traps, kidnappings, or alien viruses. Since the cards contain pictures from various episodes of *Star Trek,* the show becomes restored during the performance of the card game—where players perform within the framework of a game narrative. In the Middle-earth game (based on Tolkien's *Lord of the Rings*), players, just as in the fantasy novel, play characters, such as Frodo Baggins and Gandalf the wizard, who embark on an adventure, exploring the lands of Middle-earth as they encounter orcs and trolls, discover treasures, and go on a quest to destroy the One Ring of power. Land cards depict various locations in Middle-earth, such as Gondor and Mirkwood, and on these maps are various cities, ruins, caverns, and lairs, to which the players can take their characters.

In all of these collectible card games, players lay out their cards in front of them—in a panoptic representation of the universe, to be looked at in one sweeping view. Like *Babylon 5* ambassadors, they attempt to manipu-

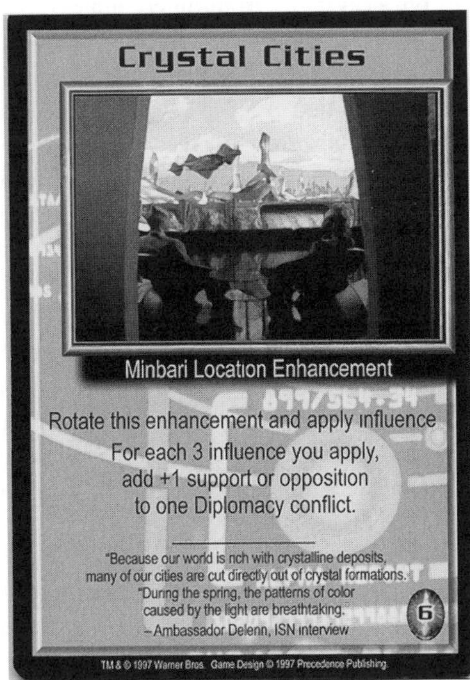

Figure 3.5.

Here, the crystal city of Minbar, in miniature, is restored for the players' sight and touch in a haptic-panoptic performance. From *Babylon 5 Collectible Card Game,* Precedence Publishing, Tempe, AZ. © 1997 Warner Bros.

late the figures in front of them in order to bring their faction into dominance. Players collect the more powerful "rare" cards in an attempt not only to increase their chance of winning the game, but to impress other players like a proud Centauri would. The laying out of cards is a means of showing one's collection in a display of fan pride and power. A player not only shows what he has in his hand but also displays what he has *collected* as memorabilia. Players can both show off a rare card and touch it and use it in a power play within the game. Through a haptic-panoptic performance, a performance of touch and sight, players become reconfigured in the *Babylon 5* universe. If eighteenth- and nineteenth-century panoramas were one means by which "[b]odily experience and cognitive understanding were . . . replaced by a reliance on vision within a simulacrum of the real" by evoking "illusory immersion in faraway places," as film scholar Scott Bukatman contends (1995:263–64), then collectible card games immerse players by combining the visual and the haptic.

The collectible card game is a new, relatively low-tech means of placing "an abundance of physical data" from ninety hours of *Babylon 5* broadcast images into a form "fitted to the epistemological desires and requirements of the public consciousness," as Bukatman says in reference to the consumers of the "Information Age" (1995:263). The desire to seek out new forms of immersion stems from the fact that some fans no longer find it enough to simply watch media shows—they want to play with those images like children playing with dolls (and I don't use this term pejoratively): they want to attain haptic-panoptic control over images (and perhaps feelings) that formerly sped past them during the viewing of *Babylon 5*. They can now slow these images down and manipulate them for their own purposes (limited as this is by a structure of game rules). Players collect cards and show off rare valuable ones in a panoptic view of the *Babylon 5* universe. A five-year show is laid out in miniature, condensed into a form that players can control, handle, and manipulate in perhaps a one- or two-hour game. Where before the show could only be seen, now it can be both observed and touched.

As Bukatman argues, the desire for displays of the "spectacular" require "a new mode of spectatorial address—essentially, *you are there* (even though you're not)—linked to new technologies of visual representation" (1995:263). Because the images are so small in the collectible card game, the means of causing the players to feel as if they are immersed in the "spectacular" arises from a set of rules that give players a goal. The visual and haptic, combined with a strategy that uses the cards in the most effective manner to win, immerses the players in the universe of *Babylon 5*. As stated above, the players' actions in the game restore the potential actions pictured on the cards, referencing scenes from the television show.

Instead of providing a panoptic view where the observer is outside looking in (as with television), the game forces players to become part of the scene. The cards—embedded as they are with strips of *Babylon 5* behavior—perform through the players. The players use the people and scenes on the cards as tangible playthings in a procedure that allows them to perform in the universe of *Babylon 5*. With the cards laid out in front of them on the table and with more in their hands, players engage in a haptic-panoptic performance where they are "capable of perceiving and comprehending the new conditions of physical reality through the projection of an almost omnipotent gaze out into the represented world" (Bukatman 1995:255).

The "conditions of physical reality" have been replaced by what I call conditions of virtual fantasies. Bukatman believes that popular culture "compensated for the lack of touch with what might be called the hyperbole of the visible" as the haptic was displaced "in favor of the visual as a source of knowledge" in the nineteenth century (1995:255). Today, objects of popular media culture—toys, games, and other artifacts of the imaginary entertainment environment—bring an almost haptic dominance to a previously singular scopic representation of fantasy. The imaginary, the virtual images of film and television, can now be touched and manipulated. They offer concrete interfaces to such imaginary environments as *Babylon 5, Star Wars, Star Trek,* and *The Lord of the Rings.*

Writing about the Renaissance, "The Age of Curiosity," in *Collectors and Curiosities,* Krzysztof Pomian describes the "major categories of beings and objects which together encompass the entire contents of the universe" (1990:49). Pomian posits:

> It would seem that the aim was not so much to create a faithful portrait of a particular room on a particular date, but rather to convey the very essence of such a room, showing it as a place where the universe, considered as a whole, became visible through the intermediary of objects intended to represent the major categories of beings and things. . . . In other words, it is here that the universe became visible as a single entity, for although it retained every single constituent part, it underwent a process of miniaturization. (50)

By touching the interface (the miniature objects of cards), not only can players see an imaginary universe, but they participate in that universe through the sense of touch. They also collect objects from that universe and display them. The collectible cards are not designed as just a game, but as a site where one can collect and view cultural artifacts from a television show, film, or novel.

Players are encouraged to keep purchasing as well as trading more cards until they have the whole set of over four hundred, with more being designed and produced. At thirty frames per second, four hundred still-shots encompass slightly over thirteen seconds of actual broadcast time out of a total of ninety hours of footage. This means that the game publisher has access to nearly ten million frames of *Babylon 5* material! It is not unreasonable to see how the designers could easily take sixty shots from each of the ninety hours, and create a stack of five thousand and four hundred cards. The ninety hours of *Babylon 5* become "visible as a single entity" through a "process of miniaturization," as Pomian might put it. Its very essence, the characters, situations, objects, and locations within the show can now be both haptically and scopically "considered as a whole." *Babylon 5*, through the collectible card game, becomes a miniature universe with its own "categories of beings and things," not meant to be a "faithful portrait" of the entire series, but rather an attempt to "convey the very essence" of such a television series—one that can be collected, viewed, touched, and performed.

Popular culture media stories become transfigured into something more powerful, "more alive," than the originating form. People who immerse themselves in these products become reconfigured into that product's fantasy environment and consequently immersed in an author's fantasy, a fantasy that they can now slow down, cut up, stop, recreate, reform, recuperate, restore, and otherwise play with. Jonathan Crary, in *Techniques of the Observer* (1992), analyzes how the nineteenth-century observer became reconfigured through such popular objects as the vision-manipulating stereoscope and kaleidoscope—but not just "for the models of representation they imply, but as sites of both knowledge and power that operate directly on the individual" (7). "An observer," Crary maintains, is "one who is embedded in a system of conventions and limitations," a "system of discursive, social, and institutional relations" (6). Furthermore, these "optical devices . . . are points of intersection where philosophical, scientific, and aesthetic discourses overlap with mechanical techniques, institutional practices, and socioeconomic forces" (8). When the observer entered the modernized age, the singular vision of the self became multifaceted as "new needs, new consumption, and new production" were created, while at the same time the "observer increasingly had to function within disjunct and defamiliarized urban spaces, the perceptual and temporal dislocations of railroad travel, telegraphy, industrial production, and flows of typographic and visual information" (11). In short, this reconfiguration was not just a fantasy—it changed how people saw themselves and how they lived.

In a similar way, images of popular culture—reproduced as miniaturized haptic objects from the panoptic displays of media images—reconfigure the participant in these games into various fictional universes. Without these technologies that allow game-play, there would be no immersion. Within these fantasies, the objects of observation and touch become the very "thickness" (to borrow Crary's term) by which the "knowledge of the observer" can be "obtained." The player can become immersed, for example, in Straczynski's fantasy universe of *Babylon 5* through game objects that create a "palpable opacity and carnal density of vision" (Crary 1992:150). The imaginary becomes concrete at the interface. An interface is the physical representation of the imaginary world—it is a virtual image, or a window, to an author's fantasy universe. Kendall Walton calls such an object a "prompter," which "coordinates the imaginings of the participants," allowing them to "imagine approximately the same things" (1990:23). Walton claims that this process is a natural extension of the imaginative games of children (11). In children's games, however, spontaneous acts of play—though governed by rules—are not bound by such regulations as found in the games of imaginary entertainment environments.

Process of Immersion

The process of immersing the player in the *Babylon 5* universe through the "palpable opacity" of the collectible card game occurs in several ways. The rules and the different types of cards provide the possible actions players may perform. A player identifies himself as performing the part of one of the four main ambassadors. This identity, whether it is G'Kar, Delenn, Londo, or Sinclair, most likely represents his favorite character and species on the show. Each character choice is designed to create a different kind of performance for the player. If the player chooses Sinclair, then he represents "the Earth Alliance, a newcomer to the galactic stage that now plays a central role in its affairs" (Ackels et al. 1997:12). The player, if she has watched *Babylon 5*, is meant to play a responsible Earth leader, as represented by the character Jeffrey Sinclair, the human who commanded *Babylon 5* in the first season.

Delenn is the ambassador for the Minbari Federation, and as this character the player is, according to the rules, a "member of an old and highly spiritual race. You possess superior knowledge and technology with which to advance your (often mysterious) causes" (Ackels et al. 1997:12). The fact remains, however, that a human plays the part of an alien, and it takes the empirical data of the cards to reflect any kind of superior technology that this fictional species has access to, as shown in the television show. The game really does not allow for the "advance" of any "mysterious causes." Like all the players, the Minbari player uses a generic set of actions that can be applied differently in attempting to win the game. The rules use a rhetoric of the mysterious in order to convey a sense of what is lacking: an embedded storyline that—when situated within a linear story—could perhaps convey this mystery, as it appears in the television series. The player is left with the *potential* to recuperate the mystery from *Babylon 5* in her own persona's performance by invoking the attitude of Delenn in the series. The player can restore the behavior of Mira Furlan's recorded performance on-screen, and thus evoke an air of the mysterious character Delenn through a recuperation of this actress's behavior. This recuperation will be absent in the body and voice if the player does not choose to mimic Furlan's behavior, however, for players may rely solely on their cards to restore the performance behavior of their characters. Suggestions in the rules by the game designers attempt to raise the game to the level of a mimetic performance found in the series, but the players do not have to enact vocal behaviors if they choose not to.

The player of the Narn ambassador G'Kar represents, the rules say, a species "born of a reptilian race, easily provoked to battle, and too often the victims of Centauri oppression. A warlike nature and supreme ability to endure hardship will help you win freedom, honor, and revenge for your longsuffering people" (Ackels et al. 1997:12). Again, the description contains certain behavioral codes that players are meant to recuperate within the performance of the card game. If a player chooses to perform the part of ambassador Londo Mollari of the Centauri Republic, the player is supposed to exemplify a "decadent and declining empire—until now. You will utilize superior guile to reverse this decay and restore your race to its former glory" (12). In all of the descriptions of these civilizations, players are given a generic psychological profile in order to motivate their play within the game. This is what causes the still-shots (cut-out, dead) of the images on the cards to come "alive" in performance.

These virtual images panoptically laid out in front of the players are supposed to evoke a story similar to the one shown on *Babylon 5*. The cards act as an interface. When players touch this interface, it activates, in their minds, the imaginary universe of *Babylon 5*. This is why the cards may be thought of as virtual images, for these images represent the imaginary, but they are not the *actual* objects from that universe, for no such objects actually exist. They are simulacra—the physicalization of this fantasy. The virtual becomes physical through the cards. The process of performing within the virtual gives players the opportunity to participate in a fantasy—an evanescent site experienced through the imagination. Interfaces allow people to enter and perform in fantasy environments. The players become reconfigured in this universe through the activation—by sight and touch—of the interface objects, the cards.

The next few pages illustrate the haptic-panoptic performance by laying out various cards in a sequence representing one turn in the game. This section shows how a visual representation helps to immerse participants in the universe of *Babylon 5*. We will see how the montage of cards is used to create its own story, and how the cards represent an interface into this fantasy universe. One player performs the part of Ambassador Londo Mollari of the Centauri Republic, the other, Ambassador G'Kar of the Narn Regime. In front of them panoptically laid out on the table are cards representing their character's faction—his associates, space fleets, and locations within his sphere of influence. These cards can be used to initiate intrigue, military conquest, or diplomatic conflicts against other players.

On the top row (figure 3.6), center, is the ambassador character, Londo Mollari. To the right is Lord Refa, representing a member of Londo's "inner circle." Characters from the inner circle can be used to initiate intrigue, diplomacy, and military campaigns. Below the inner circle are the supporting cards—the fleets of warships, characters, enhancements, and locations. To the left of the ambassador is an agenda: the Centauri have in play "Power Politics." The player plans to gain the upper hand by initiating a diplomatic conflict against the Narn.

Two cards, "Gunboat Diplomacy" and "Decisive Tactics" (figure 3.7), are brought into play when the inner-circle characters give the player enough influence points to be able to bring them into play. They represent strips of potential actions similar to dramatic scenes from *Babylon 5*. They can be used to enhance characters or fleets or an event that affects play—altering the performance as when a new character in a play enters a scene and changes its dynamics. The Narn plays "Gunboat Diplomacy" and initiates a military conflict against the Centauri at Ragesh III.

The Narns decide to attack the Centauri at Ragesh III (figure 3.8). Cards are rotated on the table to support and oppose these conflicts. The

Figure 3.6.
Centauri character playing field: "Power Politics," "Londo," "Refa," "Centauri Prime," "Centauri Captain," "Expeditionary Fleet (Centauri)," and "Ragesh III." From *Babylon 5 Collectible Card Game,* Precedence Publishing, Tempe, AZ. © 1997 Warner Bros.

Narn player puts down "Decisive Tactics" from his hand, allowing one of his characters to increase his leadership ability and ultimately increase the effectiveness of his fleet. Empirical data on the cards determines the relative strengths and weaknesses of each side—who wins the battle. This is not the way a writer would build dramatic tension in a scene. The Centauri defend with the expeditionary fleet supported by a Centauri Captain. This gives the Centauri a twelve-point defense. The Narn supports his fleet with the character of Na'Kal (four points of leadership ability) plus two from the use of "Decisive Tactics" plus the fifteen points from the two fleets. The Centauri, having less power, lose the conflict, and the Narns increase their influence in the galaxy.

During the aftermath (figure 3.9) phase, the Narn play "Assigning Blame" on the Centauri ambassador, Londo. He loses two points in his diplomacy ability for losing the battle against the Narn. The Centauri in turn play two aftermath cards, "Wear and Tear"—causing the Narn fleets to lose a point of strength; and "The Price of Power"—the Narn must "discard a character" or lose any influence he has gained from the attack. (The higher a player's influence, the closer he comes to winning.) The Narn decides to discard Na'Kal, the captain who led the attack. This "discard,"

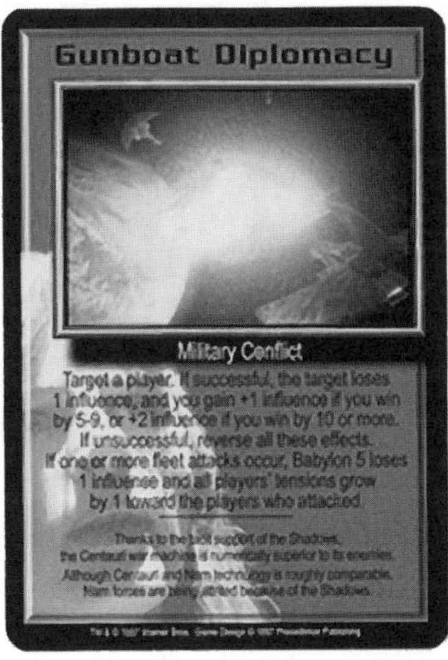

Figure 3.7.
"Gunboat Diplomacy" and "Decisive Tactics" cards. From *Babylon 5 Collectible Card Game,* Precedence Publishing, Tempe, AZ. © 1997 Warner Bros.

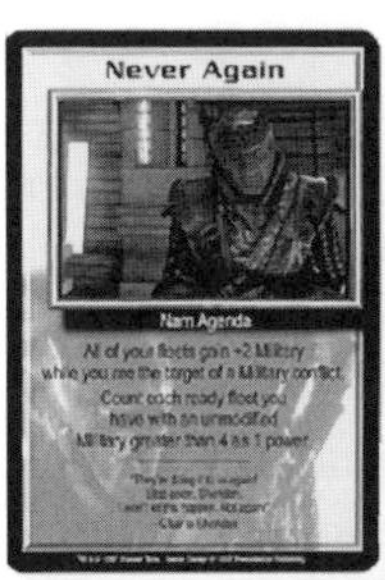

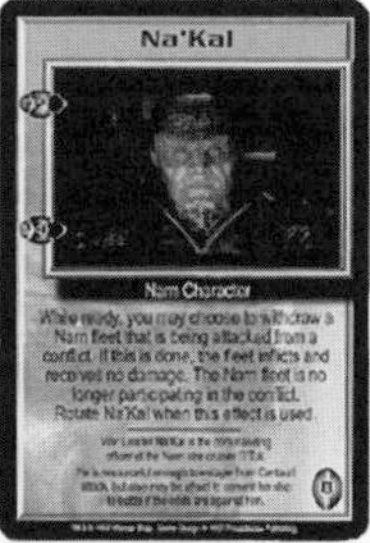

Figure 3.8.
The cards of the Narn player. From *Babylon 5 Collectible Card Game,* Precedence Publishing, Tempe, AZ. © 1997 Warner Bros.

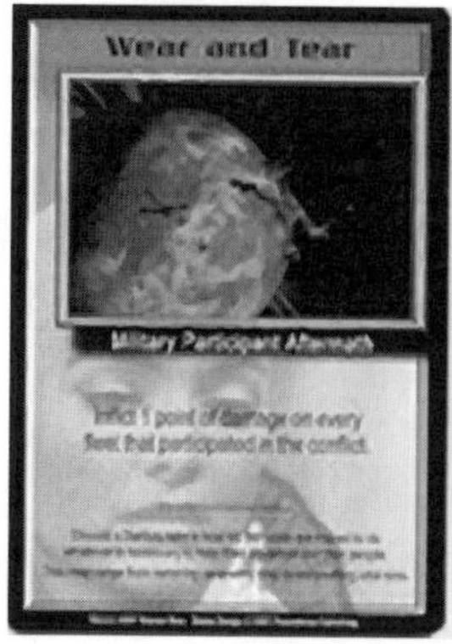

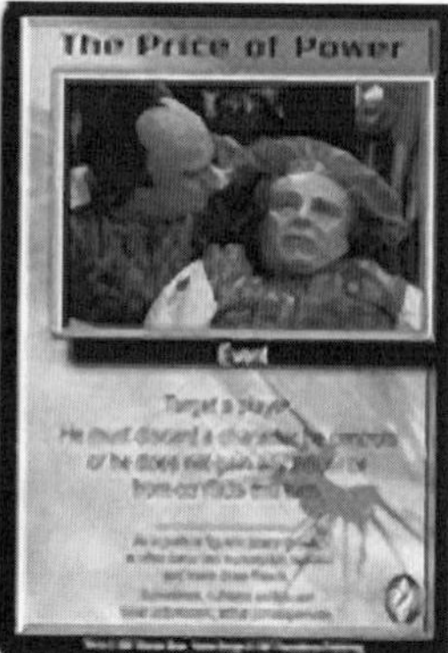

Figure 3.9.
"Aftermath" cards: "Wear and Tear," "Assigning Blame," and "The Price of Power." From *Babylon 5 Collectible Card Game,* Precedence Publishing, Tempe, AZ. © 1997 Warner Bros.

however, represents the death of that character—a fact that the rules play down. But the picture on the card says it all. This is one example of a scene from an episode of *Babylon 5* being restored as a generic representation of a character dying. The card depicts one of Londo's inner-circle members dying. However, any player may use this card to represent a similar scene, as in the case of the Centauri player using it against the Narn—who chooses which character must die (be discarded).

This example illustrates the haptic-panoptic performance of *Babylon 5*. The performance causes players to recall previous strips of performance behaviors viewed on *Babylon 5*, which become re-edited in a new story as told through the structure of the game and the montage placement of cards. The players, like characters on *Babylon 5*, are motivated to manipulate other people, events, and locations. This game becomes a panoptic system wherein players can manipulate images from *Babylon 5* through touch. The performance is controlled not just by the random stack of a deck of cards, but by how the players use these randomly dealt cards to their advantage. They physically touch them and lay them out in front of them, montage style, not to tell a story in a traditional fashion, but to perform the most powerful strategy in an attempt to win the game. This becomes the narrative. At the same time, through this very process of enacting a haptic performance, players reenact, reperform, restore scenes from *Babylon 5*. This process depicts a certain kind of narrative among the players. Television is no longer just *watched*. It is *performed*. Certainly this is not the same as textual poaching—where fans of a show take certain texts and manipulate them to express their own desires (described in more detail in Chapter 6, "Webs of Babylon: Textual Poaching Online"). Neither is the collectible card game a role-playing game, despite the fact that the rules say that players are performing a character. And certainly it does not simulate a war.

The war game allows people to simulate combat in their favorite fictions, and the role-playing game allows people to psychologically perform characters in an Aristotelian-structured narrative that recuperates tropes from a fantasy universe, while the collectible card game permits players to view, and, more important, to touch this fantasy. The card game essentially conflates the other two games into a form that allows players to perform in the universe of *Babylon 5*. They perform a semblance of characters by reenacting a simulation of various wars and intrigues from television episodes, reconfiguring them through a rules structure that allows them to perform in the *Babylon 5* universe in a different way. The game offers a surrogate for what players once could view only in a narrow-beam transmission, and the panoptic widens and slows down the television narrative in favor of a performance that restores bits of *Babylon 5* behavior through touch. The desire for space exploration and simulated battles becomes relegated to a performance of the haptic-panoptic in the collectible card game.

Chapter 4

Performing at the Interface of the High-Tech and the Bureaucratic

Taking a Tour of the *Official Guide to J. Michael Straczynski's* Babylon 5

One reviewer of the *Official Guide to J. Michael Straczynski's* Babylon 5 contends that "once you boot up the *Official Guide*, you're completely immersed within the world of *Babylon 5*" (Perenson 1998:26). High technology offers fans the potential to virtually visit the *Babylon 5* station—to see it on its own terms, rather than just watching it on television. The CD-ROM offers a kind of virtual "theme park," which fans can "enter," and they can then play in an environment on their computer—they do not need to actually travel there. Marketers and software engineers who produce high-tech devices intend to supply such fantasies. The *Official Guide to J. Michael Straczynski's* Babylon 5 (1997) attempts to take the user on a "tour" of *Babylon 5*, while the planned space combat simulator *Into the Fire* would have offered users the opportunity to fly as Starfury pilots for the Earth Alliance at *Babylon 5* and to be promoted through the various levels of command. This chapter will deal mainly with the CD-ROM guide, because the design work on the combat simulator has been discontinued, and it may never be published.

The guidebook CD-ROM offers an interesting case study of how a product can fail to immerse the participant. An important offshoot of this is the demonstration of how a company attempts, by using misleading language, to manipulate customers into purchasing a product that falls short of what is advertised. From this example readers can see how a company uses bureaucratic rhetoric in order to recover money on its investment of a product. Near the end of the chapter I will briefly examine the process by which CD-ROM games may successfully immerse participants, and I will look more closely at theories behind digital environments and how they evoke a performance.

After installing the CD-ROM into the computer, the user hears familiar music (composed by Christopher Franke) from the series as a space liner enters the vicinity of the *Babylon 5* station through a jumpgate. A shuttle flies out from this ship and enters the docking bay of the station as the user listens to verbal commands, relayed from Babylon control to the pilot of the shuttle, requesting that the pilot "please remind [her] passengers about customs procedures before debarking" (replayed from the *Babylon 5* episode "Exogenesis"). The next screen (figure 4.1) depicts a door to the Tourism Bureau with three different tour guides (digitized actors in

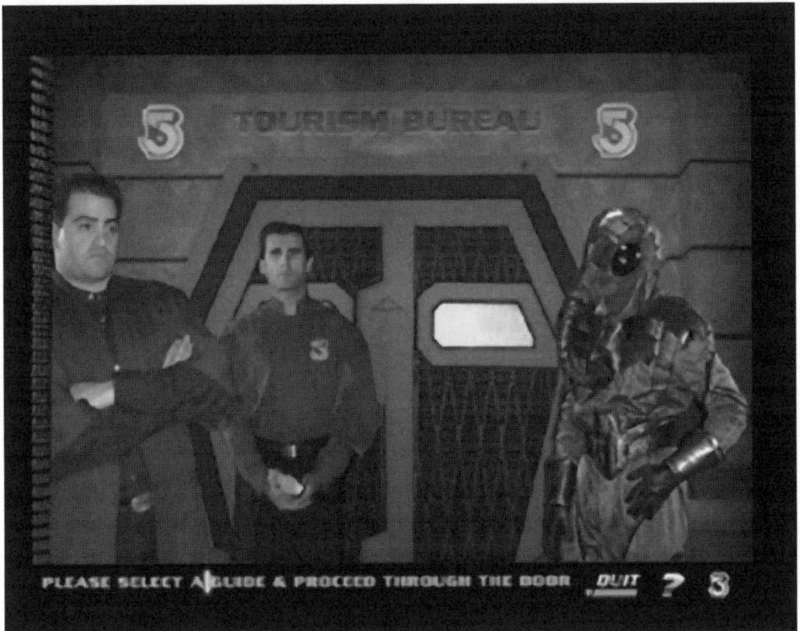

Figure 4.1.
"Explorer Drone Ja'drell at your service," the alien Gaim speaks after the user clicks on her. From the CD-ROM *The Official Guide to J. Michael Straczynski's* Babylon 5, Sierra Online, Inc., Bellevue, WA 98007. © 1997 Warner Bros.

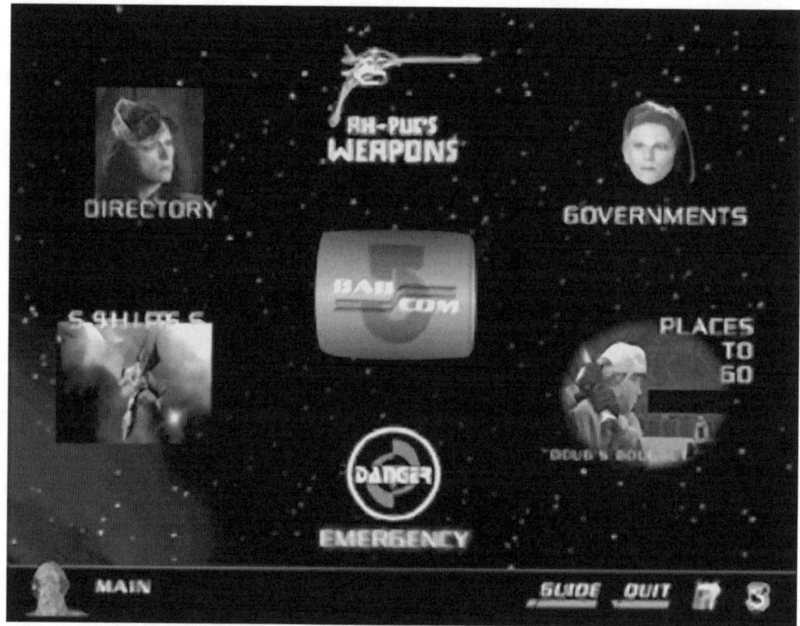

Figure 4.2.
Users go through the doors and come to a main screen page with seven icons. From the CD-ROM *The Official Guide to J. Michael Straczynski's* Babylon 5, Sierra Online, Inc., Bellevue, WA 98007. © 1997 Warner Bros.

costumes) standing by. Directions scroll across the bottom of the screen accompanied by an out-of-place sound effect of a PPG pistol warming up and firing: "Please select a guide and proceed through the door." Each guide makes different remarks about each location: a middle human performs with professional courtesy, while the other is more churlish in behavior, presenting a kind of "blue-collar" view of life on *Babylon 5*. The third guide is an alien known as a Gaim. She performs her role according to her species' perspective. The user chooses one of these guides.

Up to this point the CD-ROM is attempting to immerse the participant by putting her into a first-person view: what she sees on the screen is what she would see with own eyes if she were on the space station. Users can manipulate the environment, such as by opening doors, and they observe a scene as if the computer screen were a window into another world. CD-ROM designers make the actors look into the camera, and so when a user views the recording, it appears as if the various characters in the environment are looking at her—reconfiguring her as if she were a part of the scene on-screen (see figure 4.1). Next the user clicks on the door to

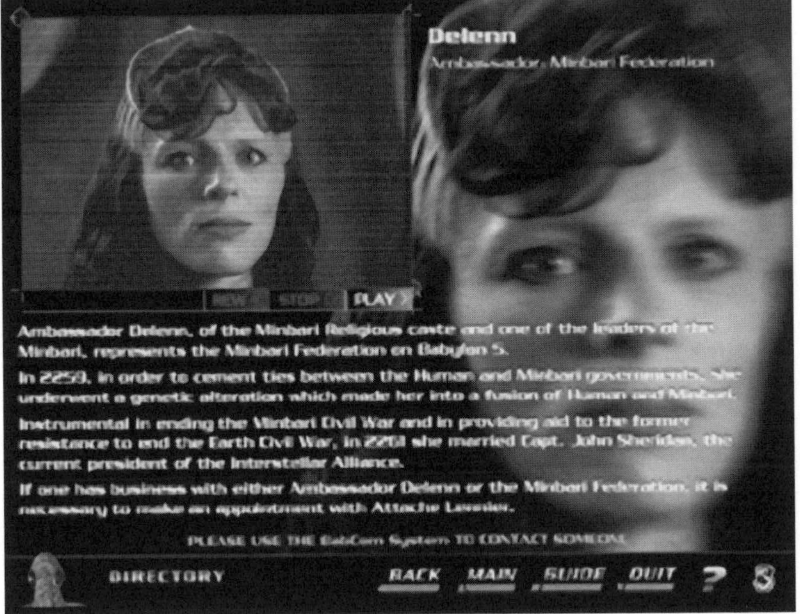

Figure 4.3.
"Ambassador Delenn" from the character directory. From the CD-ROM *The Official Guide to J. Michael Straczynski's* Babylon 5, Sierra Online, Inc., Bellevue, WA 98007. © 1997 Warner Bros.

the Tourism Bureau, and perhaps at this points expects to be able to explore, if not the entire station, at least various three-dimensional rooms that represent scenes and settings shown on episodes of *Babylon 5*. After clicking on the slate-gray door, the user is taken to a "main screen," which is accompanied by fast-beat music (see figure 4.2). Seven icons appear on the screen, each one kinetically streaming visual montage shots depicting visual information about the following categories: Directory, Ships, a gun shop called Ah-Puc's Weapons, Babcom, Emergency, Governments, and Places to Go.

All of the other "rooms" offer the same disappointingly two-dimensional experience. For example, clicking on the Directory icon (upper left corner) reveals a list of characters' names. After clicking on a character's name, the user is led to a page whereon she can read bios on various *Babylon 5* characters (see figure 4.3), which give brief historical overviews of each character. In addition, the designers have embedded the screen with a video containing a couple of brief scenes of that character in various episodes. Similar screens are designed for the Ships icon—each contains a brief description and a video clip showing the ships in action (see figure

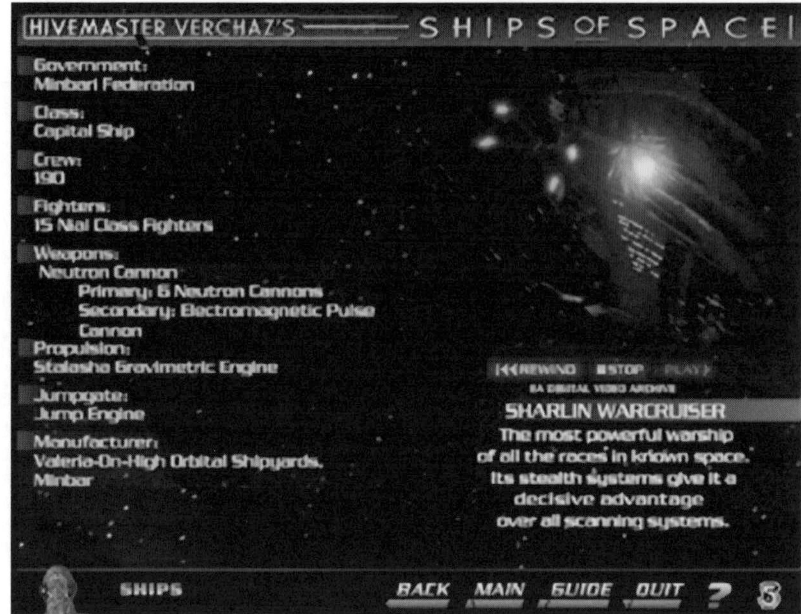

Figure 4.4.
The ship page gives statistics and video footage of ships from the *Babylon 5* universe. From the CD-ROM *The Official Guide to J. Michael Straczynski's* Babylon 5, Sierra Online, Inc., Bellevue, WA 98007. © 1997 Warner Bros.

4.4); the Weapons section has a similar set-up. Babcom is the communications system for *Babylon 5*. The bottom line on the Delenn character screen tells the user to "please use the Babcom system to contact someone." However, when the user enters the Babcom location, she sees a video monitor depicting the communication device in a state of malfunction. Static arcs across the screen, and if she clicks on it, she hears various bits of dialogue from the series. No one, in fact, can be contacted. The Emergency icon describes the different alarms for decompression alarms, fire, and so forth.

The CD-ROM gives encyclopedic background information about the various religious, political, and social factors comprising the various alien species depicted on the television series that fans may never learn by simply watching it. But this contradicts the opening scene of the CD-ROM, where the designers set up the users' expectations that they are about to embark on a virtual tour of the station. The high-tech performance of the software design never delivers what it indicates through its packaging: immersion.

In the role-playing game, character sheets provide the impetus for immersion. The war game reconfigures players into simulated roles of starship commanders riding ships into combat. The collectible card game allows players to perform narrative bits from *Babylon 5* through a haptic-panoptic interface. However, in this CD-ROM there is no nexus of immersion into the universe of *Babylon 5*. Instead, through the bureaucratic performance of press reviews, advertising, and packaging, the producers have effectively reconfigured potential participants. For example, the back of the product package states that the user will get an "in-depth tour of the immense *Babylon 5* universe." One reviewer says that this product "capitalizes on the synergy between the interactivity afforded by the CD-ROM medium and the technology depicted on the series," and the review title affirms that "You can do more than watch *Babylon 5*—now you can actually go there" (Perenson 1998:26). However, the interface of the product isn't itself designed to help bring about this immersion.

This fact discloses a bureaucratic and high-tech performance evident throughout the packaging of this product. Performance scholar Jon McKenzie calls these processes "games of performance" (1997:39). One of these bureaucratic performers is Jay Samit, a producer of the CD-ROM: "We're within the confines of 'reality,'" he explains. "This isn't a who's-the-actor-and-what-else-did-they-do. This is 'Welcome to *Babylon 5*.' You've just entered the world of *Babylon 5*." He continues with the same rhetoric: "What do you want to know, where do you want to go shopping, which restaurants do you want to go to, what do you do in case of a security problem, in case of an atmosphere problem, what do you do? It's an interactive guide book" (Perenson 1998:26). This guidebook differs from a book version in that it contains sound and video. A book uses an interface of words and pictures on paper (which a person can flip through, looking up information hypertextually from an index).

Designers who use technological tools to create consumer products intend to ensure that their products *perform* high-tech by making them *appear* high-tech. A technological performance, McKenzie says, "refers to such parameters as the efficiency, speed, and reliability of a technical system" (1997:39). One must have a high-tech computer to run this CD-ROM (Pentium 90 or Power PC 100 is the minimum processor requirement). A regular paper guidebook offers a product different from what can be distilled through a high-performance microchip accompanied by a high-performance CD-ROM. However, because viewers of science fiction (itself a high-tech genre) ostensibly want to perform in a high-tech environment, the producer of this high-tech product performs the rhetoric of a high-tech sale. Part of this sales pitch for this particular product is mention of the fact that the producers have copied images from the television series: "every piece of video was captured off the digital masters," reveals producer Samit. "None of this came off three-quarter Beta or VHS [video]. All the graphics were rendered specifically for this to give the highest possible quality level" (Perenson 1998:28). But compressed video—even if rendered specifically for a particular project—is still accompanied by pixilated dirt, making a VHS image (the lowest standard in the industry) sharper than the images attained in most current CD-ROMs on the market, including this one.

The bureaucratic performances of advertising, press reviews, and packaging override the performance of the actual product—which is essentially a high-tech book. A bureaucratic performance, McKenzie posits, is related to the high-tech performance, where the bureaucratic qualities of "profitability, flexibility, and optimization" are used to "design and then evaluate and market technologies" as well as manage bureaucratic workers (1997:39). On the outside of the CD-ROM box, one of the features promised is a "Guided Tour: Virtual shuttles leave every 10 minutes to take you on a special tour featuring key points of interest in *Babylon 5*." The producers of this reference guide mislead users into believing that they can enter a virtual space station from *Babylon 5*. So, after reading the review and advertisements for this CD-ROM and after examining its package, I assumed that there would be sites on this space station to see and explore, cultures to examine, artifacts to view and interact with. This CD-ROM is embedded in a bureaucratic rhetoric that evinces a scenario wherein users can enter a virtual *Babylon 5* station. The performance of advertising and press publicity promises an immersive environment, but the product fails to provide an interface through which immersion could occur. For example, the Places To Go icon takes the user to a screen listing all the various places on *Babylon 5* she can visit—the various restaurants, docking bays, alien sector, a view of the station core, and so on. By clicking on the Fresh Air restaurant with her mouse, the user is taken to a full-screen view (see figure 4.5) of this place. A brief textual description can also be accessed, as well as the still photograph.

And yet a full-color advertisement states that people who purchase this product will be taken on a tour: "Set course with Captain John Sheridan, Ambassador Delenn, and the dwellers of *Babylon 5* for a tour unlike any other" (*Sci-Fi* 1998:3). An article in this same magazine also describes the CD-ROM as a tour: "We wanted to give you the different perspectives so you can actually hire a virtual tour guide to take you through the same things and give you that person's perspective on various aspects," says producer Samit (Perenson 1998:26). However, besides some brief asides the "tour guide" offers as the user looks at the two-dimensional pictures before her, the product fails to perform the functions promised by the varying branches of the bureaucratic performance. The tour guide the user chooses to accompany her as she "walks" through this two-dimensional station falls far short of offering a simulated tour. Instead, a performance of bureaucracy has drawn the the user into a "language game of big money, and it is run by numerical values of profitability, cost-effectiveness, and optimization" (McKenzie 1997:47).

Language games, philosopher Jean-Francois Lyotard tells us, are a form of performance—a kind of "masquerader," to use J. L. Austin's nomenclature (1975:4). Building on Wittgenstein, Lyotard describes language games as an "utterance" with "various categories," each one "defined in terms of rules specifying their properties and the uses to which they can

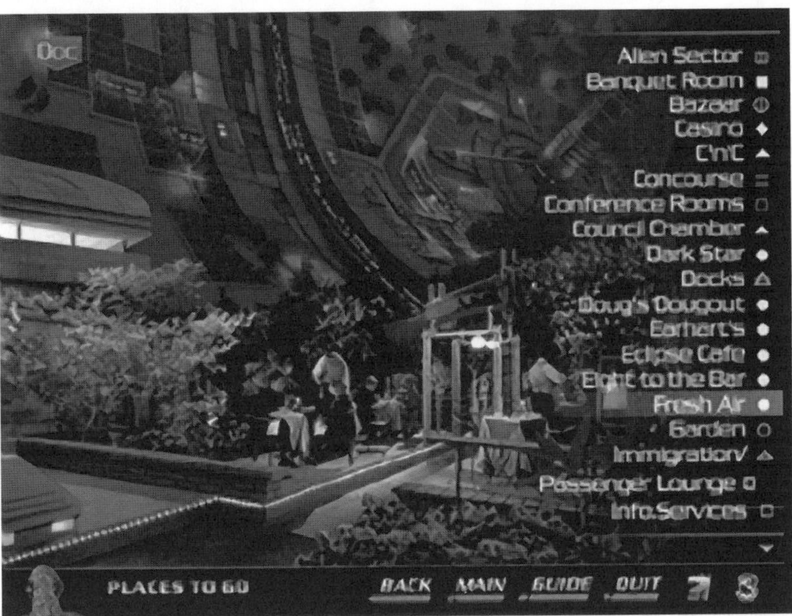

Figure 4.5.
After clicking on the "Doc" icon in the upper left corner, the user reads the following: "The finest restaurant on *Babylon 5.* Besides its extensive menu of many fine dishes, Fresh Air also offers a unique dining experience on the station: the dining area is open to the core." From the CD-ROM *The Official Guide to J. Michael Straczynski's* Babylon 5, Sierra Online, Inc., Bellevue, WA 98007. © 1997 Warner Bros.

be put" (1984:10). To issue an utterance is to engage in the "performing of an action," Austin contends (1975:6). This engagement, this utterance that initiates the performance of an action, Lyotard emphasizes, "should be thought of as a 'move' in a game" (1984:10). This "move" is an action, and action, Aristotle says—even more important than character—is the root of drama, structuring it: "Dramatic action, therefore, is not with a view to the representation of character: character comes in as subsidiary to the actions" (1961:62). The performative utterance can be seen to have its roots in the agon of drama: "to speak is to fight, in the sense of playing, and speech acts fall within the domain of general agonistics," Lyotard argues (1984:10). In the language games of bureaucratic performances, advertising is one of the chief "characters," and, in the case of the *Babylon 5* CD-ROM reference guide, it unjustly defines this product as a touristic device promising immersion into a space station viewers have watched on television for five years.

Furthermore, this same promise weaves its way into the language game of technology—uttering its Pentium processor capabilities as the optimum (if not ultimate) experience. But rather than actually making maximum use of the Pentium processor's capabilities, the designers of this CD-ROM have used its minimum ability: picture stills are incorporated instead of immersive 3-D graphics which move with the user's first-person viewpoint. Instead of rooms users can walk through, we have two-dimensional photos as in a book. "Technology is therefore a game," Lyotard assures us, "pertaining not to the true, the just, or the beautiful, etc., but to efficiency: a technical 'move' is 'good' when it does better and/or expends less energy than another" (1984:44). It is easier to place still photos on a CD-ROM than it is to design a 3-D environment. A high-tech CD-ROM book is cheaper to produce—it is more cost efficient.

However, we become immersed in an environment located in cyberspace, as technology philosopher Michael Heim says, when we "habituate ourselves to an interface" (1993:79). It is *how* the interface is designed that immerses users within virtual fantasy environments. The interface acts as a bridge between the "real" world and the fantasy world. It is the physical object or environment that translates the imaginary environment of an author's mind into a form other people can view, touch, and otherwise participate in. Authors write down words on paper in an attempt to convey a story they have imagined. Readers then participate in the author's imaginary story by perusing it. The words-on-paper of the novel comprise the interface—the point of contact between the author's invisible imagination and her audience. Without an interface there is no way an author can share the products of her imagination with someone else (unless this is done verbally).

Heim contends that an interface has a usage similar to the Greek word *prosopon:* one "face facing another face." Through mutual interaction the two faces continue to develop as they react to one another, until it is clear that they have together evolved into "a third thing or state of being" (1993:78). Whether the interface occurs through film, novels, television, audio recordings, plays, live or recorded enactments, there must be some kind of physical medium conveying an author's imagination to a spectator. The World Wide Web and CD-ROMs store computer-coded layers of text, images, and sound in a nonlinear environment called cyberspace, a location observable with a computer screen. Users "enter" this environment through an interface. Heim contends that "[w]e inhabit cyberspace when we feel ourselves moving through the interface into a relatively independent world with its own dimensions and rules" (1993:79). Despite Heim's claim that users can enter cyberspace, they really do not. Rather, they manipulate this environment by clicking (with a mouse or keyboard) icons—visual and textual images on-screen—which call up predetermined bits of visual and aural data stored on a computer, which give the illusion of space.

The interface design determines how users experience and perform in the environment. Steven Johnson, author of *Interface Culture,* believes that interfaces are "middlemen" (1997:19). They are the guides to sites in cyberspace. In the *Babylon 5* CD-ROM, this interface includes the three tour guides. But rather than have these characters take the user into various rooms and actually have them perform the role of a virtual tour guide by giving an account of the various sites on *Babylon 5,* the designers have caused the guide to speak one-liners as the user "flips" through each page of this high-tech encyclopedia. For example, the Governments icon leads the user to a screen (see figure 4.6) that lists the sixteen different species that make up the various civilizations represented on the space station, *Babylon 5.*

Each list takes the user into a textual description of the government of a particular species accompanied by a still shot of its ambassador. In each of these sites, the person the user chose to "accompany" her at the Tourism Bureau is represented on-screen as a miniature icon in the lower left corner. In each "room" she is in, if the user clicks on the tour guide, the miniature icon will expand to a larger size and make a one-line comment about what the user is viewing. In figure 4.7, the Gaim tour guide says, "The Centauri Republic is powerful."

Figure 4.6.
A booklike interface offers a list of the various alien governments represented on *Babylon 5.* From the CD-ROM *The Official Guide to J. Michael Straczynski's* Babylon 5, Sierra Online, Inc., Bellevue, WA 98007. © 1997 Warner Bros.

The tour guide's one-liners for each picture the user looks at are no different from the brief captions placed beneath pictures in a book. The user does not experience the function of an interface: the invocation of Heim's prosopon—where one face reacts with another until a third state of being or experience evolves. The user never feels as if she were "moving through the interface" into a "world" that one could visit, as Heim believes should happen.

Janet Murray, in her landmark work *Hamlet on the Holodeck* (1997), lays out an aesthetics for digital environments. The first principle is immersion—the "plunge" into a digital etherworld that William Gibson refers to as a "consensual hallucination" in *Neuromancer* (1984:5). Murray defines immersion as "the sensation of being surrounded by a completely other reality" (1997:98). The second entails the process of self-empowerment in the digital world: agency—where participants can "take meaningful action and see the results" as they attempt to solve problems and progress through a storyline (126). The third aesthetic principle Murray identifies is the process of transformation, whether physical or

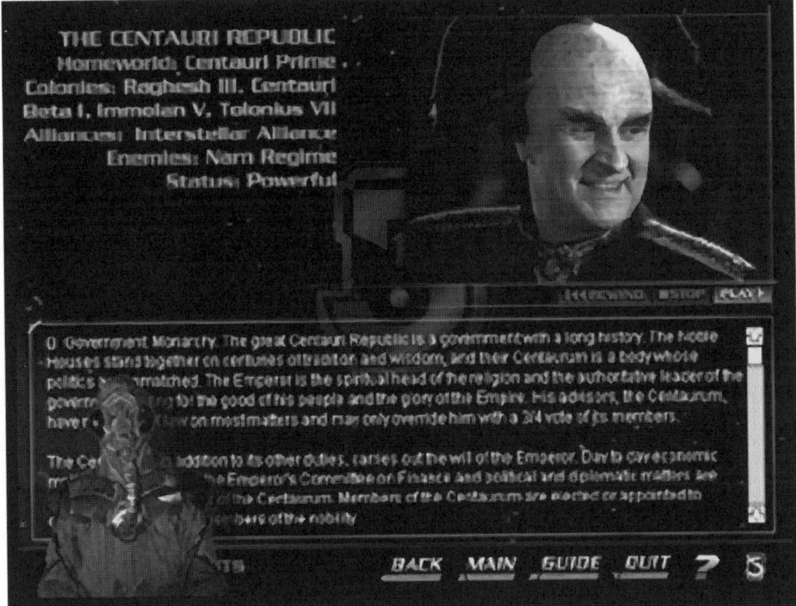

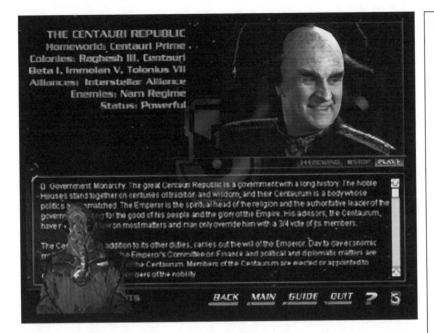

Figure 4.7.
"The Centauri Republic is powerful," says your tour guide (the alien Gaim in the lower left corner). From the CD-ROM *The Official Guide to J. Michael Straczynski's* Babylon 5, Sierra Online, Inc., Bellevue, WA 98007. © 1997 Warner Bros.

psychological (154). The aesthetics of the digital environment, Murray explains, is comprised of "essential" properties. A digital environment is interactive as a result of procedural and participatory codes, and it is immersive because of spatial and encyclopedic codes (71). Participation is governed by a procedural process: the engine of the computer, the computer code, and the rules they prescribe to the participant. Immersion comes about through information and data, which in turn help to map out the size of the universe within the digital environment (71). Thus, the interface determines how participants interact with the procedural process of the digital environments and at the same time becomes the tool by which users become immersed.

Furthermore, by examining CD-ROM games through Schechner's performance quadrilogue (1988:72), as we did with the table-top war game in chapter 2, we can further extend the analysis beyond Murray's digital aesthetics and four "essential principles" in order to show how performance is evinced through digital environments. Briefly, Schechner defines the drama as the written text—the scenario or story. The script describes how one performs this drama (such as certain movements, gestures, and vocal patterns, for example). The theater is what is performed, and the performance includes the spectators' presence in front of or within the theatrical performance.

The *Babylon 5* guidebook fails in regard to both Murray's aesthetic principles of immersion and Schechner's aesthetic principles of performance. Before I critique how and why the CD-ROM product fails, it may be easier to describe a fairly successful CD-ROM immersive environment. Through a first-person interface a player of *Star Trek: Klingon* (1996) participates—in first-person view—as a Federation officer who performs the role of a young Klingon warrior in an "immersive studies" three-dimensional holodeck program. The user learns about Klingon culture and customs after his character's father is assassinated and the young Klingon is thrown into the midst of an investigation. The designers want the user to "think like a Klingon." Through first-person mode the user is immediately immersed in the Klingon universe, because the performers in the CD-ROM talk to her and expect her to perform the actions that best convey the behavior of what it is like to be Klingon. The game literally restores certain *Star Trek* behaviors through the participant. If she fails to act like a Klingon she will flounder, and the holodeck simulation of the Klingon world will end. After it shuts off, Gowron (played by Robert O'Reilly in a reprise of his recurring *Star Trek* role), the "tutor," appears and emphasizes: "Act and ye shall *have* dinner. Think and ye shall *be* dinner." This is the theme used to help design the interface of this product. It creates the overall tone of the environment and allows the user to understand her role in order to participate in the environment.

Examining this game through Schechner's quadrilogue, we see that the *drama* is the murder mystery the player must solve (that's the scenario). The *script*—the "patterns of doing" (Schechner 1988:70)—in a CD-ROM encompasses the process of how one interacts with the realistically rendered on-screen environment through an interface of keystrokes and mouse clicks: this is *how* the participant progresses through and enacts the drama (the storyline). The *theater* is the actual playing of the game, the computer screen becoming the digital stage. The *performance* not only comprises the participant's experience in playing the game, but it encompasses the wider cultural sphere of the game, including spectators watching the player as well as reviews of the game in various magazines, and online discussion groups about the game, for example.

Furthermore, *Star Trek: Klingon* relies on all four of Murray's "essential properties" (1997:71) of an immersive digital environment: the interface shapes the *procedural* rule by which one can interact and thus *participate* with the *spatial* universe of *Star Trek* (the mise-en-scene of Klingon-style sets, costumes, and ships) and which at the same time taps into the *encyclopedic* knowledge of the participant (an understanding of the *Trek* universe gained from watching episodes of *Star Trek*). In fact, one can even apply Murray's four essential properties for digital environments (procedural, participatory, spatial, and encyclopedic) to all the various nodes of the imaginary entertainment environment, proving that digital environments are not the only place one can experience a "consensual hallucination," or immersive experience.

The digital environments tend to receive more attention because the computer screen offers realistically rendered worlds and foreshadows an immersive cinematic experience. Digital environments, because they are limited by the procedural code of the computer, have many years to go before they can reach the level of narrative freedom of choice found in role-playing games. Except for MUDs (which are essentially role-playing games on the computer), digital environments at this stage tend to offer the kind of procedural restriction found in war games and collectible card games. Similarly, in the design of the *Babylon 5: Into the Fire* combat simulator, designers created interfaces that help evoke the feel of what it may be like to fly in a Starfury, as well as the various interfaces for other commands, as one rises in rank. Because the design seemed to follow Murray's four "essential properties," it promised to offer an immersive experience that might have captured the sense of wonder, characterization, alien interactions, and intricate plot found in *Babylon 5*.

Immersion assumes a certain amount of reconfiguration between the user and the imaginary world. Interfaces are more than Johnson's "middlemen," for they are the point of contact—the window—in which the user can imagine herself sharing the same imaginary world created by its author. Immersion is more than viewing—it is participation through action. Eschewing conventional forms of authorial narrative (novels, films, and so forth), most of the sites analyzed in this book are comprised of objects wherein the point of contact—the interface—transports, temporarily alters, and otherwise allows the participant not just to experience a different state of being, but to perform within that subjectivity. The actions they take with the interface object reconfigure the participants' perceptual field, and it is as if they have become immersed in a fantasy world.

Novels, films, and other conventional forms of narrative do require spectators to participate in order to share in the creation of an author's imagination. However, participants do not necessarily become immersed to the point where they are reconfigured as *performers* in the imaginary fantasy environment. A reader may identify with a character in a novel and actually feel the emotions of the fictitious character, but she cannot make that character perform a function not delineated within the text. It seems the more an environment is realistically specified the less interactivity it offers. Role-playing games offer the most interactivity—participants have the freedom to choose what actions they take in the imaginary environment. The other end of the spectrum—novels, films, and television—offers no freedom to the viewer: what they see is what they get. They interact with the environment vicariously, experiencing it through the actions and emotions of an actor's performance or through an author's text on a page.

In the role-playing game, participants perform the part of characters in an improvisational story. The war game's ship control sheets and rules reconfigure players into the enactment of simulated fleet battles. In the collectible card game, images and data on cards, along with highly structured rules, permit players to perform the part of ambassadors who manipulate military conquests and diplomatic intrigue. CD-ROMs offer something in between the role-playing game and the restrictive media of novels and television. Participants interact with the environment, sometimes as characters or avatars, by means of an on-screen interface. The interface determines how users become immersed in the CD-ROM's environment. All these sites use different interfaces to reconfigure and immerse participants—shaping the procedural, participatory, spatial, and encyclopedic experience—which in turns allow them to perform within a make-believe world. Pictures, statistical data, and rules convey just enough information for players to restore certain *Babylon 5* behaviors in a performance that causes them to become immersed in this fantasy universe.

In the CD-ROM reference guide, however, the producers have conveyed a rhetoric of immersion without following the principles of digital immersion as laid out by Murray. Furthermore, by looking at the reference guide through Schechner's performance quadrilogue (drama, script, theater, performance), we can clearly see that the drama of this product presents the scenario of touring *Babylon 5*. However, when one enacts the script—clicks on the various icons and attempts to interact within the product on-screen—one ends up enacting a virtual book-reading experience and not the immersive tour promised. Indeed, producer Samit even mentions in an interview that this is what they have designed: "Wouldn't it be great, if you had something as if you had just checked into *Baby-*

lon 5, just like when you check into a hotel in Atlanta and they have one of those books, *What to do in Atlanta?*" (Perenson 1998:26). If the product was packaged, advertised, and presented as an electronic *What to Do on* Babylon 5 guidebook, then the drama would offer something other than taking a tour of *Babylon 5*. Instead, consumers are manipulated by a high-tech siren, which seduces them into the language game of a corporate bureaucratic performance.

Chapter 5

Webs of Babylon

Textual Poaching Online

Rewriting Unrequited Love and the Performance of Fanfic

In the episode "Endgame," Straczynski wrote a classical romantic death scene for his character Marcus Cole. This Ranger was a virgin who sacrificed his life in order to save Susan Ivanova, the woman he was in love with; he had been too proud to admit this to her. The unconsummated love is a part of Straczynski's canon. However, in "unsanctioned" fan fiction found online, this love becomes requited (see figures 5.1 and 5.2). The "Unicorn's I&M Storybook" Web page contains a list of dozens of stories fans have written based on these two characters; the page was designed by Sarah Zelechoski when she was fifteen years old. She is currently a physics major at the University of California, San Diego (Zelechoski 1999).

In the short story "The First Time," an anonymous fan-writer references a scene already viewed by fans in "The Summoning" (Straczynski 1996c). In that scene Straczynski reveals that Marcus is a virgin and had decided to save his first sexual experience for the right woman. In the fan's story, Ivanova speaks to Marcus:

> "About waiting to do things properly. I've been thinking about what you said on the *White Star* a while back about having found the right person and not letting her know it yet" [in "The Summoning"]. Ivanova's face was stern and thoughtful.
>
> "You have?" The ranger looked at her in sudden horror. Maybe he had talked in his sleep after all and she'd only been waiting to rip his lungs out in private.

"I usually don't volunteer advice to my friends, especially not advice of a personal nature, but in the last few years a lot of people have come to me looking for it, and I don't think I've been responsible for any major catastrophes to date." Susan's voice was hesitant.

"Meaning what?"

"I think you should let this woman know how you feel, Marcus. Life's too short. If you wait too long, we're going to find ourselves in the middle of some kind of deviltry again and then you might miss your chance." She punctuated her pronouncement with little affirmative shakes of her head, as though she was trying to convince both of them at the same time.

"Do you really think so?" the ranger asked her in a strangled voice.

"Yes, and I'm ready to help you in any way I can. It's the least I can do after all we've been through together."

Marcus Cole nodded mutely in shock. The woman of his dreams was offering to help him win the woman of his dreams. He suddenly found himself wishing he'd talked in his sleep. (see Appendix A)

The writer uses a narrative set-up that references the scene written by Straczynski and previously viewed by fans. This restores the behavior of

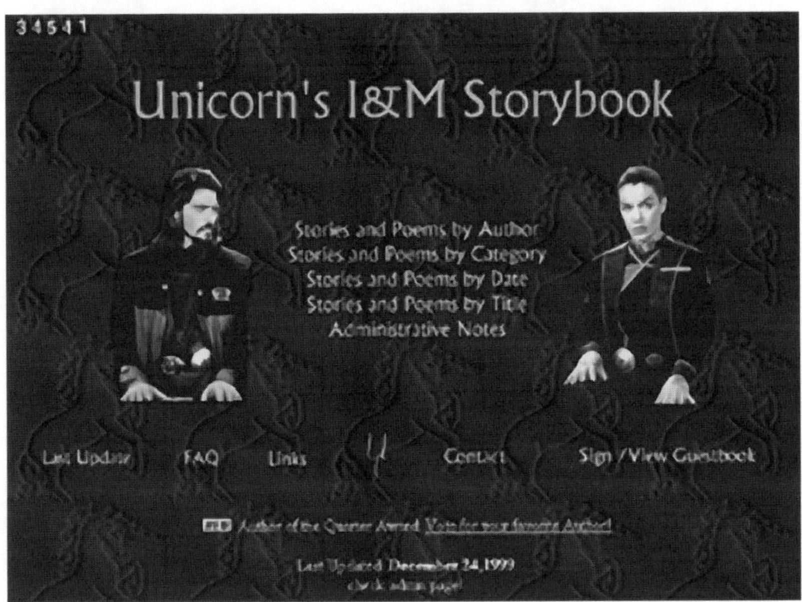

Figure 5.1.
"Unicorn's I&M Storybook": notice the tally of 34,541 hits. http://www.geocities.com/Area51/Dimension/2444/.

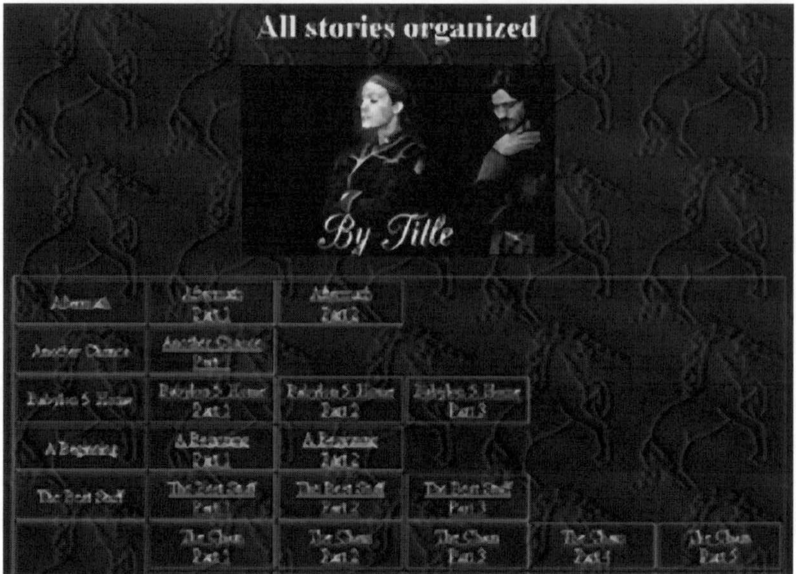

Figure 5.2.
A list of the dozens of stories fans have written about Marcus and Susan on *Babylon 5.* From "Unicorn's I&M Storybook".

the original scene and draws the fan-reader into the plausible possibilities of the scenario. The reader can imagine the scene as performed by actors Claudia Christian and Jason Carter. Later, the writer has the characters perform their first kiss—a scene that never took place on the television series *Babylon 5*, and is therefore unsanctioned and outside the saga's canon:

Susan's mouth was on his. He'd dreamt about this for so long. Well, maybe he hadn't dreamt about this exact sequence of events in this exact setting, but it was still Susan, it was still her lips covering his, and it was incredible. It might also be his only chance, he might as well do it right.

Marcus took control of the kiss, bringing one hand up to cup her head as he curled the other arm around her shoulders and shifted his mouth. He traced her lips with the tip of his tongue, willing them to open, and groaning in bliss when they eased apart. She was sweet, so sweet. The heat of her blasted straight into his soul as he explored her warm willing mouth. He possessed her thoroughly, until the contours and the taste of her were seared into his memory and both their breaths came in little ragged gasps. They sagged against each other in the aftermath.

> Her knuckles were white from her grip on his shoulders. She was breathless, warm and wobbly. "Marcus?" she breathed softly.
>
> The ranger bent his mouth to hers again. It was a gentler kiss this time. He lingered against her, tenderly brushing the spots he'd plundered the minute before and then reluctantly retreating.
>
> "Oh." He'd never thought to hear such a small, surprised voice coming out of Ivanova's mouth. (see Appendix A)

Straczynski might say that the story of unrequited love made Marcus' death that much more tragic, especially when it took a profound sense of love to willingly sacrifice his life in order to save the woman he loves.

It is not enough for fans just to wonder what it would be like if Marcus were not killed. Some fans want to know what Marcus and Ivanova's love would have been like, how they would have performed their first kiss if Straczynski hadn't killed the character. Within the canon, fans have to rely wholly on Straczynski to provide this scene, and if it is not forthcoming (which it will not be, since the character is dead), fans create their own personal texts in order to perform, enact, share in, and see scenes that the canonical author never created. Fanfic, as these fictional stories written by fans are known, revolves around such issues. The "forbidden kiss" between Marcus and Ivanova becomes the site where fans enter Straczynski's universe and shape it in *their* own image. "The idea is to change the object while preserving it," cultural scholar Constance Penley says about fan writing (1997:3). It allows them to perform Straczynski's characters in an "alternative universe." "This story is just a short speculation about what might happen," the author writes, "if Susan Ivanova decided to help Marcus Cole get his love life straightened out." The author even makes sure to give the original creator and copyright holders their due: "These wonderful people and places belong to JMS [Straczynski] and Warner Bros. I make no claim to them and have derived no profit whatsoever from their use (other than having a whole lot of fun!)." Fans are not necessarily looking for money and may not care where the stories end up—they want to have their works read. And it seems that with over 33,000 hits (as of January 2000), this Web site and these writers have gained an audience allowing them to approach "best-seller" status.

Not entirely wanting to just view someone else's story, *Babylon 5* fans write their own narratives based on characters created by Joe Straczynski. This does not necessarily reflect a lack of satisfaction with the story of *Babylon 5*, but as with other categories of the imaginary entertainment environment, fans want to participate in that universe. If fans can't live in the imaginary fantasy, they can at least participate in the culture of creation. By writing fan fiction and publishing Web pages, fans immerse themselves in the *Babylon 5* universe. One way they do this is to take favorite characters and put them into new stories. The writers become reconfigured through the stories they write and publish. Sometimes these stories go beyond the canon of Straczynski's one hundred and ten episode saga. Yet the fan writer's creations intersect with and become absorbed in Straczynski's universe.

"Fandom here," media scholar Henry Jenkins tells us, "becomes a participatory culture which transforms the experience of media consumption into the production of new texts, indeed of a new culture and a new community" (1992:46). Fans may create new cultural texts, but they do not necessarily build a new full-sized community. If anything, what evolves out of their creative productions are microcommunities. Straczynski's original narrative provides the spark for fans to create these microcommunities in which fan-created narratives circulate. Fans write new fictions and post them on Web pages, and they also create fan clubs online, which usually revolve around particular characters and the actors who perform them. Entire Web sites with multiple pages and links may be devoted to one character or theme. ("The Lurker's Guide to *Babylon 5*" lists over two hundred Web pages dedicated to the show; these range from pages about particular actors to trivia.) Web pages and fan fiction allow fans to explore the universe of *Babylon 5* on their own terms outside the original creator's authorial presence.

Fans who perform such acts, Jenkins says, enter a "realm of the fiction as if it were a tangible place they can inhabit and explore" (1992:18), and where they are "active producers and manipulators of meanings" (23). The very act of producing new texts and posting them online reconfigures the fan into the imaginary universe of *Babylon 5*. As fans restore memories of watching episodes of *Babylon 5*—by writing and reading fan fiction—they become reconfigured. To a neophyte, these texts do not mean much. In original stories, readers must delineate the characters and environment in their minds. In media tie-in stories the world and characters are already stored in participants' memory. Fans write these stories in order to immerse themselves in someone else's premade universe, previously visited vicariously when they watched episodes of, for example, *Babylon 5* on television. Now, however, they can tangibly enter this imaginary environment, inhabiting and exploring it by placing preexisting characters in new scenes. Many of the characters are already familiar. Memories of the actors' performances of these characters reside within the fan texts, and writers as well as readers restore these performances through this work.

Fans shape their texts with Schechnerian strips of behavior, applying them in new ways. The process of restoring this performance leads the reader into the act of *imagining* the actors performing in new scenes built from these stored strips of performance behavior. Mackay, writing about performances occurring in fantasy role-playing games, describes how players use "fictive blocks"—fictional tropes culled from popular culture images—as an "interface to the *immaterial* material from which a player assembles an imaginary character" (1998:90). These "fictive blocks," Mackay contends, "are stored by the potential role-player as *strips of imaginary behavior*—non-real behavior that takes place in an imaginary environment" (90). The performance is not seen. Rather, it takes place in the "imagination: not only the liminal stage, but the stages of decontextualization (of the fictive block) and of recontextualization (the strips of imaginary behavior culled from the fictive block) take place in the player's mind" (91). Mackay calls these strips immaterial, because, as opposed to a fully realized, concrete performance, role-players have to *imagine* the mise-en-scene of their performance. Through a similar process (but executed differently from the role-player), a fanfic author places strips of behavior garnered from watching episodes of *Babylon 5* into new contexts. The reader of the fanfic imagines the immaterial behaviors occurring in the story as being concrete, or *performed*. Part of this imagination is realized through the recontextualization of actors' performances from episodes of *Babylon 5*.

So, in this sense, performance scholar Peggy Phelan's contention that "Performance's only life is in the present" is wrong. "Performance cannot be saved, recorded, documented, or otherwise participate in the circulation of representations *of* representations," she contends: "once it does so, it becomes something other than performance" (1993:146). Furthermore, Phelan argues, if "performance attempts to enter the economy of reproduction it betrays and lessens the promise of its own ontology" (146). However, performances occurring within fandom—the sites that comprise the imaginary entertainment environment—rely on the circulation of the performance's originating production. Only by relying on the representation of the original—the circulation of reproduction—can fans "play" with it: reperform it (apply the strip of performance behavior) and make it into a new kind of performance. Phelan agrees that performance can be "performed again, but this repetition marks it as 'different' " (146). Yes, it is something other than the *original* performance—but it is a *per-*

formance nonetheless, despite how much it enters the "economy of reproduction," deviates, or is applied differently. In the Schechnerian sense, a recorded, documented performance—such as a media image of *Babylon 5*—can be performed again. Fans take strips of recorded performance behavior and reperform them in the present, embodied in new concrete performances.

Performing as textual nomads staking individual authorial claims, fans poach the primary text of *Babylon 5* in order to enter its universe. They do not betray and lessen the original performance's "promise of its own ontology"—they heighten it. These writers create their own characters and then place them within already familiar scenes and/or with preexisting characters. Some of these scenes may be extensions of existing histories occurring "off-screen" in episodes of *Babylon 5* that were never depicted on-screen. Fans can write new histories in Straczynski's imaginary universe. They circulate their own objects of preference in the *Babylon 5* universe and place them in an already familiar imaginary environment, like the author who wrote about Marcus and Susan's first kiss.

Rather than these stories being circulated in the traditional outlets of fanzines, magazines, or novels, online technologies allow fans to publish them with no additional cost beyond the original purchase of a computer and modem. Those who do not know how to publish their own Web sites or lack the means to build and post pages can send stories and images to already existing sites by using regular email. Users can log on and view these different Web page performances. As fans publish their own *Babylon 5* sites, they provide "a foundation for future encounters with the fiction, shaping how it will be perceived, defining how it will be used" (Jenkins 1992:45). Through a confluence of high-tech capabilities, designers of Web sites have embedded these pages with preexisting images and sounds, creating their own new texts from them.

Fans who create these kinds of sites reconfigure the master narrative of *Babylon 5* into their own vision. This is different from CD-ROMs, where official producers create official texts (or products), usually in the desire to sell as many as possible. Fanfic also contrasts with *Babylon 5*'s official canon as created by executive producer Straczynski. Scholar Michel de Certeau has argued that "official" canonical texts interpose "a frontier between the text and its readers that can be crossed only if one has a passport delivered by these official interpreters" (1984:171). The official interpretation of texts causes other readings of texts to be considered "either heretical (not 'in conformity' with the meaning of the text) or insignificant (to be forgotten)," he argues (171). And so, he continues, the "literal," correct interpretation of texts becomes a "cultural weapon" wielded by "an elite"—the "*socially* authorized professionals and intellectuals" (171). In the case of material media culture, producers want to keep control over their own creations. Profits belong to a corporate franchise. From this point of view, fandom is okay, as long as people purchase and circulate "official" products and texts created and sold by licensed manufacturers.

Due to the litigious nature of Hollywood, producers are afraid of fan-created fiction and Web pages, the belief being that a producer could be blamed for stealing a fan-writer's idea or scene and then placing it "accidentally" in a television episode—opening themselves up to a potential lawsuit. Executives also become concerned when fans take images from their copyrighted material and place it on Web pages without paying proper (and often expensive) licensing fees. Studios want to create their own sites in order to maintain tight copyright control over their images.

Yet Straczynski maintains a "don't see, don't tell" approach when it comes to fan fiction. He can't officially sanction it, but he says that the material should not be "put it in a place where I can see it or stumble over it. . . . I'm not here to be [the studio's] eyes and ears" (1994b). Executives at Paramount and Fox, for example, have been less gracious toward fandom, threatening and forcing the shut-down of many fan-created Web sites for *Star Trek* and *X-Files*. Yet, when asked outright about sanctioning such stories, Straczynski is more reluctant to side with the fans, stating that it is a "form of copyright infringement"; if he did sanction such stories, then he would be "at legal odds with [Warner Bros.], which owns the copyright" (1999b). Straczynski's ambivalent attitude is different from the attitudes of other studio executives, probably because he himself is a science fiction fan, attends science fiction conventions regularly (now as a guest speaker), and certainly understands fan culture intimately. And yet as the creator of the characters that appear on *Babylon 5*, he probably is not thrilled to see other people writing stories about his characters. He has even created sanctioned story outlines for the professional authors who write *Babylon 5* novels for Del Rey. However, fans continue to create texts and "borrow" images from copyrighted material as a way both to challenge the establishment and to circumvent its attempts to control how they participate in fictional universes.

The anonymous Critical Art Ensemble, writing in *The Electronic Disturbance* (1994), believes that plagiarism is a necessary and healthy consequence of the electronic age. (In fact, their book "may be freely pirated and quoted," the copyright page states.) Their definition of plagiarism widens the conventional definition of theft, where one takes another's work as one's own. It comes closer to what fans do with fanfic and Web pages: "Readymades, collage, found art or found text, intertexts, combines, detournment, and appropriation—all these terms represent explorations in plagiarism" (85). They believe that "no structure within a given text provides a universal and necessary meaning" (86). The Critical Art Ensemble challenges what de Certeau defines as the "official," literal, or canonical meaning of texts coming from a social elite—where the dominant interpretation is the only correct reading.

With online Web pages, fans circulate their own poached products throughout cyberspace, avoiding the dominant social structure's conventional route for circulating creative production:

author ➔ text ➔ agent ➔ editor ➔ contract ➔ publisher ➔ printer ➔ distributor ➔ sales rep ➔ bookstore ➔ —book— ➔ bookstore ➔ consumer.

In this sense, fan Web designers and fanfic writers are plagiarists, for they not only disrupt the conventional process of getting an author's text to a reader, but they give readers texts that would be considered unacceptable in the conventional bureaucratic process of publishing "official" texts. "One of the main goals of the plagiarist," the Critical Art Ensemble contends, "is to restore the dynamic and unstable drift of meaning, by appropriating and recombining fragments of culture" (1994:86). By placing strips of *Babylon 5* behavior within new contexts online, fans circumvent the cultural elite's power structure and publish their texts much more easily and quickly:

author ➔ text ➔ Web ➔ —story— ➔ web ➔ reader.

The New Plagiarism: Fan Web Sites

The official producers of television series also create Web pages, but what they publish is a regurgitation of existing texts. Circulating images and texts through a new medium does not constitute the same level of creativity or interest fans express when they poach these images and texts in designing their own Web sites. Fan sites have a feel and style different from such "official" Web sites as those created by TNT and Warner Bros. These pages are encyclopedic, formal, similar to the *Official Guide* CD-ROM described in the previous chapter. The formality of these sites lacks the creativity of fan-designed Web pages. The Official *Babylon 5* Web Site (www.b5.com) from Warner Bros. (see figure 5.3), which I visited on Feb-

Figure 5.3.
The "Official *Babylon 5* Web Site" presents old news and standard images, video, and audio files that fans can download. Web page © 1997 Warner Bros.

ruary 11, 1998, had not been updated since the previous September, as indicated by the news brief about the episode "Severed Dreams" winning the Hugo Award.

Each of the blue rectangles on this main screen is "clickable"—taking users to other screens. The communication page (see figure 5.4) offers a generic layout that is used on all of their pages. From here users can go to pages where they can read and post messages, subscribe to a newsletter, enter the chat room, or participate in the trivia section. The Image Center has a similar layout (see figure 5.5), offering images, audio, and video clips from the show. These pages represent a line of communication between producers of the show and fans. The copyright information on the bottom of the screen stresses the reservation of all rights: "*Babylon 5*, characters, names, and all related indicia are trademarks of Time Warner Entertainment Co. . . . All Rights Reserved." Most fans ignore the request that such rights be reserved only to Time Warner Entertainment, which earned $246 million in 1997 and is part of the largest media conglomerate in the world, Turner Broadcasting System (which made $5.37 billion in 1997)—which has since grown even larger after its merger with AOL. Fans poach *Babylon 5* images, indicia, characters, names, and so forth, placing them into

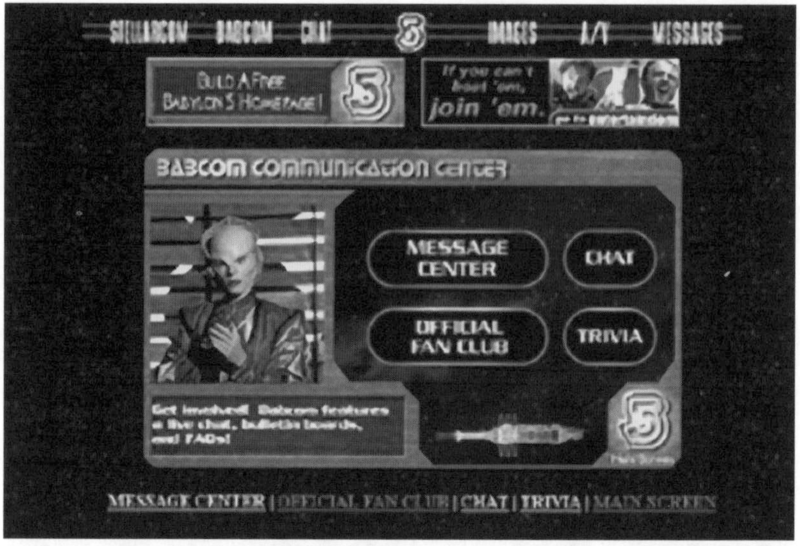

Figure 5.4.
The Communication Center of the Official B5 site. © 1997 Warner Bros.

Figure 5.5.
The Image Center is similar in appearance to the previous page. © 1997 Warner Bros.

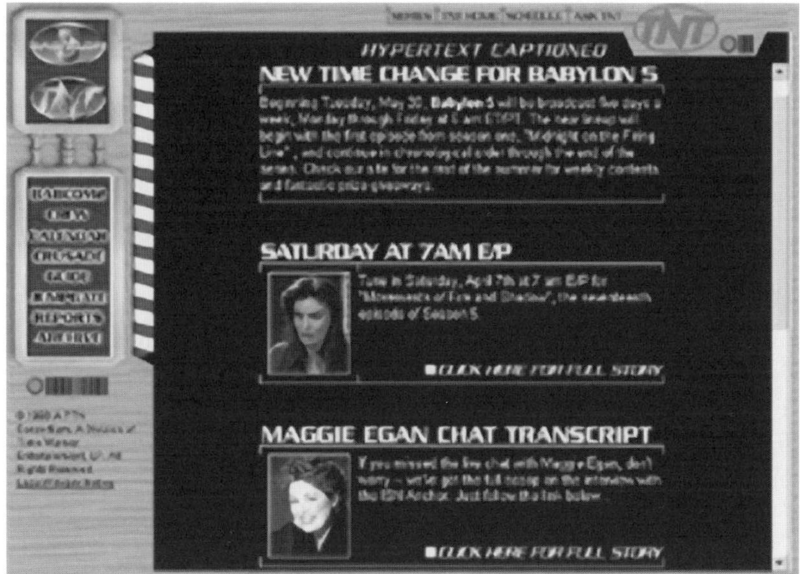

Figure 5.6.
The TNT Web site uses the frame technology, but it still lacks the creativity of fan-created sites. © 1998 TNT.

their own creations irrespective of the copyright stated by corporations. Many fans feel that without themselves, media shows such as *Babylon 5* would not exist. It was their loyal following that helped renew the show each year. Scholar John Tulloch calls fans the "powerless elite" since they are "structurally situated between producers they have little control over and the 'wider public' whose continued following of the show can never be assured, but on whom the survival of the show depends" (Tulloch and Jenkins 1995:145).

The TNT site has a different style, more up-to-date in the use of frames for its pages. As in the official Web site from Warner Bros., the TNT site has links (on the left side of the page) that take the user to a chat room, to fact pages, to news information, and to a calendar giving the title and broadcast times of *Babylon 5* episodes. In 1997 cable station TNT purchased the syndication rights for the first four seasons of the show. When the series was canceled in the first-run syndication market at the end of the fourth season, programming executives at TNT decided to purchase the fifth season in order to allow Straczynski to complete his five-year storyline. They quickly built their Web site, which is created in a style different from the Warner Bros.' Web page (see figure 5.6). But it still presents bits of generic information, news bites, and archival information concerning official views and interpretation of the material.

The Official *Babylon 5* Fan Club page (www.thestation.com) is also tied to the bureaucratic process (see figure 5.7). More glitzy in style, it offers links to its store, where fans can purchase such items as crew patches, pins, T-shirts, hats, calendars, the CD-ROM guide, scripts, and other memorabilia. It also offers a link to a print-out mail-in registration form allowing visitors to join the fan club for $12.95 (the fan club was shut down late in 1999). Members can get a discounts on store items. The third link takes users to the station, where, as in the CD-ROM guide, they can view still-shots from various locations in *Babylon 5:* the station core, main console, Zocalo, medlab, observation dome, and the Cobra fighter bay (figure 5.8). There is also a chat room, a place to post messages, and certain areas are even restricted to "members only."

Originally, Straczynski wanted the site to be designed so that

> When you come into it and you join the club, you get to hidden parts of the web page and you get your own quarters. You arrive at B5 through the docking bay, you are given an identi-card, you take a jpeg or gif [image] of your face and put it on an identi-card, get your own quarters, a Babcom unit which you furnish however you want. We'll have a chat room set up so that you can go down to The Zocalo and hang-out. And have the face of the other person you are talking with on screen with you as you talk and some fun stuff. It will be virtually like arriving at *Babylon 5*. And we'll have some online tours. We discussed for a while putting up a camera hooked into the web page by the craft services table by the set, which is where the snacks are kept. And you could see Londo munchin' down potato chips. Which I think would be a hoot! We're talking to the actors about it. We'll see how that works out. (Bruckner 1996)

Fan sites would never offer restricted-access rooms that allowed entry only after payment. Fans, on the other hand, circumvent the official channel of purchasing items from licensed producers. One fan site offers homemade toys depicting the character Kosh—the mysterious Vorlon—as well as a Ranger pin, made by fan Jennifer Morris (see figure 5.9).

When fans create such unsanctioned sites and products in direct violation of copyright laws they are "plagiarizing" under the Critical Art Ensemble's definition. But the very process of placing unlicensed objects and/or texts alongside and within official texts, objects, and images gives fans "pleasure" and a certain sense of power. Fans feel they have earned the right to "play" in the universe they helped support. Jenkins believes

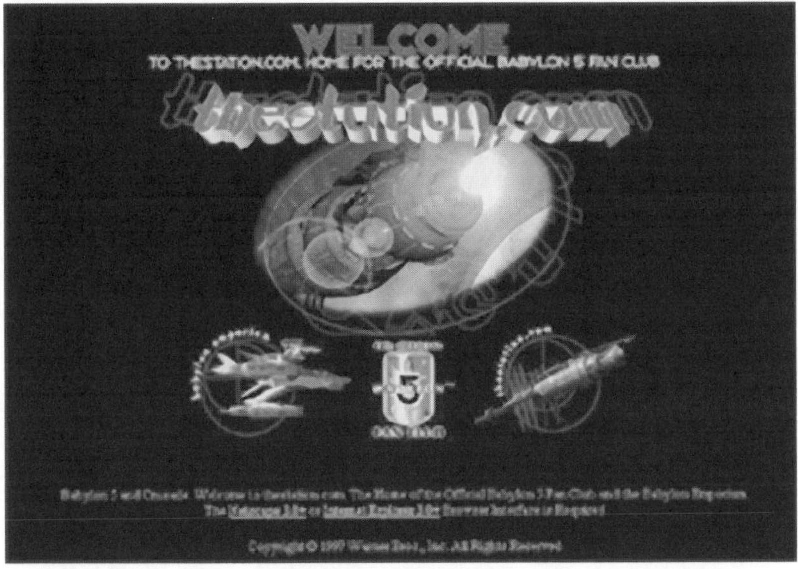

Figure 5.7.
The Official *Babylon 5* Fan Club Web page, maintained by the producers of B5. © 1998 Warner Bros.

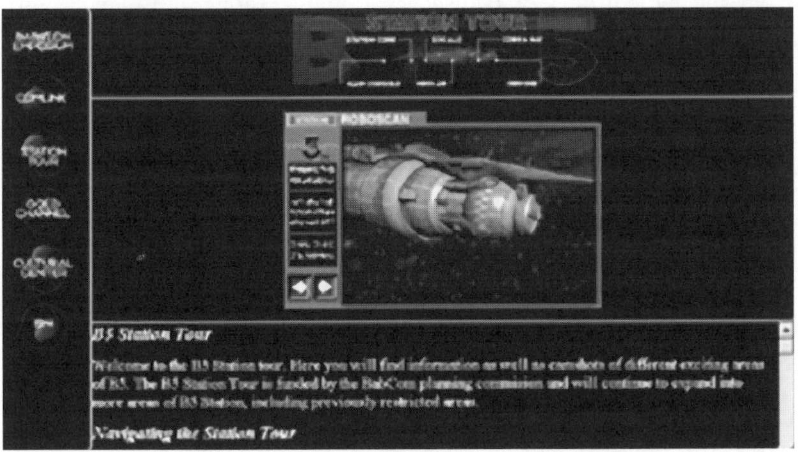

Figure 5.8.
The fan club page includes a station tour reminiscent of the CD-ROM guidebook described in the previous chapter. © 1998 Warner Bros.

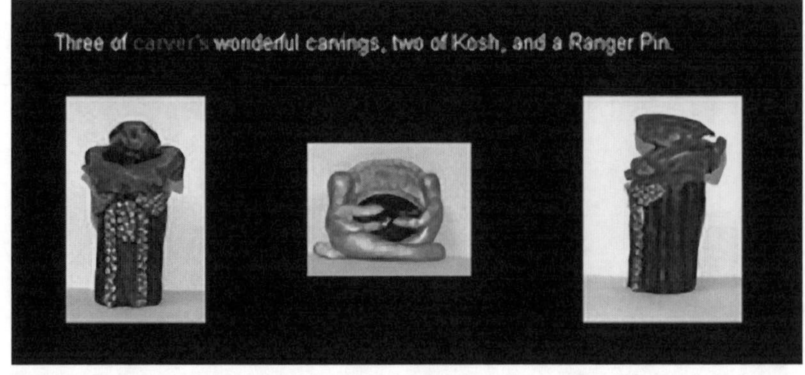

Three of carver's wonderful carvings, two of Kosh, and a Ranger Pin.

Figure 5.9.
An unofficial and unsanctioned toy of the Vorlon character Kosh and a Ranger pin from *Babylon 5.* From The Star Riders Clan Web site, Jennifer Morris.

that this "pleasure comes through the particular juxtapositions that they create between specific program content and other cultural materials" (1992:37).

For example, the Vorlon toy is a material creation representing one of this fan's favorite characters. Fans perform memories of favorite scenes from specific episodes of *Babylon 5* through creating and playing with such objects. The toy becomes a site of performed memory where fans restore potential strips of *Babylon 5* behaviors embedded within the shape of the object (causing the viewer and handler to reperform scenes from *Babylon 5* in memory). In addition, the sharing of such objects is a performance of a social act through which fans connect and build microcommunities. Around such objects fans discuss their favorite episodes and scenes, and develop friendships. Also, the creation of such objects gives fans authorial power through which they build a social community, and by which they create an interface into the fantasy of *Babylon 5*. It is the point of contact through which they connect with and become immersed into Straczynski's universe. And if they are able to do this outside official bureaucratic channels, then they see that they too can create and share their creations within this universe. Fans make another's creation their own.

The architecture of these cyberspace Web sites is embedded with *Babylon 5* behaviors. What happens in these fan Web sites is similar to what postmodern philosopher Fredric Jameson says occurs in actual architectural buildings: they provide "virtual narratives or stories, as dynamic paths and narrative paradigms which we as visitors are asked to fulfill and to complete with our own bodies and movements" (1991:42). This "narrative," however, is not to be found within the body, but in "postmodern hyperspace"—where the subject must "organize its immediate surroundings perceptually, and cognitively to map its position in a mappable external world" (44). Through objects and fiction reconstituted on Web sites, fans no longer find a "disjunction point between the body and its built environment" (44). Rather, the Web sites become the nexus where they build their own location in another's fantasy universe—making it their own: a virtual territorial place that they can visit, and where they can socialize and feel a part of Straczynski's *Babylon 5*. In the acts of creating and then circulating their desires on the web, fans become immersed in the universe of *Babylon 5* on their *own terms*. They may restore preexisting *Babylon 5* behaviors as created by Straczynski and performed by professional actors, but fanfic and fan Web pages allow people who visit these sites to see how fans have shaped strips of *Babylon 5* behaviors into forms that express their desires.

It must be remembered that, according to Schechner, "Restored behavior is 'out there,' distant from 'me.' It is separate and therefore can be 'worked on,' changed, even though it has 'already happened' " (1985:36). As long as fans are recreating, reforming these strips in new ways, the originating performance—the recorded, video performance of *Babylon 5*—cannot disappear, as Phelan believes. The performance, as she says, cannot "become itself through disappearance" (1993:146), but is manifested in the recorded longevity of itself, as can be seen in figure 5.10.

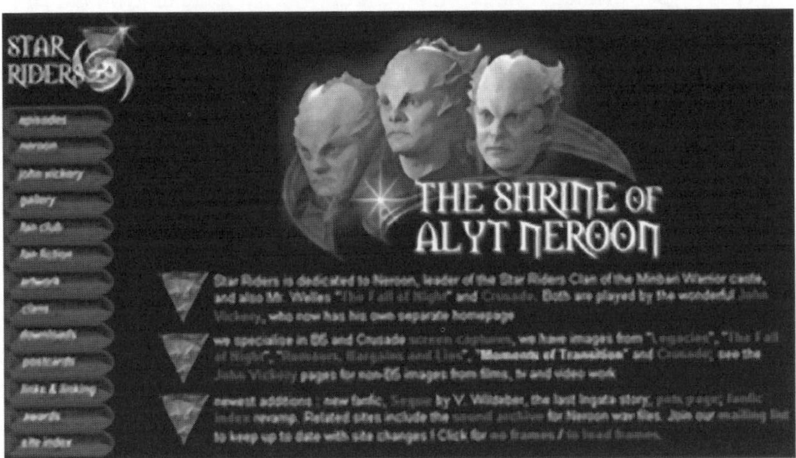

Figure 5.10.
The Shrine of Alyt Neroon is dedicated to the Minbari warrior character who died in service to his warrior caste, the Star Rider Clan. From The Star Riders Clan Web site, © 1999/2000 starriders.net.

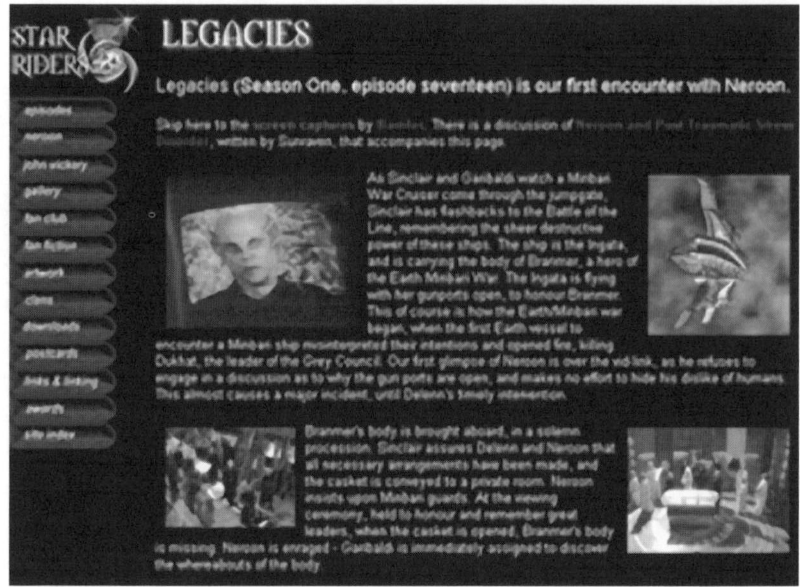

Figure 5.11.
Actor John Vickery in his role of Alyt Neroon in "Legacies." Images © 1995 Warner Bros. Web site © 1999/2000 starriders.net.

In other words, the circulation of strips of performance behavior embedded in the sites described throughout this project comprises the recuperative performance of popular culture—what Phelan would call a "substitutional economy in which equivalencies are assumed and reestablished" (1993:149). They are not equivalencies, however. *Babylon 5*, as a vehicle of popular culture performance, does leave its trace in the minds of people who recuperate it in the performances occurring in imaginary entertainment environments. A surrogate performance, as theorized by Joseph Roach, relies on a "substitutional economy." Phelan developed her thesis from performance art, which, in fact, "refuses this system of exchange and resists the circulatory economy fundamental to it" (1993:149). Popular culture performances, on the other hand, rely on just such an exchange, as can be seen in this fan-generated Web page, "The Shrine of Alyt Neroon."

A relatively "minor" character on *Babylon 5* (minor in that he is not one of the leads who appear nearly every week, but crucial in the stories in which he did appear) became a favorite of some fans. They created a fan Web page that is both a "shrine" to the Minbari character Alyt Neroon, and a tribute to the actor who played him, John Vickery—the

Figure 5.12.
Actor John Vickery, in his role of Mr. Welles in "The Fall of Night." Images © 1996 Warner Bros. Web site © 1999/2000 starriders.net.

site discusses the other role he performed on *Babylon 5*, as well as other characters on different television shows (see figure 5.10). The site is also intended as a narrative link where fans can create new stories around Neroon (who died in "Moments of Transition"). The site provides links to fifteen separate pages. The first six of these are links to the individual episodes in which John Vickery appeared in *Babylon 5* as the Minbari character Neroon (five episodes), and as the Human character Mr. Welles in the episode "The Fall of Night" (see figures 5.11 and 5.12).

These pages provide plot synopses focusing on what these two characters did in the episodes in which they appeared. The pages provide a place where fans can view images and text dedicated to this character. A shrine denotes worship, but these pages are less about personality worship and more about how circulating desires of fandom revolve around the respect given to a minor character who resonates for some reason with particular fans. The sites allow fans to "cut out" a character's image from a television episode and slow it down into a still-life which they can view and touch (click), and where they can then read about him. Each Web page is a point of confluence in which fans invest authority in this character and its actor. The pages legitimize the fans' emotional attachment to him, and they are able to learn more about the actor in a space shared with other fans (see figure 5.13).

Other pages at this site include information on the John Vickery fan club, such as how to join the Star Rider Clan and be listed at the site as a member of Neroon's clan. There are also pages dedicated to John Vickery himself, as well as images and audio files from the various episodes in which his characters appeared. One of the most interesting pages is the fan fiction page, which is devoted exclusively to the submission of original stories about Neroon, including a page listing writers' guidelines (see figure 5.14).

As in the Ivanova and Marcus fanfic pages, Neroon fanfic can cover any subject and may be used to express unsanctioned content. It may depict the character in stories in the time-line after he has died. Figure 5.15 depicts the opening scene to the fanfic story "Sleeping with the Enemy." This kind of participation in Straczynski's *Babylon 5* universe provides fans with an outlet to express—to perform—creativity within someone else's fantasy. This Web site becomes the point of contact into not just Straczynski's fantasy, but the fan's fantasy of that fantasy. Straczynski's universe becomes the stage on which fans create and perform behaviors—in new ways—previously relegated to professionals. It is a new kind of theatrical performance.

This new type of theatrical performance is made possible because *Babylon 5* is an imaginary universe comprised of certain patterns of concrete behavior. Through fanfic, fans restore these patterns that were previously viewed on television. They shape these behaviors in any way they want, because, as performance scholar Schechner believes, "Restored behavior is living behavior treated as a film director treats a strip of film. These strips of behavior can be rearranged or reconstructed; they are independent of the causal systems (social, psychological, technological) that brought them into existence. They have a life of their own" (1985:35). The fanfic writer takes the behavior expressed by the actor John Vickery (who interpreted—restored—strips of behavior located in Straczynski's scripts) and places these strips into her own stories. The strips of behavior are independent of the television broadcast: they do not have to be restored through the technology in which they first appeared. These independent performance bits can be rearranged and reconstructed into new forms, and by the juxtaposition of these individual strips of behaviors, new stories are created.

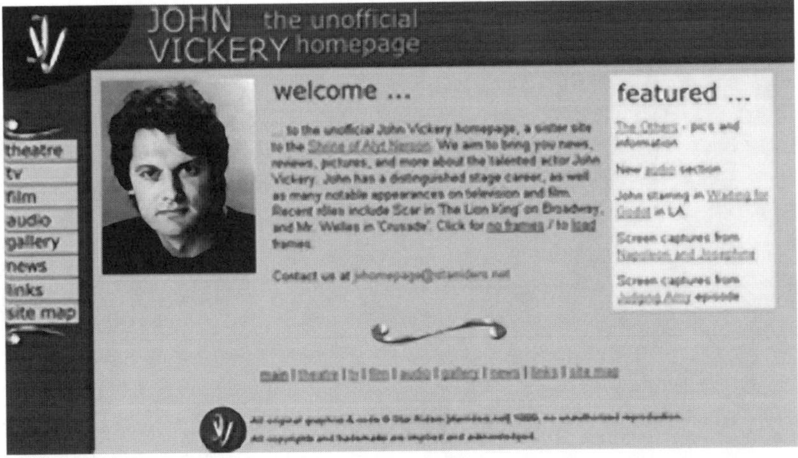

Figure 5.13.

A separate Web page is dedicated to John Vickery himself. Web site © 1999/2000 starriders.net.

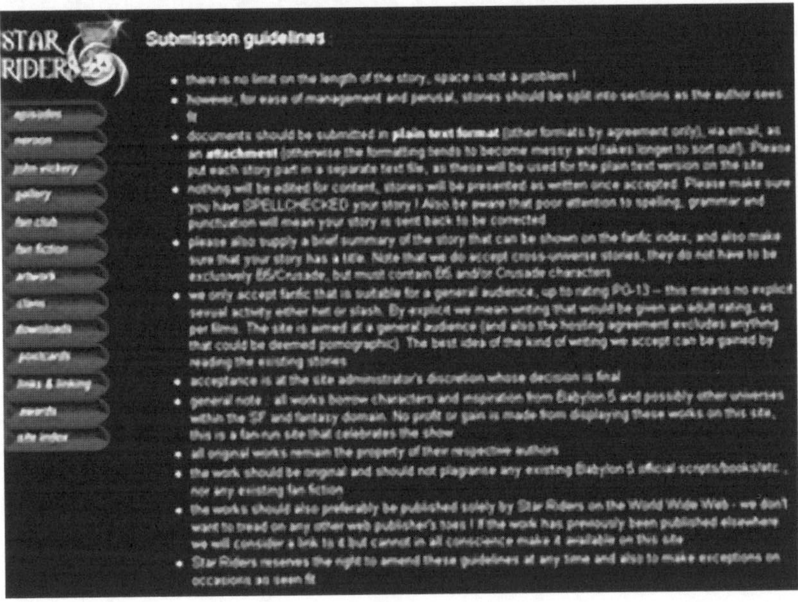

Figure 5.14.

Writers' guidelines include legal language requesting that writers not plagiarize any "official" material or other fanfic. Web site © 1999/2000 starriders.net.

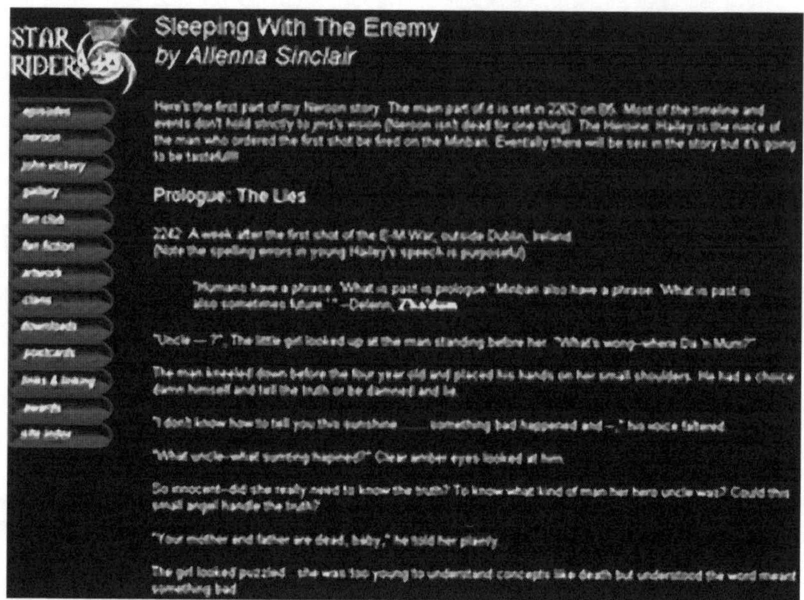

Figure 5.15.
The opening to the fanfic story "Sleeping with the Enemy" by Shaina Edmondson. © 1998. Web site © 1999/2000 starriders.net.

Fanfic authors do not need to create an original universe, setting, or characters. They take preexisting material and work on it, Schechner says, "as a film director treats a strip of film"—except for the fact that they are not manipulating actual video images from *Babylon 5:* they are working with the *memories* of the images and sounds of the television broadcast, and they count on the fact that their readers are fans who will remember the images as well. They translate these memory bits into a text that depicts a story. As Mackay says about the recuperation of these mnemonic moments, or fictive blocks, in role-playing games, they are "*strips of imaginary behavior*—non-real behavior that takes place in an imaginary environment" (1998:90). The existing scenes from episodes of *Babylon 5* are the reference points by which fans understand and appreciate fan fiction. The environment is previously textured, and fans also weave new material into this texture. The author of "Sleeping with the Enemy" has provided a drawing depicting her character and a dog she created for this fanfic (see figure 5.16). These new characters created by a fan are placed alongside preexisting characters created by Straczynski.

Fans may share the universe created by Straczynski, but the specific work—the specific way in which they restore the performance behavior—

is unique to fan writing. It is this special act of creation that reconfigures the fan in a way different from how role-playing games, collectible card games, and CD-ROMs do—and these are all products of corporate bureaucracy and licensing fees.

MUD Role-Playing Games

Besides fanfic and Web sites devoted to specific characters and actors on *Babylon 5*, another kind of online poaching occurs through MUDs (Multi-User Domains). Developed in 1978, MUDs grew out of the conventional fantasy role-playing game *Dungeons & Dragons* (1974). Performance scholar Barbara Kirshenblatt-Gimblett describes MUDs as "distributed communication environments in which players collaboratively produce a text-based fantasy world" (1996:47). This is different from Web pages that are designed to store information users can view online. These fan Web pages may include chat rooms, where fans can meet and talk together live, and chat rooms are closer to MUDs. In MUDs, people perform specific characters similar to the ones found in conventional fantasy role-playing games. They create a character and perform it textually. And, as in a role-playing game, MUDs have their own rules and character systems that help players perform certain behaviors in a particular fantasy world. "The structure, style, and ethos of these online places," Kirshenblatt-Gimblett says, "derive from their programming and script

Figure 5.16.
Shaina Edmondson's character Hailey and pet dog Orion. © 1998. Web site © 1999/2000 starriders.net.

language, database, universe rules, and premises for what kind of world the players will sustain" (47). There are many different kinds of designations for MUDs, including MOOs, MUSEs, MUSHes, and MUTTs. The original MUDs are based on text, but later ones include rendered graphical environments and graphic character icons called avatars.

A *Babylon 5* MUSH (Multi-User Shared Hallucination) is similar to fanfic in content but structurally closer to the role-playing game in execution. Instead of one author creating a work of fiction, the MUSH players create (improvise) a story together. Players perform the parts of various characters who describe their actions and dialogue to each other onscreen. Below is the opening scene from a logged (recorded) B5 MUSH called "The Rescue." A brief synopsis opens the account. Each participant plays a particular character, among which two (Sheridan and Marcus) are familiar *Babylon 5* characters, and three are new (Appendix A):

RP Log—The Rescue

Sheridan leads the Rangers on a rescue mission to save a small mining colony from the Shadows. But what they find is not what anyone expected.

Participants: Sheridan, Marcus, Sherylyne, Ralvenn, Zvedochka

Logged By: Sheridan

CO's Office—Blue Sector—*Babylon 5*

Marcus stands waiting at the office door

Sheridan strides purposely up the corridor, his features blank, and head for his office. Noticing Marcus at the door, he breaks a small lopsided smile. "Mr. Cole, just the man I was searching for." He walks into his office, motioning for you to follow.

The door to the CO's office 'shush's open, only to close after you have passed the doorframe.

Marcus says, "Yes, Captain?" He tilts his head, puzzled at Sheridan's desire to see him.'

Sheridan moves over towards his desk, placing his hands flat on the top of it, and easing himself into the chair. "Well, Marcus, Ambassador Sinclair has something that he wants us to look into." He pauses for a moment, and continues, "There seems to be quite a serious situation brewing out on a colony, one Targent VII."

Marcus says, "Mining colony . . . isn't it?"

Sheridan bits his lip, nodding. "That it is. Apparently, there had been reports of Shadow activity in the area." He pauses, looking directly at Marcus for a moment, his face grave. "The reports stopped coming a few days ago. The Ranger assigned there stopped checking in, and Sinclair seems to think that the Shadows might have attacked the colony . . ." He stops, watching Marcus's reaction closely. Marcus reaction is a

nod. His face calm, he seems almost relieved. In fact eager, "How soon can I leave . . . And should I take the White Star or a shuttle?"
Standing from the desk, he moves over towards Marcus. "Whoa there. We're/going."
Sheridan chuckles slightly, and shakes his head. "/We'll/ be taking a Whitestar. Whenever you're ready. Now is good for me."
Marcus says, "Now. Is excellent . . . mind if I use the Babcom to drop a message to Alora and Sher. Somewhat of a tradition?" without waiting for an answer he walks tot he Babcom.'

Notice the second-person designation. Players describe their actions in the present tense, indicating the immediacy of the textual performance. Where many MUDs use short descriptors to convey a sense of place and action, the *Babylon 5* MUSH uses a conventional story format to convey the scene, except for the fact that each participant helps create it. MUDs' alluring appeal stems from the fact that people create this story live, like an improvisational performance. (Typos indicate the unpolished immediate approach to this kind of interactive fiction.) "Interactivity is what intensifies presence," Kirshenblatt-Gimblett says (1996:45), and role-playing games, whether online or off, provide immersion into fantasy by means of performing a role with other participants in a live, verbally realized format.

Fan Web creators, fanfic authors, and MUD role-players circulate their desires online, rather than just accepting another's "official" creation as the only point of entry. However, without the original author's fantasy environment, fans would have no place to go, no place to create or play outside these preexisting texts. Beyond the view of producers, fans exercise what they perceive as their legitimate right to alter, express, promote, or, if they so choose, disdain the canons of culture. For it is their impressions—their lived experiences—of receiving these texts that allow official texts to be created in the first place. From the fans' point of view, they have earned the right to create their own kind of works by using another author's material, because, without the fans, the show would never have lasted beyond its first season. The original show needs the fan base. Without that, there would be no imaginary entertainment environment of *Babylon 5*. And that's what gives them the license to create new stories and Web sites based on another author's material. Through such acts, they become high-tech nomads, poaching images and texts as a means to perform in one of their favorite fantasy universes. The spectator becomes the performer.

Chapter 6

The End of Babylon

From Prelapsarian Fantasies to Postlapsarian Science Fiction

The Imaginary Entertainment Environment

Authors of imaginary environments construct alternative worlds with such detail that, as can be seen from the previous chapters, some people want to actually go and visit these fantasies. Of course, these environments do not exist—except as something imaginary, constructed from an author's imagination. In order for these fantasies to be seen and "lived," there needs to be an interface between the imaginary universe and the participant. The interface determines *how* people experience the fantasy environment, for it allows them to perceive the imaginary world in the first place. Around this nexus people write stories, play games, stake personal claims, and otherwise participate in the fantasy as well as creating something in a world originally conceived by someone else. This environment is virtual. The visual objects comprising it represent a concrete physicalization of the imaginary: a virtual fantasy.

The imaginary entertainment environment was theorized by Daniel Mackay in a 1997 master's thesis at New York University. This entertainment form, through its various manifestations, permits people to enter alternate realities as virtually real at times as the actual world. Cultures have always had storytellers who transported their listeners to other realms. Whether in print, in dramatic works and novels, aurally, through oral stories and radio dramas, or visually, in play productions, film, and television, storytelling for most of the recorded history of humanity has been fairly conventional: spectators participate through listening, imbibing the performances of others vicariously. It was really only during the latter half of the twentieth century that new entertainment forms were developed that allow people to participate as performers (at least in U.S. culture) in the immersive fantasy forms described throughout this book. The playing of war games as a form of popular entertainment began with Avalon Hill game company in 1958. The role-playing game was developed in the 1960s and early 1970s and first published by TSR in 1974. The computer text game Adventure appeared in 1976. Around the same time, Internet Protocol was developed, with Usenet postings beginning in 1979. The interactive CD-ROM movie originated in the early 1990s, a seminal work being *Quantum Gate* (1993). Wizards of the Coast released the first collectible card game in that same year. All of these forms place the consumer as a performer in another person's invented fantasy that can seem as virtually real as the actual world. Some writers even create entire histories for their fantasy worlds.

J. R. R. Tolkien spent nearly a lifetime creating Middle-earth, the fantasy world of his novels *The Hobbit* (1937) and *The Lord of the Rings* (1954–1955; 1965). He created characters that were placed within the dramatic narrative of his fiction, and he also created an entire history for them, with dates, kingdoms, stories of the rise and fall of kingdoms, much of which took place outside the narrative—the entire fictional world evolving through time as if it were a real place. Joe Straczynski, the creator, writer, and executive producer of *Babylon 5*, has created a similar history for his science fiction universe, mapping its general history one thousand years before and after the events in the show, and adding specific details for one hundred years past and future. Terry Jones compiled a chronology of events occurring in the *Babylon 5* universe that begins with the Big Bang and accounts for all the major historical events of all the major species mentioned in the show, including actual historical events from Earth history (2000: 28–41). Writing this as a fan project, Terry and his wife, Sarah, culled the information from all of the television episodes, movies, novels, and comic books and sent the information in to Fiona Avery, the reference editor for the series. Shortly afterward, their work was adopted as the official chronology for the series. The imaginary entertainment environment of *Babylon 5* fulfills the desire to enter history and become a part of it.

For each of the various immersive environments analyzed throughout this book, I have described how participants can become reconfigured through an interface allowing them in some way to behave as if they are performers in the imaginary environment of Straczynski's *Babylon 5*. The process of immersion allows them to interact with the imaginary environment. The landscape of fantasy—staking its claims in television, film, novels, comic books, games, Web pages, and CD-ROMs—encompasses the consumer desires of fans who want to participate, to immerse, themselves in their favorite fantasy worlds created from the imagination of authors. Hyperreal fictions spreading throughout the sites of many media have become the "real." People no longer escape to fantasy in order to get away from actual life. When they enter fantasyland they end up escaping from an environment already embedded by the fantasy they are entering. This reflexivity can even be seen in the *Babylon 5* episode "Epiphanies" (Straczynski 1997c).

Straczynski had one of his characters, Michael Garibaldi, speak the following lines when he resigned from his position as Security Chief: "I don't want a few days away. I don't want a vacation, a leave of absence, or a five day pass to Disneyplanet. I just want out." Through Garibaldi, Straczynski inserts a facetious aside about the expansion of the Mouse to another world in deep space. There is even a certain irony in the fact that the character Garibaldi is performed by an actor who is an ex–Wall Street executive who later ran for election in a Los Angeles congressional district in the 2000 primary. We see a certain reflexivity between two fantasy machines: Straczynski's ninety-plus-hour galactic saga is longer than Disney's combined output of its classic animated movies, yet, Straczynski knows that Disney weaves its threads through more of the contemporary social and cultural fabric. That is the significance of Garibaldi's remark about the almost imperialistic expansion of Disney throughout our culture to the point where the Mouse could swallow an entire planet. "Give 'em time, and they'll try to buy a planet," Straczynski remarked to a fan online. "It's inevitable. With Earth now in the present, that'd make two" (1997d).

Postmodern philosopher Baudrillard contends that "Disneyland exists in order to hide that it is the 'real' country, all of 'real' America that *is* Disneyland" (1994:12). He believes that America, encompassed as it is by a semiosphere (a world full of images), "belong[s] to the hyperreal order and to the order of simulation" (12). Simulation is the presence of media images representing the corporate brandishing of an imaginary fantasy. An author's creation becomes subsumed into recontextualized objects like the *Babylon 5* CD-ROM described in chapter 4. The ultimate fantasy escape, however, is to enter a kind of "theme park" that never closes, forever circulating what a group of cultural critics calls a "Spiral of Simulacra" (The Project on Disney 1995:33). They state how some visitors to Disney parks know just where to hide after closing, so that they can remain within the park of solidified imaginations, after-hours: "This fantasy has a number of liberating and subversive meanings sewn into it, not the least of which is the desire to stretch time, to live in Never-Never Land" (7). The desire to live in and among simulacra has never been so powerful as it is when propagated by the imaginary entertainment environment: where an author's imaginary fantasy coalesces into various environments, each one rendering the experience of fantasy differently, whether through a role-playing game, a starship combat simulator, a collectible card game, CD-ROMs, or fan-generated Web sites.

Media images are detached and distorted into new images—the " 'material' production . . . of the hyperreal itself," Baudrillard contends (1994: 23)—whizzing through the air and into our minds. We end up perceiving life as if it were on-screen, and these images "feed reality" through a "network of incessant, unreal circulation" (13). The Imagination Machine, Baudrillard believes, becomes a site where "the dream, phantasms, the historical, fairylike, legendary imaginary of children and adults is a waste product, the first great toxic excrement of a hyperreal civilization" (13). If hyperreal fantasies have become more real than the real, then is it such a wonder that many want to enter the imaginary worlds of fantasy? But one does not necessarily have to agree with Baudrillard's pessimistic view of simulated entertainments.

Community and Catharsis

One of the reasons fans see the same film dozens of times, perform in role-playing games, dress up in costumes, play video games, read novels based on films, and so forth is to try to capture—through participation and immersion—the original cathartic moment felt during the first viewing of a story. Rather than seeing these fantasies as the toxic waste-products of a hyperreal culture, fans desire to recapture an emotional moment through these other forms in an attempt to relive the emotion experienced in viewing the originating text. Fans inscribe their culture with performances that evoke Roach's concept of surrogation. The desire engendered by the lack of new *Babylon 5* episodes, for example, leads to the creation of new narratives in this universe.

Around the objects of fantasy, fans build microcommunities in an attempt to make social the private act of watching television. Semiotician

Marshall Blonsky believes that "in the old world you felt cleansed upon leaving a church or theater. In the new and in its theater of advertising, you feel aroused: American advertising has transformed catharsis into desire" (1992:370). The desire for the objects and the bureaucratic performance of advertising embody themselves as a form of Roach's surrogation in fans, and producers, perhaps unconsciously, know this. "The esthetic experience today, dominated by advertising," Blonsky adds, "leads you to want to possess and to do," pushing "catharsis into a corner" (370). For some, it is no longer enough to just watch television or film. Fans want to play with images from these media in order to recuperate moments of catharsis found on-screen. Fans substitute an immersive performance for the original entity, which is thus supplemented by that performance. Cultural artifacts of the imaginary entertainment environment are designed to be possessed—and the performance of these products (the doing of them) immerses participants in the universe of *Babylon 5*.

Fans create and perform within the imaginary universe they have previously absorbed through viewing and this is why they do not feel they are being taken advantage of by capitalist consumerism. "Fandom," Jenkins posits, "recognizes no clear-cut line between artists and consumers; all fans are potential writers whose talents need to be discovered, nurtured, and promoted and who may be able to make a contribution, however modest, to the cultural wealth of the larger community" (1992:280). The very nature of unprofitable fanfic, Web pages, and MUDs—which involve no costs for accessing or sharing them with other fans—"represents a critique of conventional forms of consumer culture," Jenkins adds (283). Conventional consumers may participate in the objects of fandom, but they do not give anything back to the universe they play in. Fans, on the other hand, create as much as they take. They share in a fantasy universe in order to feel a part of a larger microcommunity wherein strangers connect by participating in a shared cultural icon. By doing so, they become a part of a universe, whether from *Babylon 5, Star Wars, Star Trek,* or Middle-earth.

It could be argued that children, exposed to fantasy at a young age, become politicized into the tropes of expansionist fiction. Many science fiction tales had their birth in a post–World War II Cold War fear of nuclear war. And the 1960s movement toward a globalized transcendent Pax Americana in space waned to a great extent, its project resurfacing in works of science fiction and the desire to become immersed in them. Fantasy, on the other hand, is the desire for a prelapsarian past, where humanity is in a transcendent state before the mythological "fall," as depicted in the second creation myth in Genesis. So, the question remains, do fans become so enamored with fantasy and science fiction that they come out of an immersive experience altered? Are they participating in the metaphors of proexpansionist globalization of outer space, or is fantasy an escape to a transcendent moment where individuality is not marked outside the material bounds of a perfect Eden?

Carl Raschke in his study of satanic subcultures in society, *Painted Black* (1990), contends that four percent of a given population are "fantasy-prone personalities" who "tend to experience their fantasies as real" (cited in Stackpole 1991:6+). Michael Stackpole, who is a fantasy game designer and novelist, argues that if indeed Raschke is right and four percent of the population is fantasy-prone, then four hundred thousand people (out of a given hobby gaming population of ten million) "are unable to distinguish between fantasy and reality" (6+). Is such a large segment of our population walking our streets in a glaze of a Baudrillardian semiosphere complex—where what they have experienced in an immersive environment transforms into moments of a waking dream? Has fantasy become reality?

Taken at face value, television, film, and novels are media that isolate, failing to bring people together to form a community. Fantasy games in general—including role-playing and war games—as well as online Web sites—where fans can post stories, receive feedback on those stories, talk with other people live in chat rooms, and perform characters in MUDs—provide a viable form of community-building. Fans have taken an isolationist form of entertainment (television) and created objects around which they participate socially. Jenkins believes that this process of fan socialization is ironic in that fans "have found the very forces that work to isolate us from each other to be the ideal foundation for creating connections across traditional boundaries; that fans have found the very forces that transform many Americans into spectators to provide the resources for creating a more participatory culture" (1992:284). He certainly does not believe that this practice is necessarily a form of "empowerment" liberating fans from a dominant power structure (of an elitist-controlled television), but it does allow them to "celebrate" favored texts by "assimilating them to the particulars of their lives" (284). The question remains, however, whether these fantasy practices are pertinent to people's lives.

Umberto Eco believes that "pertinence is a function of our practices" (1985:163). We build a "signification system" in order to communicate what is pertinent to our lives. How people interact with this leads a "culture to segment the continuum of its own experience into a given form of the content" (163). Ultimately, to "know more words means to conceive of a more refined organization of content . . . acquire a more powerful world view" (165). When fans write unsanctioned stories about Neroon, Marcus, or Ivanova, for example, they are giving the *Babylon 5* universe more depth and nuance. As refined viewers, they "recode" that universe into a form through which they communicate their desires and feelings—empowering them emotionally. The fact that fans have a refined sense of viewing (and the desire to immerse themselves into a fantasy shows that they do have a refined sensibility, since they are not just consumers of fantasy but active producers and creators of it) does not make them dangerously or deliriously *fanatical* like a right-wing cult organization (for science fiction fans are not cultic), and the question is whether they are so immersed in fantasy that they lose a social awareness of the real world around them.

It is the objects of fantasy and what they do with them that determine the importance of fans' relationship to the "real" world. Immersion in imaginary entertainment environments is not a form of escapism from this world; rather, it is the concrete manifestation of an artistic and sensible appreciation of this world. The creative practice, no matter how mundane, and the sharing of that creation create a process wherein people can recuperate the objects of popular culture as a means of building communities and where they can learn about themselves and the world. Fan Jennifer Morris, mentioned in the previous chapter, practiced her own artistic skills through science fiction desires when she created the Kosh figurine and Ranger pin (see figure 5.9). Rather than escaping from the real world to fantasy, fans learn and perform the same skills—perhaps even more so—used in conventional unimaginative forms of creativity.

Psychological studies conducted on participants in fantasy role-playing games consistently conclude that "no differences were found between heavy and light involvement gamers"; "increased exposure to [role-playing games] is not positively correlated with emotional instability" (Carroll and Carolin 1989:705). Fans, rather than being subverted by dominant cultural paradigms of fantasy, play with that fantasy in an attempt to structure their lives outside the dominant paradigm of "everyday life." Scholar Kendall Walton, writing in *Mimesis as Make-Believe* (1990), believes that "viewers and readers are reflexive props in [games of make-believe], that they generate fictional truths about themselves" (213). This process takes place in a "first-person manner"—in essence "they imagine, from the inside, doing things and undergoing experiences" (214).

The performance of fantasy allows fans to see the world without from within the fantasy, allowing them to perceive the phenomenological world through the "lens" of the fantasy they inhabit for a time. This is not a condition wherein the fantasy subjunctive dominates indicative reality in such a way that fans are unable to perceive the difference between fantasy and reality, but rather the values they have absorbed subjectively from fantasy allow them to see indicative reality in "color." Through these "fictional truths," reflexively expressed in the act of being reconfigured in a fantasy universe, fans learn about themselves and their world. They come away from immersion changed—transported, but not transformed in the Schechnerian sense. A transformation occurs when the performer is permanently changed "from one status or social identity to another" (Schechner 1985:127). If any kind of transformation occurs, it is a transformation of knowledge that allows them to better understand the real world in which they live, similar to how a reader will gain a better understanding of the human condition after immersing himself in the fantasy imaginations of Shakespeare's plays.

Fans of science fiction and fantasy perform on the border between someone else's fantasy and the reality of everyday life. Along this border fans create new texts by poaching existing images, texts, and audio and video clips and making new objects and performances from them. For example, Lee Shamblin, a *Babylon 5* fan, dressed up as a Minbari warrior, like Alyt Neroon of the Star Riders clan (see figure 6.1). By "poaching" the look, the design, of an "official-looking" Minbari from the series, he transports himself to the universe of *Babylon 5*—but the fantasy does not dominate him. After he takes the costume off, he no longer has the appearance of a Minbari. The costume, however, does act as an interface to the universe of *Babylon 5*. It is embedded with strips of Minbari behavior as performed by actor John Vickery (among others) from episodes of the series. The fan stakes a claim in this fantasy universe through his costume, legitimizing his presence within a fantasy *of his own creating* through the juxtaposition of restored behavior by means of a costume. Fandom is a celebratory fact, not an escapist act.

Rather than being a danger, as Raschke seems to contend about role-playing games, popular culture, as found in the participatory sites of the imaginary entertainment environment, is important in today's society. It offers many people a surrogate for what American society lacks: the myths and rites of passages that help shape cultural and social conditions. Rites of passage once provided preadults with a smooth transition from childhood to adulthood by defining who they are and integrating them into society. Myths used to provide safety zones where people

Figure 6.1.
Fan Lee Shamblin transported into the universe of *Babylon 5.* Costume by Kit Matulich and headpiece by Josef Matulich of Dalmatian Alley Studios. Photograph by Bob Westerman. Courtesy of Kit and Josef Matulich © 1999.

could explore issues of violence, death, and mortality. However, with the loss of traditional myths in the twentieth and twenty-first centuries in the West, popular culture now provides such an outlet—a liminal place outside the strictures of society—for people to help discover their place in the cosmos. Despite the fact that some critics believe popular culture to be a negative force in society, Henry Jenkins, in testimony on media violence before the Senate Commerce Committee on May 4, 1999, contended that "cultural artifacts are not simple chemical agents like carcinogens that produce predictable results upon those who consume them" (Jenkins 1999). In fact, the "raw materials [the images and stories] given to us by the mass media," Jenkins adds, become things through which we invest meaning, a "personal mythology" reflecting "our shared experiences as part of one or another subcultural community." Thus, in a society that lacks unifying mythologies, many people end up investing deeply personal values in the imaginary entertainment environment.

Reconfiguration of Perception and Surrogate Desire

The various imaginary environments allow participants to "enter" fantasy worlds in different ways. For those who want to visit George Lucas' *Star Wars* universe, designers have created environments that allow them to participate in that universe as a virtual fighter pilot in the *X-Wing* combat simulator or as a character in a role-playing game who could, like Luke Skywalker, live on Tatooine and strike out on his own in an improvisational narrative created with other players. Through the imaginary entertainment environment of Middle-earth, fans of Tolkien's fantasy novels can play characters who explore Minas Tirith, the Lonely Mountain, Mirkwood, Bree, the Mines of Moria, and other sites, just as Tolkien's characters do in his novels. The "*Star Trek* Experience," an immersive and interactive environment located in Las Vegas, allows fans to enter the corridors, bridge, turbolifts, and landing bay of the *Enterprise* as they experience a story occurring around them. A fictional series of films, a television series, and even a novel have the potential to provide an imaginary milieu in which people desire, for a time, to participate. The particular form—coded with fantasy tropes from an originating medium—simulates the imaginary environment for the participants, immersing them in the fantasy.

Through immersion, players attempt to satiate desires for science fiction by means of the imaginary entertainment environment—packaged by various corporations who circulate objects of desire among consumers.

As shown throughout these chapters, immersion in these environments causes the subjective view of participants to become temporarily reconfigured. Television episodes of *Babylon 5* acclimated viewers—*configured* them—to Straczynski's imaginary environment. Immersive performances *reconfigure* fans as participants in different environments: character role-playing, starship battles, a deck of cards, a perceived tourist experience with a CD-ROM encyclopedia, and fan fiction. The various interfaces reconfigure participants differently. They see or experience *Babylon 5* from different perspectives.

Even in the nineteenth century "new experiments in visual representation" transformed the subjective vision of the observer, scholar Jonathan Crary tells us. This observer "is made adequate to a constellation of new events, forces, and institutions that together are loosely and perhaps tautologically definable as 'modernity' " (1992:9). The "subjective vision" of the camera obscura, for example, formerly centered on the subject's "incorporeal relations" to it, relocating the "human body" by the "empirical sciences," Crary maintains (16). The nineteenth-century visual "apparatuses are the outcome of a complex remaking of the individual observer into something calculable and regularizable" (17).

The nineteenth-century configuration of the subject through such a process seems primitive to the human subject at the beginning of the twenty-first century. Crary concludes: "If there is a revolution in the nature and function of the sign in the nineteenth century, it does not happen independently of the remaking of the subject" (1992:17). If this is so, then the nature and function of the sign have created a social and cultural state in which the configuration of the subject no longer involves the panoptic codification and normalization of the "observer within rigidly defined systems of visual consumption" (18). Rather, nineteenth-century theories of optical devices embodying "techniques for the management of attention, for imposing homogeneity, and anti-nomadic procedures" (18) have given way at the cusp of the twenty-first century to devices of performed immersion. The subject is reconfigured through the immersive performances of imaginary entertainment environments created as a consequence of such contemporary optical devices as television and film.

Babylon 5's imaginary entertainment environment, explored throughout this book, is representative of a popular new mode of entertainment that naturally evolved through a capitalist economy at the end of the twentieth century. The twenty-first century will see the extreme heightening of this form as intellectual property is shared and distributed through new as-yet-uninvented forms of entertainment. Realistically rendered virtual reality (fantasy) sites will allow participants to perform the part of fully costumed characters in an environment that has characters and settings as realistic as those seen in a movie. New Web sites will have users performing realistic-looking avatars—virtual images of various characters in live-action role-playing environments. This fantasy-illusion will allow people from around the world to interact visually, aurally, and haptically in a realistically rendered virtual space. These sites will become the reality of some people's most desired fantasies. The rudiments of such environments are already seen today in such shared online adventure games as *Ultima Online* and *Everquest*. High-technology equipment will allow fans to enter *Star Wars*- and *Babylon 5*-like environments as if the virtual on-screen images were a recording of an actual physical place.

The reconfiguration of the subject through the performance of fantasy delineates a voyage into the realm of thought—the imagination—as a site of exploration. Here, the subject evolves an alternate life wherein history, fantasy, and desire intersect among the shared identities of others. Through the objects comprising the imaginary entertainment environment, such universes as Straczynski's *Babylon 5,* Tolkien's Middle-earth, Roddenberry's *Star Trek,* and Lucas's *Star Wars* have become places people can visit and live in for a time. Formerly, these sites of the imagination could only be experienced through the scopic forms of cinema, television, and novels. However, now people can also experience an imaginary environment through other senses: sight and touch, as well as through the acts of writing and performance. Participants can exert a certain amount of control over an environment that once could be experienced only on its own terms. Whether in the role-playing game, war game, collectible card game, a CD-ROM, fanfic, or Web designs, the centrality of the scopic narrative has been replaced by immersive participation in imaginary narratives. The main difference between today's performance-entertainment forms and those of the future will be the level of realism rendered by the immersive environments.

In *Fahrenheit 451,* Ray Bradbury depicts the life of Montag, a fireman whose job it is to burn books: the State does not want any original ideas circulating within society that could upset the government's status quo. Montag, however, finally becomes aware that books are important to human culture. In one scene, the fire chief, realizing Montag's doubts about his job, comes to his home to explain the reasons behind their responsibility, and, thirty years before Baudrillard's exposition on the "toxic excrement of a hyperreal civilization" (1994:13), Bradbury gives the reader a fictional account of a culture filled with such toxic excrement. This scene has even more relevance today than it did when it was published back in 1953:

> Peace, Montag. Give the people contests they win by remembering the words to more popular songs or the names of state capitals or how much corn Iowa grew last year. Cram them full of noncombustible data, chock them so damned full of "facts" they feel stuffed, but absolutely "brilliant" with information. Then they'll feel they're thinking, they'll get a *sense* of motion without moving. And they'll be happy, because facts of that sort don't change. Don't give them any slippery stuff like philosophy or sociology to tie things up with. That way lies melancholy. Any man who can take a TV wall apart and put it back together again, and most men can, nowadays, is happier than any man who tries to slide-rule, measure, and equate the universe, which just won't be measured or equated without making man feel bestial and lonely. I know, I've tried it; to hell with it. So bring on your clubs and parties, your acrobats and magicians, your daredevils, jet cars, motorcycle helicopters, your sex and heroin, more of everything to do with automatic reflex. If the drama is bad, if the film says nothing, if the play is hollow, sting me with the theremin, loudly. I'll think I'm responding to the play, when it's only a tactile reaction to vibration. But I don't care. I just like solid entertainment. (1982:61)

Whether various imaginary entertainment environments fall within Bradbury's prophecy remains to be seen. What is clear is the ways in which people are making concrete the imaginary. These newer entertainment forms will create a classification in which historians no longer refer to the artificially created hierarchy between high art and low art: in the future the designations for art and entertainment may simply be low-tech and high-tech, nonimmersive and immersive, stand-alone art and art comprising the imaginary entertainment environment.

If these performances are a form of surrogation—an attempt to replace what has disappeared—then fantasy is a desire for a prelapsarian past and science fiction is a desire for a postlapsarian future. One never was. The other will never be.

Appendix A

Anonymous

"The First Time" 1 of 2: [SS] [AC] by Unicorn 2

http://www.geocities.com/Area51/Dimension/2444/firstt.html

These wonderful people and places belong to JMS and Warner Bros. I make no claim to them and have derived no profit whatsoever from their use.(other than having a whole lot of fun!)

This story is just a short speculation about what might happen if Susan Ivanova decided to help Marcus Cole get his love life straightened out. It contains sexual situations. with thanks to Robbie for Beta reading

Ivanova's sleep-fogged brain took a moment to recognize where she was and how she'd got there. They had taken the shuttle to Epsilon 3 this morning in response to a summons from Draal. The old Minbari had been in the midst of some crisis when they arrived—goodness know that was understandable enough, he was only running an entire planet via the great machine—so he'd told them to wait and had one of the Zathrus brothers show them into a room.

Marcus had immediately taken advantage of the chance to catch a little sleep. The ranger had just returned from a mission and openly admitted that it was at least 48 hours since he'd closed his eyes. Knowing him, that probably meant it had been even longer, he had a marked tendency to underplay the hardships he endured for Entil'zha. Susan didn't blame him for one second for collapsing on the wide divan in the corner of the room.

He didn't snore. That was one thing to his favor. What he did do however, was look completely defenseless. The shell of a trained warrior and the armor of humor fell away to leave the trusting face of a small boy. He looked so sweet and vulnerable. Ivanova had to almost forcibly remind herself that sweet and vulnerable were not traits she found appealing. As it was, she discounted the pathos of his sleeping face even as she watched it in fascination, until fatigue reached it's tentacles out for her. After all, she'd stood the midwatch herself so she was more than a little overdue for some shut eye. Other than a frail creation in the corner that Susan hadn't quite decided was sculpture or end table, the large divan was the only furniture in the room. It was wide enough that they didn't have to touch and poor Marcus was so exhausted that he'd be oblivious if a Zarg crawled in with him. At least that's what she convinced herself before she stretched out on the edge.

Susan idly wondered how many hours ago that was. It didn't seem to be terribly urgent at the moment, she was too cozy. A strong arm was curled around her, delicately cupping one breast with a bold, elegant hand. Marcus' breath played tenderly against her hair as he lay warmly spooned against her. It felt nice.

They laid there quiet, warm, and waiting for Draal's summons. She had almost dozed off to sleep again when the condition of the body laying behind her sank through to her consciousness. Either Marcus had his pike in his front pants pocket or he was in the midst of a rather intense demonstration of the fact that abstinence did not necessarily mean indifference.

Her eyes flew open. Ivanova was suddenly very much awake and very much undecided to her course of action.

For a long time after meeting Marcus, her strongest feelings towards the man had been those of pure annoyance. He was cocky, he was arrogant; he was aggravatingly, archaically noble; and at times he could be positively sanctimonious. To complicate matters, she'd strongly suspected that he was trying to gain her attention on a romantic level. Unsolicited attentions were definitely not welcome. From the day she'd left for basic training, she'd been the victim of myths about the moral and sexual behavior of women in the military. They were all supposed to be "loose" women—as eager as the randiest male troopers for shallow sexual adventures. Susan would be the first to admit that she hadn't exactly behaved like a nun over the years, but she had been far from sloppy in her personal life and she resented the stereotype. Few people, male or female, could have lived up to that expectation and still remained in Earth Force. That kind of carelessness invariably led to other pieces of ones life coming unraveled and administrative action followed, providing out and out disaster didn't occur before the authorities caught up with you. Fortunately, she was a strong person, so the abuse had mostly been of the indirect variety, but it still stung. She was used to being seen as both a challenge and an easily achievable trophy and she was pretty damned sick of it.

In the last few months however, she'd developed a grudging admiration for the man currently pressed so intimately against her. He'd become her friend, a trusted friend. As he grew in her heart, she found herself replaying some of his earlier flirting, almost trying to read more into it. Some of the remembered remarks would have been encouraging, if not for his recent confession that he had been waiting for the right person all his life and that he had finally found her.

Ivanova sighed softly as she gingerly displaced Marcus' hand from its cozy rest and slipped carefully out of his embrace. Whoever this mystery woman was, she'd better treat him right or else little Miss Right would find herself answering to Commander Susan Ivanova at her worst. He was warm and funny, brave and noble, and he deserved someone who would see all that and value it. Someone who would appreciate him for the treasure he truly was.

Someone better than a not so old soldier who was currently fighting the urge to do something so intensely pleasurable with that bulge in the front of his britches that he'd forget the faceless little Miss Perfect ever drew breath.

It had been a long time since she'd taken a lover, too long perhaps, and she knew instinctively that making love to Marcus would be more than just a union of the flesh. It would be nice to have someone cherish her soul as thoroughly as he worshipped her body, but she admired and respected the ranger far too much to use him. Long ago, when she was young and gullible, her cousin Magda had sat her down and explained the facts of life to her.

The climax of the presentation had been the assurance that somewhere out there was the one person that God intended for her. As the years went by, Susan grew in the certainty that she'd missed the chance to meet the other half of her soul—providing he'd ever truly existed in the first place. She could live with that, but if there was still a chance for Marcus to find happiness, she wanted him to have it.

It came to her in a sudden rush—she loved him. More importantly, she loved and respected him enough to want him to be happy, even if that meant putting his needs above her own.

Susan sat on the floor, drew her legs to her chest, wrapped her arms around her shins and rested her head on her knees. Marcus' brow creased in a frown as he mumbled and moved in his sleep, obviously missing her warmth as much as she missed his. Maybe he had been dreaming of his mystery woman while he caressed her in his sleep? To the best of her knowledge, she'd never been groped in lieu of someone else before. The possibility was a melancholy thought. She examined it briefly before setting it aside with sudden resolution.

Ivanova was going to see that Marcus Cole got the woman he wanted or die trying.

Marcus glanced awkwardly at the woman in the pilot's seat of the shuttle. Ivanova had been strangely quiet ever since he'd woken in Draal's guest room. He was used to her moods by now, but there was something different about this one. She looked truly vulnerable, as though something had pierced her careful defenses and wounded her to the quick. Had she received some unwelcome news? The ranger briefly revisited the paranoid speculation that he talked in his sleep. He didn't think he could bear it if some muzzy disclosure of his true feelings for her had caused her to spiral down into this blue funk.

"That Draal's a strange old bird," he ventured to break the silence.

Her only answer was a smile.

"Can you believe he insisted that we come down there—even to the point of asking for us by name—kept us waiting all day, and then forgot what he wanted to talk to us about?" He eyed her anxiously, hoping to see some flash of something in her eyes.

"Well, at least you got a good nap for your trouble," she reminded him.

Oh, yes, his nap. It had been a long lovely sleep, visited by one of the most intensely erotic dreams in his recollection. He had the memory of her warmth grinding gently into his engorged groin and the feel of her nipple coming to attention against the palm of his hand. It had been so real, he still ached with the sweetness of it. He surely hadn't talked in his sleep about * that *, had he? Probably not. After all, he was still breathing.

"I'm really looking forward to a shower and a bit of supper," he advised her.

"Well, you'll get it soon enough. We're almost home," she assured him. She adjusted a switch on the console and glanced at a relay. "Want to call ahead and order a pizza?"

He glanced at her with relief. As suspected, her eyes were dancing with amusement. Here was his wonderful, funny, brave, sarcastic Ivanova.

"Any chance of getting them to meet us at the docking bay with a pint?" he asked with a grin.

"Not much," she returned.

"Oh, well, I guess I'll just wait and do it properly then." He leaned back against the seat, stretching his long legs out in front of him.

The Russian drew a deep breath, squared her shoulders and turned from the controls to address him. "I've been meaning to talk to you about that, Marcus."

"About what?" he asked, suddenly suspicious.

"About waiting to do things properly. I've been thinking about what you said on the White Star a while back about having found the right person and not letting her know it yet." Ivanova's face was stern and thoughtful.

"You have?" The ranger looked at her in sudden horror. Maybe he had talked in his sleep after all and she'd only been waiting to rip his lungs out in private.

"I usually don't volunteer advice to my friends, especially not advice of a personal nature, but in the last few years a lot of people have come to me looking for it, and I don't think I've been responsible for any major catastrophes to date." Susan's voice was hesitant.

"Meaning what?"

"I think you should let this woman know how you feel, Marcus. Life's too short. If you wait too long, we're going to find ourselves in the middle of some kind of deviltry again and then you might miss your chance." She punctuated her pronouncement with little affirmative shakes of her head, as though she was trying to convince both of them at the same time.

"Do you really think so?" the ranger asked her in a strangled voice.

"Yes, and I'm ready to help you in any way I can. It's the least I can do after all we've been through together."

Marcus Cole nodded mutely in shock. The woman of his dreams was offering to help him win the woman of his dreams. He suddenly found himself wishing he'd talked in his sleep.

It was decent beer, considering the trouble it took to get any kind of beer at all in this forsaken place. Marcus stared down at the dregs in his glass and wondered if he ought to have another. Eventually he decided against attempting to drown his sorrows, left a credit chip on the bar to pay for his drink, and turned to go.

For the last week and a half, Susan had repeatedly told him that she was not going to pressure him to take the plunge with Miss Right. He didn't think he could take the pressure much longer. He could face Neroon with a pike, why couldn't he bring himself to face Susan Ivanova with an "I love you"?

Maybe because Neroon would have just beaten him slowly and painfully to death. Susan would rip out his heart, stomp on it, and then leave him to walk around empty. He'd always harbored the fantasy that there was some chance she'd fall into his arms with delight when he finally got up the nerve to confess his true feelings. In the light of her recent efforts to further his love life, that didn't seem too likely at the moment.

Absorbed in his misery, Marcus literally walked straight into Betsy Prue.

If there was an exact opposite of Susan Ivanova, it would be Betsy. She was petite, blond, and perky past all human endurance. Her perpetual good humor even got on his nerves after a while. Betsy worked for the docking guild. Officially she was a clerk, unofficially she was there to keep the boys on the loading dock in a good mood. She was better at the second part of her job than the first.

"Sorry," he muttered, pushing her away from him.

"Hi, Marcus!" she greeted him cheerfully, apparently oblivious to the fact that he'd almost run her over.

"Hello, Betsy."

"Why, you're not leaving, are you?" She grabbed his arm and steered him back towards the bar. "I just got here."

"But, I have to go," he protested.

"Don't be silly. You can keep me company until Gideon gets here."

Marcus sighed. Gideon was a young ranger who actually found this little airhead fascinating. Oh well, the least he could do for the lad was make sure someone else didn't pick the silly thing up before he got here. Marcus ordered a round of drinks for them and settled down to nurse his beer and listen to her babble.

He was mentally reciting the Minbari alphabet backwards in an effort to keep his eyes from glazing over in boredom when Susan walked into the bar. He sensed her immediately, he always did. Her hair was hanging soft around her shoulders and the top of her uniform jacket was undone, displaying a glimpse of skin beneath. She looked so wonderful to him.

Marcus froze in panic when he realized that she'd spotted him. Ivanova raised one perfectly shaped brow in question and nodded towards the woman chattering away beside him.

Was she asking if this was the woman they'd been discussing? Damn. Surely she thought his standards were a little higher than * this.*

Deciding that jumping up and yelling * Hell no, give me credit for some taste * would be considered even more rude than letting his eyes glaze over, Marcus settled for a sheepish smile and a shrug. He'd explain himself later when he had a chance to talk to Susan alone. It looked like he wouldn't have too long to wait. Gideon was on Susan's heels. Betsy greeted him enthusiastically and Marcus beat a hasty retreat.

The Commander intercepted him before he reached the door. "That wasn't *her*, was it?" she demanded in a whisper.

"Oh, no," Marcus quickly assured her.

Ivanova heaved a sigh of relief and surveyed the crowded bar thoughtfully. "But she's here, isn't she?"

There was no denying it. Marcus nodded.

"You were trying to make her jealous." There was an unpleasant twinkle in Susan's blue eyes. He wasn't sure he was going to like where this was going.

"Not necessarily," he mumbled.

"No, actually that's probably not a bad idea." She grabbed his arm and steered him towards a quiet spot of the room. "But you should probably do it right."

"Any suggestions?" The ranger regarded her dubiously.

The Russian regarded him silently for a long minute. "Well, I guess it's all in a good cause," she finally muttered.

"What's in a good cause?" Marcus asked in confusion.

"This," she responded as she placed a hand on each of his shoulders and leaned towards him.

In the first second he was too shocked to move away. In the following seconds, he rapidly lost all desire to do so.

Susan's mouth was on his. He'd dreamt about this for so long. Well, maybe he hadn't dreamt about this exact sequence of events in this exact setting, but it was still Susan, it was still her lips covering his, and it was incredible. It might also be his only chance, he might as well do it right.

Marcus took control of the kiss, bringing one hand up to cup her head as he curled the other arm around her shoulders and shifted his mouth. He traced her lips with the tip of his tongue, willing them to open, and groaning in bliss when they eased apart. She was sweet, so sweet. The heat of her blasted straight into his soul as he explored her warm willing mouth. He possessed her thoroughly, until the contours and the taste of her were seared into his memory and both their breaths came in little ragged gasps. They sagged against each other in the aftermath.

Her knuckles were white from her grip on his shoulders. She was breathless, warm and wobbly. "Marcus?" she breathed softly.

The ranger bent his mouth to hers again. It was a gentler kiss this time. He lingered against her, tenderly brushing the spots he'd plundered the minute before and then reluctantly retreating.

"Oh." He'd never thought to hear such a small, surprised voice coming out of Ivanova's mouth.

"For the cause," he whispered in a voice made rough by passion.

She nodded at him in mute amazement as he spun away and all but ran from the bar.

Okay, what was going on here?

Ivanova sat on the couch, staring at the untouched glass of vodka in her hand and resisting the urge to jump up and start pacing around her quarters again. She'd retreated from the bar almost as rapidly as Marcus, and made damned sure she left in the opposite direction. She needed time to think before she spoke with the lovelorn ranger again.

A lot of strange things had happened to Susan Ivanova in her life, but this was moving rapidly to the top of the list. Men did not practically suck the tonsils out of her throat in the middle of a public place and then run off without comment or explanation. At least they never had until now. Until Marcus.

What was there about Marcus Cole? She tried valiantly to remind herself for the hundredth time that they were just friends. That's all it was, wasn't it? He had found some sweet meek person that would laugh at all his jokes and devote her existence to making him happy. Susan was only helping him get her. It didn't matter that she'd gradually realized she wanted him, he wasn't for her. She was too bitter and shop worn for that kind of story book romance.

Except what was that kiss about? Maybe he'd never kissed anyone like that before and his lack of experience had caused his body to get a little more involved than his brain intended? Surely that was the case. He'd said he'd never made love with anyone before. In her experience, that was not the kind of kiss you walked away from without finishing the job. Perhaps Marcus had been embarrassed by his response? After all, she'd been around the block a time or too, and she was still a little rattled by the intensity of their union. Actually what she was, was throbbing. Her lips ached for the return of his. He'd curled her toes and they still hadn't straightened out yet.

This selflessly helping him fix his love life was rapidly becoming impossible. If Little Miss Right didn't haul her derriere over here and stake her claim immediately, Ivanova was going to do something about it herself.

What she was going to do now was take a shower—a nice cold shower

—and maybe light a few of those scented candles Delenn had given her. They were supposed to emit a soothing scent for meditation. She could definitely use a little soothing at the moment. She had a feeling that Marcus would eventually show up to apologize and explain his actions, if not tonight then in the near future, and she had better get all this throbbing out of her system before then or she was going to make a fool of herself.

He'd been walking the corridors for hours. At first he'd brushed past the station's residents with alarming speed, but after an hour or so he'd slowed down. The crowds had thinned by now. It was very late.

Maybe it was too late for him. Unless the woman was dense, she should have figured out what had happened in the bar tonight. There were a lot of words to describe Susan Ivanova, dense was most assuredly not one of them. He'd lied to her—not lied directly, but let her assumptions go without correction up to the point where the final effect was the same. She'd been confused when he left her. Surely she'd had enough time to get over her confusion and work her way up to a good strong snit while he'd been out here trying to wear the soles off his boots.

His feet must have realized what his head did not. Marcus was in her corridor, just a few steps away from her door. It was time to pay the piper.

He regretted pushing the door chime the instant he did it. She was probably in bed. The thought of her lying warm and soft in sleep was arousing, the thought of her response to an unwelcome visitor was not. It all balanced out to a cold knot of dread in the pit of his stomach.

"Who is it?" came the soft voice from the speaker.

"It's Marcus," he sighed resignedly.

"Come in." There was only a moment's hesitation in her response.

He entered cautiously, unsure of his welcome. He wouldn't have been completely surprised to find her waiting with a weapon of some sort. What met his eyes was a total shock.

The negligee was very plain, but it suited her. A robe of unadorned black silk covered a long straight gown of the same material. It shimmered in the flicker of the candle lit apartment. His heart caught in his throat.

"Hello, Susan," he smiled nervously.

"I wondered if you'd come by tonight," she replied.

"I wanted to discuss what happened," he stammered.

"Yes, I think we should," Ivanova agreed firmly.

"I don't know where to start," he sighed miserably.

"Was the woman . . . was she there?" Susan asked.

"Yes, she was." Marcus could be firm about that response.

"Did you make her jealous when we . . . uh . . ." Susan seemed to be having some difficulty looking him in the eye.

"I don't know," he answered with a timid smile. "Did we make you jealous?"

If his whole life hadn't been hanging in the balance, the emotions playing across her face would have been funny. She was surprised, baffled, shocked and suddenly relieved.

"Oh, Marcus," she finally sighed.

"Well, you told me to speak up. Now what happens next?" He couldn't bear to look at her and yet he couldn't bear to take his eyes off her.

"It's me? You've been waiting for me? All this time you've been saying all those wonderful things about me?" she sputtered in disbelief.

"Why are you surprised? You are wonderful. You're the most extraordinary person I've ever met." His voice was earnest and aching.

"I've been worried all along that this woman might not be good enough for you," she sighed.

"Now you know."

"Yes, now I know." Susan smiled nervously.

Marcus moved towards her in desperation. "I don't mean to put any pressure on you. I know this is a shock, I'm just hoping that maybe you could warm up to the idea." He stopped two steps short of her.

Ivanova took those two steps.

"Oh God, Susan," he gasped.

"Hush," she whispered, moving into his arms and pressing her lips against his.

If the kiss in the bar had been beginner's luck, he had apparently not lost his amateur standing. It was even better this time, she sought him out aggressively. Fed by the added intensity of reaching out and touching silk and skin instead of heavy uniform material, his pulse raced. He felt like the top of his head was going to come off, unless, of course, his pounding heart burst first. It was beyond his wildest dreams that this woman would be warm and willing in his arms.

Susan shuddered as she pulled back to catch her breath. Her body was not as surprised as her brain had been. Suddenly it all fell into place. It had all been one long silly game—not based on malice but on the fear of rejection. That kind of fear was well within her understanding. Now that they were suddenly at this point it didn't matter whether or not they could turn back. She didn't want to turn back. She wasn't going to let him turn away from her.

Her hands worked between them as he moved to recapture her mouth.

Trembling fingers undid the clasp of his tunic, pushing aside the edges and laying the base of his throat bare to her attentions. When she regained possession of her lips, she pressed them there and savored the feel of his pulse and the warm male scent of him.

His head fell back in ecstasy. "Susan?" he gasped with great difficulty.

"What," she murmured against his skin.

"I don't . . . I don't just want to be inside your body. I want to be inside your life. This can't just be about . . ." He struggled for the words, the slender remnant of his brain that had not been overtaken by lust attempting to plead for reason.

Strong, slender hands came up to cup his face and turn it back down to hers. "Marcus, can you promise me that we'll both be alive in a year?"

"No," he whispered miserably, gazing deeply into her eyes.

"Then take * now *. You * are * in my life now, and this is all we know for sure that we'll ever have." The words seemed so sensible, even if they did admit defeat to the whims of fate.

He groaned in acceptance, letting her hands resume the torturous process of laying his skin bare to her ministrations. The ranger pin on his jacket made a melodic click against the edge of the end table as it fell softly to the floor, his tunic followed quickly, leaving his bare chest to quiver under the intensity of her gaze, the brush of her lips, and the gentle stroking of her palms.

Marcus covered her hands with his own and leaned forward to reclaim her mouth. He traced the length of her arms, roughened fingers catching against the silk, until he reached the top edge of the robe and peeled it away from her shoulders. The long pale column of her neck swayed sweetly under the pressure of his lips, giving him access to the perfect shell of her ear above and the smooth skin of her shoulder below. He examined the territory thoroughly as her arms moved up to gather him closer, her fingers trailing paths of fire up and down his spine. After a long moment, the delicate sensation of her hands burned it's way along the waistband of his trousers, moving to the front and resting on the clasp.

She pulled back and gazed into his passion clouded eyes. This was his first time. She didn't treasure the memory of her first sexual encounter. It had been a fumbled skirmish with a classmate on a musty mattress in his attic—an act based more on curiosity and teen-aged defiance than mutual passion. She could never go back and make it right. That was why she couldn't let this be any less than what he deserved. If he'd been waiting his whole life—waiting for her his whole life—she owed it to him to do this right.

"Your call," she whispered with a shaky smile.

"Huh?" he asked dazedly.

"What next? This is your fantasy. Make it right. Couch, floor, bed, up against the wall . . . ? Where do we go from here?" she offered huskily.

"I think I'm shaking too hard for up against the wall," he laughed softly. "The bed. Your bed. I want to go to your bed, Susan."

Ivanova started to back up to lead him toward the bedroom when he startled her by stopping. His arms reached down to circle her thighs and she suddenly found herself lifted high against his chest. The contact of their bodies displaced her nightgown, pulling the thin strap down her shoulder to partially reveal one dusky nipple. His mouth fastened on it, pulsing the contradictory sensation of warm, wet stimulation against bare skin and silk at the same time directly to her fevered brain. She arched back to give him better access and shuddered as he staggered towards the door of her bedroom.

The ranger lowered her to the satin sheets with a frustrating reverence. She burned with the need to feel the weight of his warmth pressing her into the bed, not the gentle stroking of his hands as he pushed the strap from her opposite shoulder and sat back to admire her body as it was revealed.

"Oh, my." His voice shook. The awe of his tone struck a fire deep within her, the sound setting off a coil of warmth deep in her body.

She lifted her hips, mutely encouraging him to pull the gown from the rest of her body, which he did with trembling hands.

"I don't know if I can last long enough to do this properly," he whispered.

Susan examined the face looking down at her with a lazy smile. He was flushed, fighting to control his ragged breathing. It was obvious that he was in immediate danger of being over run by this new flood of sensations. She knew a dozen tricks that might prolong their pleasure, but somehow it didn't seem right to use them. It would be like bringing her old lovers into bed with them. This time was his. There'd be a next time. Patience was not the sole province of the Rangers. She replied by silently undoing the fastener of his trousers.

He stood to strip, the candlelight flickered off his slim, well-muscled body. A few scars marred his perfection. She felt the urge to trace them with her lips, to ease away the memory of all his old hurts, but that could wait. At the moment her attention was drawn to the length of silken steel twitching with a life of its own. She sat up and leaned towards the edge of the bed, placing a teasing kiss against his flat belly as she tempted his shaft with the delicate brush of her fingers.

Marcus groaned again. She smiled softly at the musical sound and reached up to lace the fingers of both hands with his trembling fingers. As she leaned back against the pillows, he followed her down.

At long last, she finally had the glorious warm weight of him against her. She sighed in pleasure as he buried his face into her neck. Their bodies fit perfectly. She savored the sensation for a long sweet minute before opening for him.

His body automatically adjusted to the invitation, nestling within the cradle of her thighs. Marcus lifted his head, eyes wide with surprise, as he realized that he was suddenly exactly where he wanted to be. "Susan?" he sighed.

She breathlessly resisted the urge to laugh. Surely he couldn't be asking permission at this belated point in the proceedings. "Yes," she replied softly.

He raised himself slightly, transfixing her with his stare as he shifted his position, and then slowly lowering his body as he sank home.

Considering his inexperience and the level of his arousal, she knew that this would not be a prolonged encounter. What surprised her was the intensity of her own sensations. His impassioned gaze filled her as slowly and surely as his body, pushing away reason and rational thought with a slow, steady surge of heat. Their sighs mingled as they reached their rhythm. Embracing the heat and then moving away so they could have the bliss of meeting it again. She could tell he was rapidly tumbling over the edge.

To her great surprise, he took her with him. She cried out as she arched against him, desperately absorbing the pleasure into the core of her being even as he shuddered into her in release.

When she returned to conscious thought, Marcus was pressed limply against her in warm completion. She lightly caressed his back, willing him not to pull away from the warm nest of satisfaction they'd created.

"I love you," he murmured drowsily into her ear before he slipped softly into slumber.

She smiled lazily in response. Secure in the knowledge that her life had somehow managed to become a little more hopelessly complicated, Susan Ivanova slowly closed her eyes and followed her lover into sleep.

Appendix B

"The Rescue"

B5 MUSH

RP Log—The Rescue

Sheridan leads the Rangers on a rescue mission to save a small mining colony from the Shadows. But what they find is not what anyone expected.

Participants: Sheridan, Marcus, Sherylyne, Ralvenn, Zvedochka

Logged By: Sheridan

CO's Office—Blue Sector—*Babylon 5*

Marcus stands waiting at the office door

Sheridan strides purposely up the corridor, his features blank, and head for his office. Noticing Marcus at the door, he breaks a small lopsided smile. "Mr. Cole, just the man I was searching for." He walks into his office, motioning for you to follow.

The door to the CO's office *shush*s open, only to close after you have passed the doorframe.

Marcus says, "Yes, Captain?" He tilts his head, puzzled at Sheridan's desire to see him"

Sheridan moves over towards his desk, placing his hands flat on the top of it, and easing himself into the chair. "Well, Marcus, Ambassador Sinclair has something that he wants us to look into." He pauses for a moment, and continues, "There seems to be quite a serious situation brewing out on a colony, one Targent VII.

Marcus says, "Mining colony. . . isn't it?"

Sheridan bites his lip, nodding. "That it is. Apparently, there had been reports of Shadow activity in the area." He pauses, looking directly at Marcus for a moment, his face grave. "The reports stopped coming a few days ago. The Ranger assigned there stopped checking in, and Sinclair seems to think that the Shadows might have attacked the colony . . ." He stops, watching Marcus's reaction closely.

Marcus reaction is a nod. His face calm, he seems almost relieved. In fact eager, "How soon can I leave. . . And should I take the White Star or a shuttle?"

Standing from the desk, he moves over towards Marcus. "Whoa there. /We're/ going." Sheridan chuckles slightly, and shakes his head. "/We'll/ be taking a Whitestar. Whenever you're ready. Now is good for me."

Marcus says, "Now. Is excellent. . . mind if I use the Babcom to drop a message to Alora and Sher. Somewhat of a tradition?" without waiting for an answer he walks tot he Babcom"

Shrugging slightly, he moves towards the door, standing straight motionless, his eyes filled with anticipation.

Marcus pages Alora and Sheridan: Message from Marcus Cole: A business trip has come up . . . No time to say good bye in Person . . . see you upon my return Marcus says, "I'm ready lets go." Marcus passes through the doorway, the door *swish*ing closed behind him.

The door *swish*es open at your prompting, just before you pass through. It then *swish*es closed a moment later.

Whitestar

The exterior of the ship is forgotten, sleek and gleaming with a hull that could have never been made on Earth or Minbar. But the interior is if anything . . . more spectacular in its quiet fashion. The technology a mixture of Minbari and Vorlon . . . melding the two into an elegant whole. An engineer would drool over her . . . a pilot simple cracks his knuckles and moves to the strange command consoles with the light sensitive controls. The stations are manned by religious caste Minbari.

Marcus moves tot he controls and his hand shifts over the crystal controls, "Course laid in.," he looks to the Captain for the order to go. Marcus looks to Ralvenn, bows in Minbari fashion

Ralvenn bows back to Marcus, lowering his gaze with respect.

Sheridan moves through the bridge, taking the chair at the helm. He turns to what he assumes to be the navigator, his voice filled with forced confidence, "Take us to sector 192x8x12."

Ralvenn takes up a position near the computer displays regulating power levels for the primary weapons systems, off to the left of the command chair.

Marcus takes the helm. his hands move over the controls. The Whitestar moves smoothly onto course and accelerates, Space warping as the aperture opens into hyperspace. Marcus says, "Speed?"

Sheridan turns, looking over his right shoulder. "As fast as we can get there, Marcus." His face concerned, he turns to face forward again, ankle resting on his knee, seemingly mesmerized by the eddies of hyperspace.

Ralvenn quickly scans the weapons power level outputs and nods, apparently satisfied with what he sees. He presses down on several crystalline indicators and they flash with alternating colours of blue and green. The tall Minbari turns his attention back to the command area, watching and waiting for further instructions. He glances at the forward display and his eyes are wide with wonder.

Marcus says, "As fast as we can speed . . . Set.," he smiles. as his hand moves the Whitestar to the edge of her outer limit of speed. Racing towards their goal. He seems to relax. walking away from the control, even as he does a Minbari moves into his stead, "Any idea if the colony has been. attacked?" Marcus looks to Ralvenn Marcus says, (in a language you don't recognize) ". . ."

Ralvenn (in a language you don't recognize) bows to Marcus and replies, Yes, although I am slightly concerned about a power regulation in the neutron cannon. I would like to have permission to run a full test diagnostic before we arrive at our destination."

Sheridan shakes his head, pulling his gaze from the window, and letting it rest on Marcus. "Sinclair seems to think it was . . . But he really isn't sure. But apparently the Ranger who was there isn't the type to just 'not check in', you know?"

Marcus looks to Sheridan, "I can understand his concern. The technicians would like to run a diagnostic on the neutron cannon . . . before we leave jump space . . . just to be . . . safe."

Sheridan tilts his head slightly, running an open palm across his forehead, and loses himself in thought for a moment. "Wouldn't that just be plain foolish to do in hyperspace? Shouldn't we perhaps jump out, and test them, and then jump back in?"

Marcus says, (in a language you don't recognize) ". . ."

Ralvenn ponders for a moment. Ralvenn (in a language you don't recognize) replies to Marcus with only a slight hesitation, ". . .". Marcus says, "Captain. circuit testing and power throughput checks only. No firing would be required." Marcus says, "But the cannon would be offline"

Sheridan chuckles low, and shakes his head, rolling his eyes. He's slightly uncomfortable, this ship still overwhelms him at times. "Then proceed, Marcus."

Marcus says, (in a language you don't recognize)" . . ." Marcus bows to the Minbari Tech

Ralvenn nods to Marcus, also bowing from the waist and then turns to approach the weapons panel. His fingers fly over the controls for a moment, then he steps back and watches as the diagnostic proceeds to run.

The Whitestar speed through hyperspace . . . drawing closer to its destination.

Sheridan leans back in the chair, his arm resting on the left rail, holding his chin as he continues to think, his brows furrowed deep. "Marcus?" Lights flash and a gentle tone sound directs Ralvenn to reapproach his panel, where he presses a few more input selectors and then turns to another Minbari technician nearby. The two whisper something to one another, pointing at another display unit across the way. The second Minbari nods and then approaches the display, reads something from it and then returns to murmur something back to Ralvenn. He nods in understanding and then presses a final selector switch.

Marcus says, "Yes Captain?" Marcus moves to be in the Captain's vision

"Another thing that Sinclair said, was something about a family, the name was Shushunov." Sheridan unzips his jacket, and reaches into his pocket, producing a data crystal that he hands to Marcus. "It's all here, if you want to take a look."

Near the very back of the command bridge, the entire weapons monitoring array section of wall lights up with a beautiful rainbow array of lights emitting from the crystalline components. Some type of power surge draws into it but then subsides rapidly, the light along with it. Ralvenn and now two other Minbari technicians, the third a female, watch it carefully and then confer amongst themselves with hushed tones. Marcus accepts the crystal, "Yes. I shall.," he walks over and drops it into a reader and scans over the data. As he reads his face, grows expressionless. his jaw clenches., "Bloody Hell.," he says under his breath.as he finishes scanning the data, he sighs, "Children . . . that had children that close to the Shadows."

Ralvenn (in a language you don't recognize) walks briskly back to the front of the command bridge after speaking with the two Minbari. There he waits for Marcus to make eye contact with him. He nods with a satisfied smile. ". . ."

Marcus says, (in a language you don't recognize) ". . ." Marcus bows to Ralvenn then looks to the Captain, All weapons systems are available Ralvenn bows in return, then turns and walks back to where he and the female technician continue monitoring the incoming data. Marcus says, "Should be there in about an hour. shouldn't take long.," he smiles, "Unless of course we're killed. then it takes a great deal longer"

Sheridan nods, his stance in the chair unchanging, but his voice takes on an authoritative tone as he turns to Marcus. "Make sure that when we jump out the weapon systems are charged up and ready to fire. We've go no clue what to expect out there." As if that was a cue to him, he sits upright in the chair, back straight, hands clasped around the ends of the chair arms. He looks straight ahead, as if willing space and time to move faster. Perhaps it does. who knows. but time passes and the emerge from jumpspace . . .

Marcus says, "Docking bay is on the surface. Fits the average size freighter. we might bet a wingtip in there. shuttle flight. Down. for me and an one more."

Sheridan stands from the chair as the ship comes out of hyperspace. "Marcus, have then scan for -any- ships in the area." His voice commanding, he moves towards the windows to get a better look at the colony, even if from a distance. Marcus says, (in a language you don't recognize) ". . ."

Ralvenn (in a language you don't recognize) turns briskly around from his weapons control panel and reports to Marcus, ". . ." he says. ". . ."

Sheridan looks back to Marcus. "Anything?"

Marcus says, "Nothing Yet . . ." Marcus says, "Shall we try to hail the colony" "Please do so." Sheridan walks back to the command chair, retaking his ready posture.

Marcus opens the channel, "Targent VII. Targent VII. Identify please

The only answer is silence.

Marcus says, "No response." Marcus says, "I'll take the shuttle down with your permission"

Ralvenn finishes a final inspection of the weapons array and steps back into view, his hands folded neatly at his waist, awaiting instructions. Sheridan looks out the window, almost as if he's willing the colony to communicate. "Scan the surface for any signs of life, before you do that Marcus. And I'm coming with you. By the way." His gaze out the window remains steady.

The comm system flares into life, the signal. broken, the language. broken "Zvezdochka. . Walks. in Walls." A scream and then static. Sheridan looks to Marcus, pointing at the controls. "Track that signal, get a lock on it!"

Marcus says, (in a language you don't recognize) ". . ." Marcus speaks quickly to the Minbari as he moves to a set of controls Ralvenn steps quickly over to another panel and moves his hand slowly up a long purple crystal. "Boosting power to comm tracking." he says, turning back to look at Marcus.

Marcus says, "Signal. acquired. and located. Looks like its coming from the C&C of the complex."

The comm system flares into life, the signal. broken, the language. broken "Zvezdochka . . . Walks. in Walls." A scream and then static.

Marcus blinks, looking up, "That's exactly the same.

"A recording?" Sheridan's gaze still locked on Marcus, his questions the transmission, and looks towards Ralvenn. "Could you verify?"

Marcus nods, "Yes. only answer.

Ralvenn's demeanor seems to turn somewhat more worried as he stares into a communications panel before nodding his head up and down. "Signal strength nominal, looks to be the same broadcast Captain. We will need another repetition to verify."

Marcus says, "Life signs on that rock are extremely hard to get, the complex is mostly tunnels in indigenous rock. through nickel iron ore. I can't say if there is anyone at the point of origin."

The comm flares again "Zvezdochka . . . Walks. in Walls." A scream and then static.

"Move us in closer, we might not have time. Make sure the shuttle is prepared for immediate launch." Sheridan nods to Marcus and adds, "And make sure they load the weapons that I brought as well."

Marcus says, "Yes Sir."

Ralvenn shakes his head, looking perplexed. "Cross section analysis confirms repeated broadcast Captain."

Marcus says, (in a language you don't recognize) ". . ."

Marcus speaks to one of the Minbari and moves from his position stepping back and making quick statements in the elegant language,

"How long till we get in range to launch the Shuttle?" Sheridan still looks to Ralvenn, his face and voice calm, but tense.

Ralvenn shakes his head again, still looking at the comm panel and then returns with increased vigor to a scanner bank. He carefully scans each detail of the crystalline controls, moving his hands delicately over their glowing surfaces. "Two minutes Captain." he says, turning back to look at the Captain with eyes alert and attentive.

Marcus says, "Shuttle is ready. weapons are aboard"

Sheridan stands from the chair, descending from the small dais. "Ready Mr. Cole?"

Marcus says, "To quote an old saying. The games afoot" Marcus says, ". . . or tentacle."

Sheridan chuckles, and pats Marcus on the back as he walks by. "Let go then."

Marcus leads them to the shuttle and enters the small two man craft. sliding tot he co-pilots seat in expectation of the captain wanting to fly the ship himself. With jolt they are free of White Star

Ralvenn raises an eye-ridge and watches the two Humans as they prepare to leave for the shuttle. He nods with an appreciative look on his face, then turns back to continue monitoring.

Sheridan moves into the shuttle, slightly surprised at the empty Pilot seat. Cracking his knuckles, he sits, fastening the belts. "It's been a while since I piloted one of these things . . ." As they clear they bay of the Whitestar, he deftly maneuvers the shuttle through space, towards the colony below.

The shuttle moves towards the surface, and hovers for a moment over the landing pad, before settling down with a slight jolt. Marcus says, "Zvezdochka. What does it mean?" Marcus says, "Docking bay doors have a good seal. we have atmosphere"

"Shuttle one to Whitestar, we've arrived." Sheridan turns to Marcus, and shrugs. "I was thinking about that . . . Susan would know." He takes a deep breath as his eyes darken for a moment, remembering the past. "Little . . . Little something, I think."

"Shuttle One, we have you on scanners." Ralvenn's voice crackles back over the command system.

Marcus says, "Yes. She would know. But she is _gone_"

Shaking his head, he moves to unbuckle from the seat. "Not now, Marcus. I need to concentrate on this. I don't need to think about it, i'm sorry I brought it up." The sadness in his voice weights in the air, as reaches back, grabbing a PPG pistol and a holster. He checks the cap, the telltale noise informing him that it's indeed charged, puts the holster on his belt. Reaching back again, he grabs a rifle as well. "I brought enough for you, if you feel the need, even thought I doubted it." His voice is all professional again, and he moves out of the shuttle.

Docking Bay: The mining colony docking bay is as common as such prefab construction usually is. The landing pad is in the airless vacuum of the asteroids and has a run in. the runway covered in metal sheeting that leads to a set of airlock doors into a hollowed out cave that is the actually airlock.

Its a good use of the tunnels that requires a minimum of equipment and little to no high tech and management. In short just what you expect in a shoestring operation in the middle of nowhere. Inside, the hanger has that reddish light that emergency lights cast. Shadows seem deep enough to hide arms and the rest of the room is cold and quiet. Sparks and fires died long ago in this room.

Marcus picks up a PPG pistol and slides it away inside his coat, "Common sense. Marcus seems to have forgotten any reference to Susan as he steps out into the darkness of the docking bay and the red lights glow, Marcus says, "Emergency power. primary power was cut. manual locks engaged on the doors."

Sheridan nods, following Marcus, the rifle balanced in his hands.

Marcus moves to the door, bypass the circuit and mech. of the lock with an ease that would be frightening in man of less morals. "We're in. C&C should be just up the hallway . . .

"Whi . . . to . . . Sheridan . . . communications . . . king up . . . energy . . ." Ralvenn's voice crackles again over the comm system, this time the signal much weaker and distorted.

"Ok, let's get a move on then, we need to find out what the Whitestar is trying to say, we'll probably have a better chance of communication once we get there." He moves down the hallway, gun slightly relaxed at his side.

Marcus moves down the hallway. quiet as a ghost. . he takes the point without question. and the skills make it obvious that this was. is what he is trained for.

At the door of the control room, Marcus draws his PPG, "On . three? 1 . 2 . . . 3.

Sheridan moves to the other side of the door, rifle raised, and nods, preparing to enter. Marcus swings in, scanning the room. "Hell. we look a bit late.

Bibliography

Ackels, Ran, Edi Birsan, Paul W. Brown III, John Hart, David Hewitt, and John Myler. 1997. *Babylon 5 Collectible Card Game,* ver. 1.1. Philadelphia: Precedence Publishing.

Aristotle. 1961. *Aristotle's Poetics.* Translated by S. H. Butcher. New York: Hill and Wang.

Austin, J. L. 1975. *How to Do Things with Words.* Cambridge: Harvard University Press.

———. 1971. "Performative-Constative." In *The Philosophy of Language,* edited by J. R. Searle. London: Oxford University Press, 13–22.

Barthes, Roland. 1985. "Textual Analysis of a Tale of Poe." In *On Signs,* edited by Marshall Blonsky. Baltimore: Johns Hopkins University Press, 84–97.

———. 1972. *Mythologies.* Translated by Annette Lavers. New York: Hill and Wang.

Baudrillard, Jean. 1995. *The Gulf War Did Not Take Place.* Translated by Paul Patton. Bloomington: Indiana University Press.

———. *Simulacra and Simulation.* 1994. Translated by Sheila Faria Glaser. Ann Arbor: University of Michigan Press.

Bernardi, Daniel Leonard. 1998. *Star Trek and History: Race-ing Toward a White Future.* New Brunswick, NJ: Rutgers University Press.

Blonsky, Marshall. 1992. *American Mythologies.* New York: Oxford University Press.

Bradbury, Ray. 1982. *Fahrenheit 451.* New York: Ballantine Books.

———. 1979. *The Martian Chronicles.* New York: Bantam Books.

Brecht, Bertolt. 1992. *Brecht on Theatre: The Development of an Aesthetic.* Edited and translated by John Willett. New York: Hill and Wang.

Bruckner, Sandra. 1996. "DC Gathering." *The Zocalo* 50 (26 February).

Bukatman, Scott. 1995. "The Artificial Infinite: On Special Effects and the Sublime." In *Visual Display: Culture beyond Appearances,* edited by Lynne Cooke and Peter Wollen. Seattle: Bay Press, 254–89.

Campbell, Joseph. 1968. *The Hero with a Thousand Faces.* Princeton: Princeton University Press.

Carroll, James L., and Paul M. Carolin. 1989. "Relationship between Fantasy Game Playing and Personality." *Psychological Reports* 64: 705–6.

Certeau, Michel de. 1984. *The Practice of Everyday Life.* Translated by Steven Rendall. Berkeley: University of California Press.

Cochran, Joseph. 1997. *The Babylon Project*. Blacksburg, VA: Chameleon Eclectic Entertainment, Inc.

Crary, Jonathan. 1992. *Techniques of the Observer*. Cambridge, MA: MIT Press.

Critical Art Ensemble. 1994. *The Electronic Disturbance*. New York: Autonomedia.

David, Peter. 1998. Babylon 5: *In the Beginning*. New York: Ballantine Books.

Dery, Mark, ed. 1994. *Flame Wars: The Discourse of Cyberculture*. Durham: Duke University Press.

Diller, Elizabeth, and Ricardo Scofidio, eds. 1994. *Back to the Front: Tourisms of War*. New York: Princeton Architectural Press.

Eco, Umberto. 1986. *Travels in Hyperreality*. Translated by William Weaver. New York: Harcourt Brace & Company.

———. 1985. "How Culture Conditions the Colours We See." In *On Signs*, edited by Marshall Blonsky. Baltimore: Johns Hopkins University Press, 157–75.

Edmondson, Shaina. 2000. "Sleeping with the Enemy." http://starriders.net/neroon.

Eisenstein, Sergei. 1975. *The Film Sense*. Translated by Jay Leyda. New York: Harcourt Brace Jovanovich.

Ellison, Harlan. 1997. "Harlan Ellison on Heaven's Gate." http://harlanellison.com/text/ellicult.htm (4 April). (A version of this essay appeared in *Newsweek* [5 April 1997].)

Fannon, Sean Patrick. 1996. *The Fantasy Role-Playing Gamer's Bible*. Rocklin, CA: Prima Publishing.

Fine, Gary Alan. 1983. *Shared Fantasy: Role-Playing Games as Social Worlds*. Chicago: University of Chicago Press.

"The First Time" (author anonymous) in "Unicorn's I&M Storybook." http://www.geocities.com/Area51/Dimension/2444/firstt.html.

Geertz, Clifford. 1973. *The Interpretation of Cultures*. New York: Basic Books.

Gibson, William. 1984. *Neuromancer*. New York: Ace Books.

Goffman, Erving. 1974. *Frame Analysis*. Cambridge: Harvard University Press.

———. 1959. *The Presentation of Self in Everyday Life*. New York: Doubleday.

Gorchakov, Nikolai M. 1994. *Stanislavsky Directs*. New York: Limelight Editions.

Graw, Bruce H., and Robert N. Glass. 1997. Babylon 5 *Wars*. Dayton, OH: Agents of Gaming.

Haraway, Donna J. 1991. *Simians, Cyborgs, and Women: The Reinvention of Nature*. New York: Routledge.

Heim, Michael. 1993. *The Metaphysics of Virtual Reality*. New York: Oxford University Press.

Henderson, Mary. 1997. *Star Wars: The Making of Myth*. New York: Bantam Books.

Huizinga, Johan. 1955. *Homo Ludens: The Study of the Play-Element in Culture*. Boston: Beacon Press.

Jameson, Fredric. 1991. *Postmodernism, or, The Cultural Logic of Late Capitalism*. Durham: Duke University Press.

Jenkins, Henry. 1999. "Congressional Testimony on Media Violence." Presented before the United States Senate Commerce Committee, Washington, D.C., on May 4. Testimony archived at: http://media-in-transition.mit.edu/articles/indexdc.html.

———. 1992. *Textual Poachers: Television Fans and Participatory Culture*. New York: Routledge.

Johnson, Steven. 1997. *Interface Culture*. New York: HarperCollins.

Jones, Terry. 2000. "The *Babylon 5* Official Chronology." In *The Official* Babylon 5 *Magazine* 18 (January): 28–41.

Kellman, Jerold L. "Games to Magazines to Children's Books Is the Multimillion-Dollar Wisconsin Saga of TSR." *Publishers Weekly* 8 July 1983: 34–35.

Killick, Jane. 1998. Babylon 5: *Signs and Portents*. New York: Del Rey.

Kirshenblatt-Gimblett, Barbara. 1996. "The Electronic Vernacular." In *Connected: Engagements with Media*, edited by George E. Marcus. Chicago: University of Chicago Press, 21–65.

Lancaster, Kurt. 1997. "Epic Story of *Babylon 5* Takes On the 'Big Questions.'" In *Christian Science Monitor* (5 June): 13.

————. 1994. "Do Role-Playing Games Promote Crime, Satanism, and Suicide among Players as Critics Claim?" *Journal of Popular Culture* 28:2 (fall): 67–79.

Landay, Jonathan S. 1997. "Dawn of Laser Weapons Draws Near." *Christian Science Monitor* (20 October): 1, 4.

Levine, Lawrence W. 1988. *Highbrow/Lowbrow: The Emergence of Cultural Hierarchy in America*. Cambridge: Harvard University Press.

"The Lurker's Guide to *Babylon 5*." Maintained by Steven Grimm.

————. www.midwinter.com/lurk/guide/113.html.

————. www.midwinter.com/lurk/making/awards.html.

Lyotard, Jean-Francois. 1984. *The Postmodern Condition*. Translated by Geoff Bennington and Brian Massumi. Minneapolis: University of Minnesota Press.

Mackay, Daniel. 1998. *The Dolorous Role: Towards an Aesthetics of the Role-Playing Game*. Master's thesis, New York University, Department of Performance Studies.

McCurdy, Howard E. 1997. *Space and the American Imagination*. Washington and London: Smithsonian Institution Press.

McKenzie, Jon. 1997. "Laurie Anderson for Dummies." *TDR* 41:2 (T154; summer): 30–50.

Mendlesohn, Farah. 1997. Email interview with Lancaster for "Epic Story of *Babylon 5* Takes On the Big Questions" in *Christian Science Monitor* 5 June: 13.

Murray, Janet. 1997. *Hamlet on the Holodeck: The Future of Narrative in Cyberspace*. New York: The Free Press.

"News in Brief." 1998. *Christian Science Monitor* (28 April): 2.

Penley, Constance. 1997. NASA/*Trek: Popular Science and Sex in America*. London and New York: Verso.

Perenson, Milissa J. 1998. "You Can Do More Than Watch *Babylon 5*—Now You Can Actually Go There." *Sci-Fi Entertainment* (January): 26–29.

Phelan, Peggy. 1993. *Unmarked: The Politics of Performance*. London and New York: Routledge.

Pomian, Krzysztof. 1990. *Collectors and Curiosities: Paris and Venice, 1500–1800*. Translated by Elizabeth Wiles-Portier. Cambridge: Polity Press.

The Project on Disney. 1995. *Inside the Mouse: Work and Play at Disney World*. Durham: Duke University Press.

Raschke, Carl. 1990. *Painted Black*. San Francisco: Harper and Row.

Roach, Joseph. 1996. *Cities of the Dead*. New York: Columbia University Press.

Salkever, Alex. 1998. "Dust Off the Moon Suite, Honey, It's Time for a Space Vacation." *Christian Science Monitor* (16 January): 1, 8.

Samit, Jay, producer. 1997. *The Official Guide to J. Michael Straczynski's* Babylon 5. Bellevue: Sierra On-Line.

Schechner, Richard. 1990. "Performance Studies: The Broad-Spectrum Approach." *Phi Kappa Phi Journal* (summer): 15–16.

———. 1988. *Performance Theory.* New York: Routledge.

———. 1985. *Between Theater and Anthropology.* Philadelphia: University of Pennsylvania Press.

———. 1969. *Public Domain: Essays on the Theater.* Indianapolis and New York: Bobbs-Merrill Company.

Schivelbusch, Wolfgang. 1986. *The Railway Journey: The Industrialization of Time and Space in the Nineteenth Century.* Berkeley: University of California Press.

Stackpole, Michael. 1991. "Role-Playing and the Real World." Editorial. *Dragon* July: 6+.

Star Riders Clan. 2000. http://starriders.net/neroon.

Straczynski, J. Michael. 1999a. "Beginnings and Endings." Last Word column in *The Official* Babylon 5 *Magazine* 2:9 (April): 66.

———. 1999b. "JMS Usenet messages." www.midwinter.com/b5/Usenet/latest.

———. 1998a. "JMS Usenet messages." www.midwinter.com/b5/Usenet/jms98-01-usenet.

———. 1998b. "JMS Usenet messages." www.midwinter.com/b5/Usenet/jms98-03-usenet.

———. 1998c. "JMS Usenet messages." www.midwinter.com/b5/Usenet/jms98-04-usenet.

———. 1998d. "JMS Usenet messages." www.midwinter.com/b5/Usenet/jms1998-05.

———. 1997a. "Approaching Babylon." In *The Babylon File* by Andy Lane. London: Virgin Publishing, 7–27.

———. 1997b. "Endgame." *Babylon 5* episode. Directed by John Copeland. Warner Brothers.

———. 1997c. "Epiphanies." *Babylon 5* episode. Directed by John Flinn. Warner Brothers.

———. 1997d. " 'Epiphanies' jms speaks" www.midwinter.com/lurk/countries/master/guide/073.html.

———. 1997e. Interview. Email with author.

———. 1997f. "JMS Usenet messages." www.midwinter.com/b5/Usenet/jms97-10-usenet.

———. 1997g. Westercon science fiction convention, Seattle, Washington, July. Personal notes.

———. 1996a. "The Coming of Shadows" (script) in *The Complete Book of Scriptwriting.* Cincinnati: Writer's Digest Books.

———. 1996b. "Severed Dreams." *Babylon 5* episode. Directed by David Eagle. Warner Brothers.

———. 1996c. "The Summoning." *Babylon 5* episode. Directed by John McPherson. Warner Brothers.

———. 1995a. "JMS Usenet messages." www.midwinter.com/b5/Usenet/jms95-01-usenet.

———. 1995b. "The Long, Twilight Struggle." *Babylon 5* episode. Directed by John Flinn. Warner Brothers.

———. 1995c. "Z'ha'dum." *Babylon 5* episode. Directed by Adam Nimoy. Warner Brothers.

————. 1994a. "JMS Usenet messages." www.midwinter.com/b5/Usenet/jms94-01-usenet.

————. 1994b. "JMS Usenet messages." www.midwinter.com/b5/Usenet/jms94-02-usenet.

————. 1994c. "JMS Usenet messages." www.midwinter.com/b5/Usenet/jms94-08-usenet.

————. 1994d. "JMS Usenet messages." www.midwinter.com/b5/Usenet/jms94-09-usenet.

————. 1994e. "JMS Usenet messages." www.midwinter.com/b5/Usenet/jms94-11-usenet.

————. 1994f. "Mind War." *Babylon 5* episode. Directed by Bruce Seth Green. Warner Brothers.

————. 1994g. " 'Mind War': jms speaks." "The Lurker's Guide to *Babylon 5*." www.midwinter.com/lurk/countries/master/guide/006.html.

————. 1994h. "Holographic Storytelling." In *Alternative Universe Today.*

————. 1993a. "JMS Usenet messages." www.midwinter.com/b5/Usenet/jms93-08-usenet.

————. 1993b. *The Gathering*. Directed by Richard Compton. Warner Brothers.

Tulloch, John, and Henry Jenkins. 1995. *Science Fiction Audiences*. London: Routledge.

Virilio, Paul. 1989. *War and Cinema: The Logistics of Perception*. New York: Verso.

Walton, Kendall L. 1990. *Mimesis as Make-Believe*. Cambridge: Harvard University Press.

Zavatta, Sylvie. 1994. "The Past Perfect(ed) or The Creation of an Historical Space." In *Back to the Front: Tourisms of War,* edited by Elizabeth Diller and Ricardo Scofidio. New York: Princeton Architectural Press.

Zelechoski, Sarah, designer. 1999. "Unicorn's I&M Storybook." www.geocities.com/Area51/Dimension/2444/admin.html.

Index